The Digital Economy

The Digital Economy

TIM JORDAN

polity

First published in 2020 by Polity Press

Polity Press
65 Bridge Street
Cambridge CB2 1UR, UK

Polity Press
101 Station Landing
Suite 300
Medford, MA 02155, USA

ISBN-13: 978-1-5095-1755-8
ISBN-13: 978-1-5095-1756-5(pb)

A catalogue record for this book is available from the British Library.

Typeset in 11 on 13pt Adobe Garamond Pro
by Fakenham Prepress Solutions, Fakenham, Norfolk, NR21 8NL
Printed and bound in Great Britain by CPI Group (UK) Ltd, Croydon

The publisher has used its best endeavours to ensure that the URLs for external websites referred to in this book are correct and active at the time of going to press. However, the publisher has no responsibility for the websites and can make no guarantee that a site will remain live or that the content is or will remain appropriate.

Every effort has been made to trace all copyright holders, but if any have been overlooked the publisher will be pleased to include any necessary credits in any subsequent reprint or edition.

For further information on Polity, visit our website:
politybooks.com

Contents

Acknowledgements

The ideas in this book are in part a result of teaching-led research, in which students initially taught me that what I thought was a well-analysed subject (the digital economy) was problematic, and then helped with identifying the issues this book addresses. Thanks goes to all the students at the University of Sussex and at King's College London who took the course 'Digital Industries and Internet Cultures'. Colleagues at Polity Press were not only sympathetic but very helpful when the manuscript was delayed, and have been highly efficient in refining and producing the book; many thanks to Ellen MacDonald-Kramer and Mary Savigar as editors, Tim Clark for a thorough copy edit and Evie Deavall for production. Two anonymous reviewers provided feedback, much of which was helpful and I thank them for their time.

I had further and essential help from a wonderful network of scholars I meet at conferences, seminars, dinners and more; unfortunately there are too many to name but my thanks goes out to them all. The Society for the Advancement of Socio-Economics' annual conference, the Centre for Digital Culture at King's College London, and the Klein School of Media and Communication at Temple University all offered a chance to present my ideas about the digital economy, and the discussions at each were very helpful.

A few individuals helped particularly and I'd like to thank them: Tarleton Gillespie and Hector Postigo and all who attended the Philadelphia Culture Digitally meeting at which I presented some of these ideas in a confused way; Kim Humphery, particularly for her help on ideas about consumption politics; King's College London colleagues in both Digital Humanities and Culture, Media and Creative Industries (including those like me who left); Joss Hands, Jodi Dean and David Castle for discussions as part of the Pluto's Digital Barricades series; the dinners that have offered emotional and intellectual support with Kath Woodward, Mark Banks and Richard Collins; and colleagues at the University of Sussex, particularly those who helped during some very difficult issues there.

My children offer both a window into living the digital economy and huge amounts of fun; love to them both.

During the final stages of preparation of this manuscript my older brother Campbell died suddenly and unexpectedly. He was an example of someone who made the world better through daily acts of kindness and commitment, particularly in his work with the local life-saving club. Over a hundred people turned out when we scattered his ashes in the bay outside the home we grew up in – and that he lived in for much of his life – and the life-saving club that runs as a central thread through our family. I dedicate this book to him and to all those who make the world better though everyday moments; those who make the world a better place one everyday act at a time, or in Campbell's case (among other sessions) one nippers' session at a time.

1 The Meaning of the Digital Economy

Hype and #Hyper-hype

The digital economy has been an object of fear, fascination and greedy hope for over thirty years. The rise of the digital economy has been marked by a number of companies that are both hugely influential on society and are hugely financially successful. As the names roll off the tongue – Google, Facebook, Alibaba, Amazon, Tencent, Apple, etc. – who could deny the digital economy's importance? But what is the digital economy? And how does it relate to wider social changes marked by the rise of the internet and the digital?

A start to answering these questions is to acknowledge the fog of hype that has so often surrounded and obscured them. And one thing the internet and the digital economy have never been short of is hype. From being the greatest revolution in humanity since, variously, the Gutenberg Press, the invention of language, the invention of the wheel and the taming of fire, the internet and the digital have not lacked boosters willing to proclaim their fundamentally transformative effects. This is not only true for the digital economy but is frequently true for it in a more intense way, often because of the great financial gain that seems possible. For the hashtag generation, the economic effects of the digital could easily be expressed as #hyper-hype. The over-reaching of some commentators – such as Anderson's (2013) positing of a 'second industrial revolution' based on email, 3D printing and offshore factories, or Zuboff's (2019) claim of a new stage of capitalism based on surveillance – should not blind us to changes that are important to the ways twenty-first century economies function.

There is, also, an opposite and just as unenlightening position about the digital economy to #hyper-hype that amounts to a shrug, expressed in various forms of the claim: 'it's really just the same old capitalism'. It is important in understanding the digital economy to see past claims it is a fundamental revolution or really nothing new at all. One way to turn down the brightness of #hyper-hype and disperse the fog of the anti-capitalist shrug is to define the question being asked more clearly and proceed to specify a path toward understanding the digital economy. This will be the task of this introductory chapter, starting with a question.

1

Either hyping or rejecting claims that there is a 'digital economy' all too often presuppose a question that is left implicit: When referring to the 'new' digital economy are we referring to changes that digital and internet socio-technologies have brought to the existing economy, turning the whole economy into a 'digital economy', or does the latter refer to a new kind of .economic activity that can be called digital? For example, a McKinsey report into China's digital economy placed heavy emphasis on the fast take-up of mobile payments as evidence of a quickly growing Chinese digital economy, but if we pause and think about mobile payments it is not clear whether they are indicators of the effect of digital mobility on the whole economy or are part of new economic practices which require such mobility (Woetzel et al. 2017). Any analysis that effectively collapses the digital economy into the whole economy will have a strong tendency to miss two things: first, the distinctiveness of the digital compared to prior economic processes; second, how much of the preceding economy remains non-digital. The danger is of a kind of selective blindness that sees digital processes everywhere but misses already existing practices, such as buying things in a supermarket, that remain a key part of the economy. To grasp what may be new and distinctive about the digital and the economy without giving in to either hyper-hype or dismissal of the digital as new, means accepting the premise that there was complex economic activity prior to the digital which may or may not have been affected by any new kinds of economic activity related to the internet and the digital. The issue then becomes one of identifying if there is any distinctively new economic activity. The simplest way to explore this question is through a sectoral analysis that looks for a new digital sector existing alongside and intersecting with the sectors that already existed. If such digital economic activity can be identified it will then be possible to consider what effect such new activities might have on other economic activities. Knowing what is specific to the digital economy is the first step to understanding its effects on the economy.

The first attempt at identifying an economic sector that is distinctively digital will be to review statistical evidence for a digital economy, hoping to establish if such an economy can be counted and, if so, how significant it is. The initial hypothesised picture of the economy is then that it is made up of distinct yet interacting economic sectors, one of which is relatively new and is called the digital. Counting this can be done by determining which existing companies operate in the digital sector. A first approximation may be possible by developing existing definitions and using these to help establish what a digital company might look like; for example by looking at the difference between an Apple, Tencent or Google compared to a Petrobas, China Bank or Walmart.

To develop this strategy while also offering something more substantial than common sense, I will present a view first through the work of the Organisation for Economic Co-operation and Development (OECD) analysis of what it called the 'information economy'. It is not entirely clear that an information economy is the same as a digital economy – though all companies usually thought of as digital were included by the OECD within the information economy – but for the purposes of this initial discussion it can be taken as an indicator of the potential scale of the economic activity under analysis. Second, I will develop an analysis based on the 500 largest companies by market value looked at in relation to key indicators: revenue, assets, profit (net income) and employment (numbers of workers employed). Centring on market value allows for a direct comparison between different kinds of economic activity, which is crucial for the case being made here. Market value is also less subject to short-term economic tactics when compared to indicators like revenue or profit. For example, profit can be affected by a company working on its figures by writing-down costs; similarly revenue does not adequately allow for a comparison between different industrial sectors (with the financial sector being particularly different here) (Dullforce 2015).

An understanding of the size and value of the digital economy can appropriately, if cautiously, begin from the market value of existing companies. Of course, caution should be taken here as market value reflects what buyers are willing to pay for the shares of a company, and accordingly, especially during booms and busts, it may reflect a market view not necessarily connected to other ways of understanding economic activity. Limiting my analysis to the top 500 companies creates a workable statistical base that is generally considered to cover around two-thirds of economic activity. Despite these limitations, the point is to create a first view through OECD and top 500 company statistics; for reasons that will become clear while exploring these numbers it is not worth undertaking any more substantial work.

The Digital Economy as Seen Through the OECD and Market Values

In 2014, an OECD report addressed the extent to which the information economy had survived the global financial crisis of 2008 and whether it was contributing to increased economic activity after the crisis. In reviewing its results, I will set aside the question of the difference between an information and a digital economy, partly because the digital is folded within the OECD's statistical definition of the information economy and partly because definitions are a topic that will be discussed further below. The report judges the information economy both to have survived the 2008 crisis relatively well, though with a drop in research and development expenditure, and to be a key contributor to innovation in other economic sectors. 'While the role of ICTs in science has become pervasive and demand for products from the information industries has increased significantly over the last decade, the aggregate weight of these activities declined slightly in the average of OECD economies, to little less than 6% of total value added and 3.7–3.8% of employment' (OECD 2014: 37). In these terms, the information/digital economy is smaller than might have been thought; however, the OECD measures also emphasise how central ICT and the information economy is to other industries, making it difficult to separate a specific sector out.

Another measure is the international trade in ICT goods: 'Between 2000 and 2012 world exports of manufactured ICT goods grew by 65% to more than USD 1.5 trillion. However, their share in total world exports of goods decreased by about 5 percentage points, partly due to widespread falls in unit prices' (OECD 2014: 144). In other words, while the sale of goods deemed informational or digital grew rapidly, it still fell as a proportion of the overall economy, hovering at around 4 per cent of total world exports, varying from over 12 per cent in India down to negligible figures for some nations (OECD 2014: 145). Depending on where in the world the measure is taken, the information economy fluctuates between just over 10 per cent of an economy down to zero.

The next sets of figures draw on the categorisations underpinning the *Financial Times* and *Fortune*[1] analyses of the 500 most highly valued

Table 1.1 Economic Sectors – Total Market Value (USD millions)

	Manufacturing	Financial	Retail	Service	Digital	Extractive	Total
2017							
Market Value	3,885,168	3,400,038	1,462,153	4,329,598	6,650,784	1,865,371	21,593,112
% of Total	17.99	15.75	6.77	20.05	30.80	8.64	
2015							
Market Value	9,146,439	7,979,289	2,393,507	2,676,982	6,547,547	3,643,449	32,387,214
% of Total	28.24	24.64	7.39	8.27	20.22	11.25	
2006							
Market Value	5,249,680	5,955,721	1,247,266	1,723,698	4,233,769	3,979,554	22,389,688
% of Total	23.45	26.60	5.57	7.70	18.91	17.77	

companies in the world at three points: 2006, 2015 and 2017[2] (Fortune 2017; FT 2015, 2006). These figures (see Table 1.1) suggest that the digital economy makes up around 20 per cent of the total economy – possibly up to 30 per cent – and is worth around 6.5 trillion US dollars. There are discrepancies between the methods for the 2017 (Fortune) and the 2015/2006 (both FT) figures, with the significant increase in the percentage of the digital in 2017 related to values decreasing in other sectors to such an extent they are likely to be definition related. These figures also suggest that the proportion the digital sector occupies expanded slightly during the period after the 2008 financial crash, though not by an amount that seems overly significant or that is comparable to fluctuations in other sectors (the 5 per cent increase in manufacturing for example). Broadly, the digital sector appears to be as important as the financial and manufacturing sectors and roughly twice as important as the retail, service and extractive sectors.

Given what looks like a possible discrepancy in classification, and the aim here being only an initial rather than detailed look, the next analysis examines only the most recent 2017 numbers and some additional measures: revenue, net income or profit, total assets and number of employees (see Table 1.2).[3] This comparison helps develop a sense of the differences between sectors. In terms of a pattern, the digital is relatively high in profit while being low in assets and moderate on employment. The fact that the sector has roughly 28 per cent of profits with only 16 per cent of revenue, 9 per cent of assets and 15 per cent of employees might be a starting point for understanding the high valuation of digital companies, which come out with 30 per cent of total market value. Retail having 28 per cent of employees but less than 8 per cent of profit suggests the importance of employment in this sector while also perhaps explaining its low market value of only 7 per cent of the total.

It may be that such differences are indications of different kinds of economic activity, and it is tempting to immediately connect these findings to existing discussions about the digital economy. For example, to what extent is its very strong profit–asset relationship due to digital companies disintermediating government regulations and so avoiding asset costs that others must incur? Likewise, while the financial sector's relation between profit and employee numbers may have an intuitive basis in the intangibility and large size of the commodities it deals with – shares, futures, derivatives and so on – it is tempting to connect the digital sector's relatively moderate employment and high profit to the way many digital products benefit from extensive 'free' labour provided by the users of those products. Before being seduced by such numbers, however, it is important to face up

Table 1.2 Economic Sectors (2017) – Other Measures (USD millions)

	Market Value	Profit	Revenue	Asset	Employees (total number)
Manufacturing	3,885,168	155,430	2,350,529	3,496,514	5,479,283
% of Total	17.99	15.47	18.34	8.30	19.41
Financial	3,400,038	228,481	2,232,306	27,909,063	3,198,268
% of Total	15.75	22.74	17.42	66.26	11.33
Retail	1,462,153	77,704	2,641,316	1,184,934	7,933,952
% of Total	6.77	7.73	20.61	2.81	28.10
Service	4,329,598	181,381	2,144,832	2,826,420	6,538,487
% of Total	20.05	18.05	16.74	6.71	23.16
Digital	6,650,784	276,929	2,047,313	3,821,682	4,254,320
% of Total	30.80	27.56	15.98	9.07	15.07
Extractive	1,865,371	84,876	1,398,194	2,879,857	827,529
% of Total	8.64	8.45	10.91	6.84	2.93
Total	21,593,112	1,004,802	12,814,490	42,118,470	28,231,839

to the more fundamental difficulty – which these and the OECD analyses both point to – of coming up with a clear definition of the digital economy.

Numbers do not speak. It is only through a conceptual framework that they appear to talk, even if we often forget that and instead take numbers as the gift-horse whose mouth it would be impolite to examine. From one perspective, the evidence suggests there is a digital sector of significant size, around 20 or perhaps even 30 per cent of the total economy, with a distinct pattern, while from the OECD perspective it is much smaller. These differences raise the question of what has been done to the numbers to get them to say these things? For example, while the FT and Fortune figures can be manipulated to produce the same sectoral division of the economy, the variation between them suggests that different definitions may be affecting the results, given the dramatic changes between 2015 and 2017. The definition of the digital economy as a statistical category resulted from the allocation of companies to particular sectors, the principles of which have not been clearly articulated. There is then no point in seeking more precise statistical results, or trusting anything but the most general results, until the definition of the digital economy is clearer.

Digital Economic Practices and the Problem of Definition

The problem of defining the digital economy can be articulated by asking what may seem an odd question: are Apple, Microsoft, Google and Facebook all part of the digital economy? This may seem an odd question, as for so many analyses of the digital economy Apple and Microsoft are not just part of the digital economy but are exemplars of it. However, in the case of Apple and Microsoft, it is possible to argue that they are essentially old-fashioned manufacturing industries – they make stuff and sell it, and what they sell happens to be digital or informational products (Bruns 2008: 2). After all, an operating system or an iPhone are commodities for sale. Of course, both companies are more complex than this and include a range of other economic practices, but at their heart their profits and ability to survive and thrive derive principally from creating a commodity and selling it. Google and Facebook cannot be described in this way. Both offer a free service – search, sociality – that allows them to generate information about their users and then profit from advertising that is targeted on the basis of that information (Turrow 2011). I will return to these practices later, but here their relevance is to question how I and the OECD made the numbers speak, because in both cases the assumption was made that Apple, Microsoft, Google and Facebook were all part of the digital or information economy. Yet both Apple and Microsoft's revenues come out at over 80 per cent on selling 'things'. In the case of Apple, iPhones, iPads, Macs and 'other' products made up 83 per cent of its revenue in the final financial quarter of 2017, with 'services' such as iTunes, AppleCare, ApplePay and so on accounting for most of the rest. Microsoft's top four revenue streams in 2017 were Office, server products, the Windows operating system and the Xbox, amounting to around 80 per cent of all revenue. Both companies have long histories of inventing digital commodities and then selling them, in economic terms not entirely unlike Ford inventing and selling cars (Bishop 2017; Apple 2017).

In attempting to untangle these issues, the OECD's definition is problematic. The report cited above is based on an earlier OECD paper that defined how it would measure the information economy (OECD 2011). Conceptually this is presented as two linked diagrams, both of which assume what they are trying to explain. The first diagram links the following groups: ICT supply, ICT infrastructure, ICT demand, ICT products, Information and electronic content, and ICT in a wider context. Rather than explaining what is meant by 'ICT', information, communication and technology are simply imported with it as concepts prior to their definition, creating a circularity. The second diagram outlines what is called the S curve, which conceptualises preparedness for e-commerce in three stages: e-readiness (the infrastructures needed for e-commerce); e-intensity (the state of use, value, nature of e-commerce); and e-impact (the value added potentially by e-commerce). Again, explaining what 'e' means is avoided by assuming it. From here the OECD falls back into prior categorisations and, employing the rather vague diagrammatic concepts just outlined, designates some existing statistical categories as measures of the information society.

Similarly, the top 500 company statistics from FT and Fortune build on existing sectoral definitions which were re-grouped to create a new sector. With only a couple of individual companies excepted, the digital economy sector was made up of the following categories: computer software; computers; office equipment; entertainment; information technology services; internet services and retailing; network and other communications equipment; semiconductors and other electronic components; telecommunications; and wholesalers in electronics and office equipment. This list should immediately throw up uneasiness about whether it is grasping a 'digital sector' or even any one kind of economic activity. Similarly, the existing categorisation of companies under these headings likewise raises as many questions as answers. Netflix is categorised as an information technology service but Disney and Time Warner are treated as entertainment companies. While the latter pre-date the former and the digital economy, they are closely related to Netflix in their developing economic activities. The network equipment category includes Cisco, which rather like Apple might be considered more a company that 'makes products that happen to look digital and sells them' than a company with a specific digital activity. Without a better understanding of what digital economic activity is, then, it is difficult to separate out companies in order to generate sectoral statistics. With such difficulties, it is hard to make numbers talk about the digital economy.

What is the standard that would allow the classification of companies as digital? Making the numbers speak is not easy because the skills required to manipulate them are not always the same as those needed to give them a framework which creates their voice. And it is that framework that is missing. In short there is a definitional problem; neither the OECD nor the existing economic sectoral categories answer the core question: how is the economic practised in such a way that it might be considered digital?

While there is a significant populist literature on the digital economy, this work is light on theorisation of what constitutes digital economic practice. The work of Tapscott is perhaps the most famous here, in particular his book *The Digital Economy*. First published in 1995 and updated twenty years later, this was originally, and remains, a series of anecdotes in search of a theory, offering no real framework or appreciation of what the digital economy might mean other than having something to do with computers, the internet and money (Tapscott 2015). A number of Marxist theorists have argued that the digital economy is based on a new type of rent or on the extraction of surplus value (the latter particularly in relation to free labour). These arguments will be returned to in Chapter 7, as there are some useful ideas here, but because it posits the same capitalism operating across all sectors, the Marxist attempt to understand a digital sector presupposes that surplus value or rent will be found to be the sources of profit and the drivers of economic activity. As such, this is not so much a theory of the digital economy as a presumption that extending Marxist economics to digital interactions will be sufficient to theorise that economy (Fuchs 2014; Dean 2012). Zuboff (2019) claims a new stage in capitalism that succeeds the Fordist period has arisen with digital technologies. Her account will also be drawn on but because it focuses entirely on the economic practices associated with advertising online and does not examine other potential economic practices it is a restricted view. Her claim that there is a 'surveillance capitalism' – echoing Balkin (2008) and others who have identified the rise of the 'surveillance state' – accordingly both assumes the digital economy has restructured the whole economy and limits what practices might make up the digital economy to those Google relies on (meaning also that surveillance and advertising developments in the digital and the internet prior to Google are not given appropriate attention, as they are for example in Turrow's (2011) work).

What the problem of statistics makes clear is that a theory encompassing and connecting the elements of the digital economy and defining its specificity is missing. The remainder of this book will take up the task of providing such a theory, beginning with a clearer articulation of the question being asked.

Digital Economic Practices

A starting point is the work already built up in the related areas of cultural economy and of creative economy and cultural industries. While some distinctions may be drawn between them, for the purposes of relating to the digital economy their key innovations are similar enough to be taken together, just as are their key weaknesses. Where cultural economy addresses the cultural dimensions of all economic activity, work on the cultural and creative industries addresses those industries that have creativity at their core. Both then address culture in economic settings and read this as requiring attention to specific kinds of activities. As Pryke and du Gay argue: 'Common to those within the broad church of cultural economy' is therefore a shared focus on (material) practices, orderings and discourses which produce economically relevant activity' (2007: 340).

What is helpful here is the initial point that identifying an economy will involve the identification of practices and culture. An economic sector, then, may be understood as having at its core cultural and social practices that constitute the production, exchange and consumption dynamics specific to that sector. However, the quotation from Pryke and Du Gay also throws up a key issue, not so much for cultural economy or creative industries work, but for the present argument, because following this idea of defining a sector also entails working out what 'economy' and 'practice' mean (Amin and Thrift 2004). The project of analysing the digital economy becomes one of building an understanding of whether there are any particular digital economic activities and, if so, what constitutes them. The aim here is not grand, in the sense of arguing that analysis of economic life should all be based on economic practices, but rather is specific; the argument is that to understand a new region of economic life looking at how it is lived and practised is an important way to grasp it. In the following chapters this will be done through a series of case studies focusing on particular digital economic practices. To undertake these studies we first need an understanding of 'economic practice'.

Practices are the repeated actions taken to construct everyday life-worlds, or what Schatzki calls 'a nexus of doings and sayings' (cited in Reckwitz 2002: 250). While practice as a concept is often closely associated with Bourdieu, Schatzki and others (Bourdieu 1977; Schatzki 2008; Cetina et al. 2005), one way of applying such ideas to digital economics is to draw a parallel with Couldry's attempt to use the sociology of practice to change how media is studied. Couldry sought to move media studies from a study of texts and effects toward a study of media practices; in doing so he emphasised three things. First, in the analysis of practice, culture is recentred on routine, often unconscious, actions and on the structures of meaning that allow something to be said (rather than on the thing said). Second, the analysis is open to following what people are doing in relation to media, and should not presume prior existing categories of media, such as 'the audience'. Finally, there is a focus on the kinds of practices that produce categorisations or identities that are enduring (Couldry 2004: 121–2).

> The value of practice theory ... is to ask open questions about what people are doing and how they categorise what they are doing, avoiding the disciplinary or other preconceptions that would automatically read their actions as, say, 'consumption' or 'being-an-audience', whether or not that is how the actors see their actions. (Couldry 2004: 125)

While Couldry here addresses media, his focus on following the routine, the everyday and repeated actions and the meanings of and within media is strongly indicative of the way I wish to use 'practice' to open up the phenomena of the digital economy. In this regard, a cognate conceptual ally is the feminist materialist focus on the 'trouble' or the 'mess' of life. As with Couldry's extensive work, there is insufficient space here to outline all that is relevant, but it is worth noting the connection here to Haraway's notion of the 'trouble' inherent in becoming-with each other, from microbes to humans. As she says when discussing partners in making life's troubles: 'The partners do not precede the knotting' (Haraway 2016: 13; see also Barad 2007).

In the following chapters, practices are understood as entanglements of meaning and action in which various actors appear and are formed, or disappear and are deformed, and which are in some sense repetitive, iterative and patterned. 'A "practice" (Praktik) is a routinized type of behaviour that consists of several elements' (Reckwitz 2002: 249). We might think of practices as habits, like using an ATM to obtain cash, or clicking to register our agreement to an end-user licence online; in such ways we become habituated in the habitus. 'The paradox of habit', as Deleuze puts it, 'is that it is formed by degrees and also that it is a principle of nature ... The principle is the principle of contracting habits' (1991: 66). Habits and repetitions are important because if a set of meanings and actions is simply a one-off then it does not form a practice; the principle of habit and iteration is that it forms habits by degrees. If practice seems to focus on meaningful actions then the latter are meaningful only because they have been replicated in order to be part of a practice.[4]

From Couldry in media studies to Haraway on troubling boundaries, I could also have looked at Barnes's (1988) collective action theory, Butler's (1997) theory of performativity, and Latour's (2007) actor network theory, which broadly and similarly demonstrate how practice encompasses the myriad interactions and entanglements between many different kinds of actors (human and non-human) that create patterned forms of life. Drawing inspiration from these sources but focusing on the digital economy, the aim is to follow the practices; paraphrasing Touraine, when analysing the digital economy it is important to 'pass on the side of actors' practices' (2002: 89).

Economic practices, then, are the habits, actions and meanings, formed into repeated routines, that sustain how we produce and exchange the goods that provide for life, wealth and their reproduction. Adam Smith famously, and broadly, enquired into the 'wealth of nations', and particularly into the peculiarly human 'truck, bartering and exchanging' of one thing for another, while Marx enquired into humans who, in producing their subsistence, 'are definitely producing their actual material life' (Smith 1982; Marx 1978). To these we can add Marshall's view that the economy is the 'social action which is most closely connected with the attainment and with the use of the material requisites of wellbeing' (1890: 6). As Keynes emphasised, this attention to social life and its production and reproduction makes economics a moral and therefore imprecise science, and one that requires the observation of economics in action (Keynes 1938). Feminist accounts have ensured that such a view of the economy is not just about the production of goods and labour but also their reproduction (Jarrett 2016). The economy connects the production and reproduction of life to the creation, exchange and consumption of the goods and commodities of all kinds that constitute wealth. Furthermore, because these complex inter-relations between creation, exchange and consumption are embedded in ways of life, they have to gain meaning within practices: an economy of exchange of food and shelter for sheer subsistence is very different to an IT-enabled, app-focused economy of attention, but both are economies embedded in and gaining meaning from the ways people live. Whatever it is that is created, exchanged or consumed, it can only derive its meaning from being embedded in social worlds which give meaning to goods or commodities themselves.

The definition of economic practices employed here follows this, perhaps more classical, understanding of the economy, while also drawing inspiration from revisions of economics in the light of the 2008 financial crisis (e.g. Piketty 2014), and from the work of contemporary cultural economists and analysts of the creative industries (Core 2018; Hesmondhalgh 2010; Banks 2017). This is important, for being open to finding a new phenomenon requires attention to what is occurring, since it is all too easy to see what is already known. Economic practices are then the practices that create and sustain the wealth of a society, seen in its exchanges of goods or commodities, and the organisation of the production and reproduction of life through everyday practices. These two sides are closely connected and ensure that various cultures in society are attended to, something that will be crucial in understanding the digital economy.

This book treats digital economic practices as repeated and patterned habits of creating, exchanging and consuming a huge range of goods and commodities that make up the wealth of society, while understanding that often the meanings of these commodities must themselves emerge from within those practices. This entails paying close attention to the practices that produce and reproduce social life. My approach is then a materialist and a qualitative one. The numbers can only speak when we know what they are talking about, and, when confronted by what seems to be a new form of economy, we can only reach that understanding by following and examining its economic practices and particularly its distinctive causal mechanisms. If the digital economy is powerful and fast growing – at least according to the faulty numbers I have presented – then it is important to examine the economic practices that constitute it.

Plan of the Book

> Any self-respecting university course or textbook on industry economics spends some time at the outset discussing the difficulties of defining an industry – i.e. whether the concept of industry can be delineated according to groupings of producers, product classifications, factors of production, types of consumers, location, etc. What is problematical for industries in general is especially so in the cultural sphere because of uncertainties in the definition of cultural goods and services. (Throsby 2014: 112)

The opening to this book has conformed to Throsby's concerns about the difficulties of definition; indeed, the main aim of this introduction has involved the contradictory purposes of establishing the importance of the digital economy while noting that it is hard to know what 'digital economy' means. The statistical data I have presented broadly suggests that there is something about the digital economy that deserves serious attention. Many other indications point toward the need to grasp what has happened since the 1970s in economic terms, with the rise of digital and internet socio-technologies. For example, in 2018, first Apple and then Amazon became the first companies ever to be valued at over 1 trillion US dollars (Axon 2018). The difference between Amazon and Apple is again illustrative of the difficulties of deciding what kind of economic activity constitutes the digital economy, given the former's origins as a digital and internet company and the latter's as a design and manufacturing company.

What is missing is a definition and model of the digital economy as a sector within the wider economy. Modelling the digital as a sector is key to discovering if there is anything distinctive about the digital amid the complexity of the everyday, in which all kinds of different and hybrid economic practices will be present. The qualitative method adopted here is to follow digital economic practices in their patterned interactions until there is a strong enough base to posit a model. This conforms to Keynes's suggestion regarding economic thought:

> one cannot get very far except by devising new and improved models. This requires … 'a vigilant observation of the actual working of our system'. Progress in economics consists almost entirely in a progressive improvement in the choice of models … The object of statistical study is not so much to fill in missing variables with a view to prediction, as to test the relevance and validity of the model. (Keynes 1938)

The plan of this book is to move from the questions posed by this introduction, and more generally by the hype surrounding the significance of digital economic activities, to examine a range of ways the digital economy operates in practice. This will be achieved in two phases: in the next five chapters case studies of digital economic practices will be presented; following this, three chapters will provide concepts for, a model of, and policy questions about the digital economy.

The five case studies will cover search, social media, disintermediation, free digital economic practices and games. Chapter 2, on search, will examine Google as well as Baidu and other search engines. The importance of the collective activities that construct the World Wide Web (WWW) – which are then 'read' to produce search results that are combined with subsequent personalisation based on data collected from users – will be stressed in order to demonstrate how the value of Google's search results depends on the community of practice that it 'reads'. Monetisation will be examined to show how the search engine platform privatises the information it collects, generates new information, and then monetises that information through targeted advertising. Chapter 3, on social media, identifies a similar economic practice, though here the 'value' resides in the very stuff of emotional and social life. This is explored in relation to Facebook, Snapchat and WeChat, among other social media sites. Again, the way in which a set of collective activities is created and then 'read' in order to be monetised will be demonstrated.

The third case study examines disintermediation, looking primarily at Uber, Airbnb and blockchain technologies. Here the economic practice involves a digital platform intervening into an existing service in a society (taxis for example) by disintermediating existing service providers and the various regulatory requirements imposed on them. Monetisation then occurs as the platform sits between the service user who pays and the service provider who is paid, allowing the platform to dip into that monetary flow.

The fourth case study looks at not-for-profit digital economic practices, including free software, the World Wide Web Consortium and Wikipedia. These offer a contrast to the previous case studies in demonstrating that, while digital economic practices create a kind of value which is realised by the collective activities of users, this value can exist separately from its monetisation for profit. Digital economic practices that refuse monetisation produce different conceptions of information as property, in particular how information may be treated as a property that is distributed freely by right, instead of one that is privately and exclusively owned.

The final case study is of online, computerised and networked gaming. Here the economic practice of renting and not buying a commodity is examined more closely, having been mentioned briefly in prior case studies. This practice is one in which what appears to have been bought by a consumer is in fact rented to them and may be withdrawn by the digital company that has been paid. It is also closely related to subscriptions for access to digital platforms. Moreover, the study of gaming allows different digital economic practices to be seen operating together, particularly in the rise of 'free to play' models of monetisation, and in the intersection of digital with non-digital economic practices – after all, many games are bought in much the same way as a book is bought online. Massive multi-player online games, including *World of Warcraft*, are examined here, as are a range of other games, in particular mobile games like *Candy Crush* and 'battle royale' games like *Fortnite* and PlayerUnknown's *Battleground*.

While these case studies do not comprehensively map digital economic companies – neither Amazon nor Spotify, for example, are addressed in detail – they do qualitatively examine a multiplicity of digital economic practices, both successful and unsuccessful. This case study work will then be developed with concepts drawn from key debates in existing digital economy theory. The three debates examined are free labour, information surpluses as exploitation, and the breakdown of the producer/consumer divide. All three have substantial existing literatures, but Chapter 7 will show that, in the face of case study evidence and conceptual analysis, all three have significant failings needing further theorisation. Such a plan, it should be noted, means that there will be a significant shift in tone as the argument moves into theoretical debates. Whereas the case study chapters engage with the daily matters of digital economic practices, attempting to both follow and excavate how such practices are formed from different actions and perspectives among users, platform owners, platform workers and so on, examining existing theories of these practices involves conceptualisation. Issues such as the information drawn from freely given activities that users provide to social media, that in turn underpin revenue through advertising, will be repeatedly mentioned within the complexity and materiality of practices, and it requires a shift of emphasis to start drawing out such issues by exploring conceptualisations of them. Practices always involve ideas about what is happening within them, and ideas always refer to (even if obliquely) and rely on a sense of relevant practices; in this sense the shift is one of emphasis from primarily diagnosing the meaning of economic actions in digital contexts to theorising across such contexts how recurrent actions are structured and may be conceived.

This move to conceptualisation will provide the basis for a model of digital economic practices to be proposed through three linked divisions – value, property and profit – to be set out in Chapter 8. The first two divisions address the creation of a value that is realised by collective activities, such as search or gaming, linked to different forms of information property. Once a digital platform instantiates such a connection, it becomes possible for the third division of profit to be added through a monetisation strategy. Three main monetisation strategies are identified: targeted advertising, disintermediation and reintermediation, and rent not buy. Within this model, the possibility always remains that a digital economic practice may refuse to seek monetisation for profit and instead offer information as a distributed property. In the latter case, radical options open up for digital economic practices that offer information able to be used simultaneously and completely by everyone who can access it.

Following this modelling of the digital economy, Chapter 9 will consider broad policy questions. The first key issue is to establish where a digital economic practice exists: what is the jurisdiction appropriate to any digital economic company? The argument is made that location can be defined by using the activities of platform users as these are located in places, instead of the information flows resulting from these activities as these are transferable across boundaries. Following this, policy issues around tax are examined, particularly in relation to taxes that derive from the places in which digital economic activities occur. The discussion also includes an examination of the possibility of micro-taxation. Third, the chapter addresses labour issues, particularly those arising in relation to platforms that monetise users freely given time in activities on a platform and to disintermediation monetisation strategies that avoid regulation (particularly regulation of the service providers associated with each platform). Finally, the more radical possibilities offered by information as a distributed property are explored in the context of debates over the information commons.

The final arguments of the book address how the evidence of the case studies and the model of the digital economy fit into wider discussions of the nature of twenty-first-century global economies. Digital economic practices depend on the collective activities and communities of users, and have managed to insert profit-making into the most intimate spaces of everyday life through these collective moments. The challenge and urgency of digital economic practices is to address this takeover, for profit, of socially essential and intimate activities, such as searching for information or making friends.

2 Search and Advertise

Let me start with wealth. In the first three months of 2018, Google[1] had a total income of 31.1 billion US dollars (a 26 per cent increase compared to the first three months of 2017), 85 per cent of which, or $26.6 billion, was brought in by advertising. In the same period Google's net income, or profit, was $9.4 billion (Alphabet Inc. 2018b). In the second three months of 2018, the company's total income was $32.7 billion, advertising brought in $28 billion (86 per cent), and net income was $3.1 billion (or $8.2 billion excluding fines) (Alphabet Inc. 2018a). A surplus or profit of $12.5 billion in six months is wealth.

Google's profit has always been dependent on revenue from advertising that is driven from its search engine. Formed in 1998, the company began as a website with one feature, its search engine. The first ever Google webpage was just the name Google and a box in which a search query could be entered. Its distinctive search capabilities attracted the attention of investors, who funded its losses in the early years. In 2000 Google lost $14.1 million, double its previous year's losses, but was soon to launch an advertising program called 'Adwords'. In 2001 the company showed a profit of $7 million, its first ever profit, rising to $100 million the following year, and then steadily upward to a yearly profit $19.5 billion in 2016, $12.6 billion in 2017, and $12.5 billion in the first half of 2018 (Auletta 2011; Levy 2011; Alphabet Inc. 2017).

Such figures sometimes lead to the judgement that 'Google is an advertising company', but while the source of revenue and profit is undeniable, advertising hardly defines Google's economic practice. It is also not alone as a search engine – before it were Alta Vista, Ask Jeeves and others, alongside it are Baidu, Bing, DuckDuckGo, Mojeek and others. Google is also not alone in monetising a service through advertising – Facebook, many computer games, web portals and other sites also take this route. While there are other search engines and other online advertisers, in examining a specific digital economic practice it helps to focus on just one, and it makes sense to start with Google given its position as a pioneer of online advertising and one of the largest profit-generators in the digital economy.

Following an examination of Google's economic practice, this chapter will pursue two directions. First, Google's economic practice will be abstracted to try to identify its key elements. Particular attention will be paid to its digital elements – those which might signify a specifically digital economic practice – and to how this practice might have a possible wider applicability. Second, I will explore whether Google's practice can be applied to or found in other search engine companies.

Googling as an Economic Practice

To examine a specific practice, it needs to be acknowledged that practices come from points of view. A practice is always with or from someone or something. Points of view come with intentions and meanings, with authors, actants and actors aiming to do certain things, even if sometimes they achieve only related or different things. Points of view are necessary entanglements with other points of view, not all of which are visible to each other. The individual who searches does not necessarily see the algorithm forming the answer, nor does the algorithm necessarily account for the computers it requires, which themselves alter environments through their hunger for electricity, rare metals and so on. The points of view can never all be collated; the 'god's eye view' misleads with a false promise of totality (Haraway 1991: 189–98). Yet, points of view can anchor an analysis of a web of intersections though a focus on a certain perspective that brings into view economically significant practices.

Practices are materialised in repeated actions, ideas and relations, each practice making a particular context material. When a practice is performed, one materiality is realised leaving behind other possibilities. While the previous discussion established the importance of habits amid differing activities for understanding practices generally, moving to a specific set of practices (here those of searching) requires taking into account points of view and understanding the materiality and the moment of activities. When a practice is performed, for example when a search is made, a reality is cut – in Barad's sense – out of the mess of entanglements that intersect in each specific moment and place. And in each cut where a materiality is made there will be multiple points of view, different ways of performing in the complexity of an overall practice (Barad 2007: 148–70). One matter realised once is still matter, but it only transforms into a socially, culturally, politically or economically significant matter when the cut is repeated across a range of points of view and the same matter is realised. To understand Google's economic practices, then, the points of view from which such repeated practices create and rely on materialities need to be followed. Three such points of view will be examined: those of the searcher or user; of the advertiser; and of Google itself, particularly in relation to its algorithms and datasets and the demands on these created by its commitment to a for-profit corporate logic.

A caveat to this analysis is that Google search has changed and continues to change, becoming more complex over its development. This case study will simplify somewhat by focusing on Google relatively early in its advertising days, at the point broadly speaking when its two key ad programs – Adwords and Adsense – and personalisation through data were established.

In 2016 around 2 trillion searches were conducted using Google's search engine. To explore user practices, I will follow one user finding an answer (Sullivan 2016). Imagine you are writing a book about the digital economy based on following economic practices in specific digital contexts, rather like this book. As part of this project, you wish to outline the various practices related to searching for information using Google, and, as you write that, you realise it might be helpful to locate those practices in a broader context, perhaps by establishing how many Google searches are made. Practices then follow.

First, your practices have a material context. This will include working on a desktop computer from home, rather than in the office your employer provides, or on a phone while moving around, or on a tablet while commuting to work on a train. There are a range of taken-for-granted practices here: using a mouse and the Microsoft operating system, using alt-tab to switch to an already open browser (Firefox) and knowing that typing a string of words – 'Google search enquiries 2017 total number' – into what looks like the address box of the browser will invoke the Google search engine. Underpinning even these unthought and semi-automatic practices are a range of things like electricity, broadband access, light and so on, which create a material context in which our user can sit and quickly bash out an enquiry, hitting return to initiate the search.

Taking most of this material context for granted, our user is now looking at a computer screen on which a window organised by the Firefox browser has opened up. The window is very familiar. At the top are buttons, an address window, and various customisations (Zotero for referencing, for example), which control the actions that can be taken in the browser. Just below this ribbon of buttons is the Google logo, the search box in which the words used in the search reappear, reminding the user what the initial action was. Below that is a list of responses to the query, with a blank space to the side of these answers, though the user knows that sometimes advertisements or summaries will appear there. The list of entries is each an address (a URL) linking to another site on the World Wide Web, with the first two to three lines of each site being shown. From this our user realises that their search words were not the best, as the second entry is for the UK's Her Majesty's Land Registry, which records land ownership in the UK and has nothing to do with the number of Google search queries. Scrolling over the entry box for a new search brings up a suggestion – 'how many Google searches per day 2017' – which our user clicks on to generate a second set of results. The result that was first on the first search is now second, but our user clicks on that result as it has now shown up twice, and in their experience (that is, in the practices they have developed to search for information using Google), this is a reasonable indication that the answer they want may be found there. Disappointingly, the article linked to is from 2016 but it is from a search engine analysis site and seems reasonably sourced, so our user lifts the 2 trillion a year figure and adds it to their text.

From here our user may move in several directions, perhaps diving more deeply by looking at the top result in the second search, which purports to record live how many Google searches are being made (www. internetlivestats.com/google-search-statistics). Or they may restrain the impulse to dive deeper into the topic and return to the writing at hand. The practice of searching is closely connected to other practices that make up this working life. Our user has one last reflection as they notice that accompanying the second site they looked at there are advertisements for paintings by indigenous Australian artists, and they remember that similar ads have been following them as they visited different websites at other times. These paintings indicate the practices of Google advertising, which we can turn to next.

Many readers will have guessed immediately what happened in relation to the searcher finding ads for indigenous Australians' art on various websites that have nothing to do with such art, because ads that follow a searcher have become a common experience. The user must at some point have looked at or searched for such art, and tracking mechanisms on the internet have recorded this and used it to target ads. Similarly, some years ago, I booked a trip to Walt Disney World online, which led to Mickey Mouse and his friends stalking me across the Web amid the often noted, and ongoing, irony of being shown ads to go somewhere I could no longer afford to go because I had just paid to go there.

In following the practices of a user engaged in materialising an answer to a question, a second set of practices that can be followed has emerged with advertising, which implies an advertiser. For an advertiser, economic practices, at their crudest, involve trying to persuade people to buy the goods the advertiser has been paid to get them to buy (though it should be noted that advertising strategies may be complex, such as building brand loyalty or gaining attention). The question is, how does an advertiser end up in profit by being paid to boost a company's sales? Let us assume this advertiser decides to work with online advertising and goes to Google. The magnet Google has to attract potential buyers is its search engine. In the period of Google's development focused on here, two broad routes are offered. One is that when someone searches for a term related to a product being advertised, then the websites our advertiser has designated show up in the advertising sections of the Google page on which the search query is returned. The second is that Google facilitates ads appearing on other companies' websites and, again, our advertiser can pay for their products and related sites to show up on sites other than Google's.

To appear on the search page is to directly draw on the magnet of Google search. Ads appearing here are marked out in slightly different colours and with words indicating that they are ads – 'sponsored' often appears – ensuring that they remain distinct from the search results. If our advertiser works for a business that sells package holidays, they may want their site to be advertised to anyone searching for terms like 'Disney', 'beach' and so on. To do this they have to decide what kinds of words a user might type into search that would indicate they might be interested in holiday products. Google runs an auction on keywords and advertisers bid according to how much they are willing to pay each time someone clicks on the advertisement. The way Google's auction is set up guarantees that the winner only pays just above whatever the second highest bid was. Once the auction is won, the ads our advertiser wishes to be seen will appear on Google's search page when the words are used in a search. If a user then clicks on the ad, the advertiser pays Google. There are complications to this simple scenario – such as Google rating good or bad ads, the standards ads must meet, and the information Google offers advertisers to improve their ads and so on – but the fundamentals are in this practice of buying words at auctions which result in ads being served to users of Google search (Turrow 2011: 67; Levy 2011: 87–93).

The second process – in which ads appear on websites other than Google's search page – runs in a similar way to the first. For example, a fan of model railroads might run a website and seek to gain some funding by signing up with Google to host ads. Our advertiser might then think that people who are interested in model railroads might also be interested in holidays featuring rail travel (and when I say 'think' that probably means research into the demographics and holiday habits of model railroaders). Having come to this conclusion, the advertiser bids for the relevant words and then pays in various ways. One key form of payment is what is called 'cost per mille', or what an advertiser will pay for 1,000 views of their ad on various sites. Google is paid by the advertiser and then pays the hosting website a percentage based on the ads served up and viewed. Again, there are many complications here and there have been developments over time, but the core practices of advertisers should by now be clear.

The third set of intersecting activities, or third point of view, making up the economic practices of Google search are those of Google itself. These activities split between the structures set up by the company that allow it to offer services and mediate between search users and advertisers, and the implementation of those structures in the software/hardware that allows practices to be automated. This connection transformed Google and established one kind of digital economic practice as a money gusher, as noted earlier in the company's turn from loss to profit once Adwords was implemented. To sustain this, Google's economic practices have a dual character, with a never-ending process of improving search alongside never-ending developments in advertising.

We have followed a single search from the point of view of the individual searcher, but from Google's point of view things appear differently. Instead of the individual who searches, Google has to first see the collective and its social relations, which it can read to judge what search results to deliver. From this point of view, a search question is the last point of a search enquiry; it is what leads up to the delivery of certain results in a certain order that determines whether a search engine will be good or bad. This also highlights a recurrent frustration in trying to follow digital economic practices, as the algorithms and programs that fuel search engines are generally industry (or government) secrets. In the case of Google, however, the broad principles are known because its theoretical foundation, the PageRank algorithm, is publicly available (Page et al. 1999).

PageRank was the first method Google used to generate search results and was the basis of its early success, on which everything else depended. The fundamental insight was that the World Wide Web could be read through techniques modelled on academic citation practices. Citations are a means of judging how important an article is by measuring how many people cite that article in later papers; it is in this sense a 'backlink' because the links, here in the form of citations, appear after the article is published. To read the World Wide Web in this way, Google's founders Larry Page and Sergey Brin developed a model that treats the links from one website to another as a backlink similar to an academic citation and then judges the importance of a site in relation to a particular subject by the number of backlinks. Further, they created a recursion through which, having worked out what sites were important on a particular topic (by reading the numbers of links to that site), they could weight those sites more heavily. This meant

23

that their model generated complexity, as many links from unimportant sites might be balanced by a site having only a few links if those few links came from important sites (Page et al. 1999).

To fully grasp the significance of this use of the World Wide Web we need to remember that what Google were (and are) reading through PageRank is a collectively created store of information to which anyone with access to the internet can add on topics of their choosing, including linking as website creators feel is appropriate. The WWW is created by following a set of formal standards that define how you have to form information and load it on a networked computer for it to be visible to other sites (as will be discussed further in Chapter 5). Once a website is visible other sites can link to that site just as anyone can link to their sites. The standards were released to be freely available and are maintained by a not-for-profit consortium. Much of the content that was created was done so freely by ordinary users with internet access and computing resources, though over time corporate and government sites run by paid employees have played a greater role. The WWW is then a collective creation formed of a series of groups that link to each other because they choose to do so in order to ensure that relevant information is connected and available. Although it was heavily commercialised once it became popular, the WWW preceded the birth of Google, and remains a space in which groups of people with similar interests can generate and share information resources (Berners-Lee 2000; Gillies and Cailliau 2000).

PageRank was a means of reading these linked groups and their social relations. Once PageRank had read, for example, sites devoted to surfing it had evidence of the most important sites based on those who loved surfing and had created sites on the subject, including what those people thought were the most important sites and topics. This was the key work done in the initial Google search engine which can be drawn on when someone makes a surf-related search query. In this sense, any search query comes last in the practices of answering it, after the work has been done to read the relevant topics represented on the WWW.

The PageRank algorithm did not, however, last long in its original form. As Google gained a reputation as a good search engine and traffic to it began to increase, it became possible to raise a site up the search rankings by adding fake links to it. Large farms of sites which did nothing but try to game Google's rankings by faking links appeared in the first rounds of the then emerging and now never-ending struggle between Google's attempts to deliver the search results it deems best and the attempts of individual sites to ensure they are returned as high as possible in the results. As one information expert in search put it: 'there's definitely a kind of, ah, a kind of a war going on between the search engine and the marketers, marketers are pressuring the search engines to be more crafty, more authentic in how they rank' (cited in Mager 2012: 777). Google then has to commit considerable labour to constantly monitoring and then upgrading its search mechanisms, which then feeds through to changes in advertising. This leads to the second set of practices necessary to understand Google search, which involves the elaboration of the original algorithm with more algorithms (Hillis et al. 2012).

One of the best-known early additions to PageRank was the Random Surfer Model, which injected, as its name implies, randomness by assuming that at certain points anyone following web links would randomly jump to some other link. Further improvements were made, some in response to attempts to game the system and others to improve search results. For example, the Hilltop algorithm aims to divide the Web up into thematic sections and then judge if a site has links to it from experts who are not connected to that site. If many independent experts link to the site, then it is deemed an authority in its thematic area and can be used to judge the importance of other sites. Hilltop thus builds on citation practices while developing them in a specific direction. This algorithm was initially developed independently of Google and was bought by them to be integrated into its own set of tools. There are no doubt many other adjustments and wholly new algorithms integrated into PageRank and because of trade secrecy there will be more than we know about. But these examples are enough to establish the basic principle that, however it is implemented, Google's successful search – successful both in terms of delivering useful results and in terms of popularity – derives from reading the creations of the pre-existing community of the World Wide Web (Turrow 2011: 64–8; Vaidhyanathan 2012: 60–4; Hillis et al. 2012).

The second key area of search development was opened up by Google only after the first algorithms for reading the WWW proved successful. This second area was that of personalisation, which only became possible once Google became big enough to start collecting significant datasets on those using its search engine. Exploring these datasets enabled the targeting of search results, with different users receiving different search results. This is particularly the case if the searcher uses other Google services, such as Gmail, and has a Google account. Personalisation appears to many to be the process whereby Google judges whether a searcher who uses a term like 'surf' is interested in surfing on water, musical channels, or the Web and so on. It also seems to identify users individually, each having a certain age, location, gender, race and so on, bringing users the results that are judged appropriate to their demographics. However, reading personalisation in this way is to read it from the point of view of the user's practices rather than Google's. For the latter, the key is not so much each individual but the correlations between many individuals; it is the inter-relations that are key to producing a useful result for an individual, not the other way around. This is because the inference has to be constantly made that if many individuals of a certain type favour a particular search result then this can be delivered to individuals who fit that type. It is these kinds of mass correlations that allow for the targeting of particular groups of people – assuming, for example, that men of a particular age group might prefer the Burt Reynolds version of the film *The Longest Yard*, whereas those from a younger age group might be looking for the Adam Sandler remake with the same name, and those of a different nationality may be interested in the Vinnie Jones-led soccer version called *The Mean Machine* (Feuz et al. 2011; Hillis et al. 2012).

Personalisation achieved by building correlations between categories, or profiling as it is sometimes known, is a second way to mine social relations to create Google search (Elmer 2004). The results delivered to individuals are partially based on correlations which are meant to mathematically capture what social and cultural life means. This is not a totalising analysis which posits one set of internally consistent social dynamics, but a tracing or mapping of whatever social relations can be found from analysing the data Google collects. In this way, Google's practices of delivering search results and generating data on which ads can be based include various ways algorithms can read the relations between people.

Starting with the social relations that can be read from the structure of the WWW, Google search then progresses through various means of manipulating and extending that reading. Once enough data has been collected, it can progress to reading the kinds of correlations that measure social relations, which may then be used to personalise search results. Google search practices intertwine different kinds of people, algorithms, datasets and constant updating and storing processes to deliver an answer to a question. These algorithmic logics, that are interweaving different kinds of actors in people, software, data, hardware and so on, must continue to deliver a successful search engine, but they must also conform to the corporate logics Google has embraced as a for-profit company.

For example, one of Google's initial problems in profiting financially from its search engine was how to generate trust in its very different way of selling advertisements (Auletta 2011: 3–6). As already mentioned, Google runs automated auctions to allocate search words. From the advertiser's point of view, this is about connecting their ad with the best search query or term on the best site, while for Google it is about balancing income with advertiser trust and ease of use. These interests are resolved in the specific auction practice in which the winner does not pay what they bid but only a small amount more than the second-placed bid. While this is usually less than Google might have earned, the process has the advantage of building long-term trust with advertisers. At the same time, the process removes the advertiser's interest in bidding lower than they might otherwise due to worries about over-bidding (Levy 2011: 89–91). Here is a specific kind of practice, again automated through algorithms and networks, that mediates the search result into an advertising program that generates revenue for Google and, possibly, for the advertiser. But search had to come first: the value of Google had to be established by the practices of creating a functioning, free and attractive search engine, so that practices could then be generated connecting the value of search to the value of money.

The corporate logics of revenue and profit have to be implemented after the practices of search as value, but these logics also find that the practices of creating search can themselves be translated into and reused as practices of revenue and profit. In particular, the processes of personalisation can develop closely with those of profits derived from advertising, because in both the issue is one of using datasets to generate ways of grouping users together. The same clues that allow personalisation can be moulded to deliver targeted advertising. These Google practices consist of translating both advertiser trust and dollars through the prism of profiling users, similar to personalisation. This is not to say that personalisation and targeted advertising are exactly the same processes, only that they draw on the same idea that correlations and profiling can be generated from Google's vast datasets of its users' behaviour (Hillis et al. 2012). In this way, Google's algorithmic and corporate logics intertwine.

Essential to Google's practices is a set of algorithms that distributes ads, according to words won at auction, onto its own or other websites. It should be particularly noted that Google has access to recursions within its data, recursion being the process of creating infinite information by returning the results of an information process to itself: when the output serves as input to create a different output then information may increase exponentially and infinitely (Jordan 2015: 29–44). Here we catch sight of a corporate reason for the mass information storage and processing, because a core recursion involves using the information collected to refine searching and so to refine the delivery of advertisements. In this sense, Google's advertising practices are essentially a recursion of some of their search practices, particularly personalisation, but with the information being delivered in the form of advertisements rather than as answers to search queries. While we know this, the nature and specificity of these practices are obfuscated as a trade secret, leading to the 'Search Engine Optimisation' industry, which seeks to find ways to improve clients' ranking in search engine results by analysing and manipulating their secret algorithms (Havalais 2009).

The obfuscation of algorithms and networks will be a repeated issue when analysing digital economic practices, but it should not be over-emphasised. As demonstrated above, while we cannot follow the details, we can follow the nature of the practices that create search, partly because we know what users, in this case searchers or advertisers, are doing, and because we know the nature of what the company is doing. Closer work would have value, but in defining digital economic practices generally, or Google's practices specifically, the level of detail that is available is more than adequate.

With this analysis of Google's economic practices, we have thoroughly examined a leading example of digital economic practice in which the searcher, the advertiser, the advertising site and Google itself each have different practices that intersect to create the overall practice. At its core, we see that while the money comes from advertising, this revenue is dependent on prior search processes. Advertising is then second both temporally – the search engine has to first be established to attract users, whom the company can then use to attract advertisers – and existentially, in the sense that without a successful search engine advertising is irrelevant since no company will survive for very long. Once Google had learned how to read the community of the WWW and ally this to the data flow derived from its searchers, it could then make the profitable leap to advertising, while still offering its core 'value' of search as a free service. At Google, the addition of monetisation is materialised in new practices of analysing users, as well as in auctions, money transfers and bookkeeping. Fundamentally, Google's digital economic practice is based on its ability to read a community and then pass that reading through recursions that both identify better search results and deliver targeted advertising.

Search as an Economic Practice

If Google is not the only search company, and not the only digital economy company, then is this understanding of its economic practices being dependent on and deriving their primary value from communities, groups or collectives specific to Google or to search companies? In relation to digital economic practices generally, subsequent chapters will examine cases other than search in order to both complicate and confirm how far Google is an exemplar of more general practices. But here it will be worth looking briefly at a number of other search engines.

Bing is the next in line for the most search queries in many parts of the world, with around 10 per cent of all search queries worldwide, though this varies according to region, from around 30 per cent in North America to 3 per cent in the Asia Pacific (Statista 2017). Bing is different to Google in a number of ways, though it retains the element of reading the World Wide Web, with somewhat different strategies for achieving a good read. Primarily, Bing aims to be a semantic search engine by building rankings related to keywords. Once a complex set of rankings is created it is supplemented with a measurement of links to deliver an answer to a query. While not a great deal of detail is available, it seems Bing's keyword table is generated by looking at the nature of websites and how many links there are to their semantic content, creating a hierarchy based on a particular kind of web linking. Indicative of this is Bing's advice to websites about how to make themselves more visible to its search, which includes providing clear and discrete keywords that are strongly related to the site's content (Moffit 2014). Though implemented differently, Bing maintains a strategy of reading the WWW. Once read through keywords the semantic content is supplemented with further backlink searches, not entirely unlike Google's processes, to generate answers to search queries. Bing notably uses this system to provide search that takes on non-text content, attempting to provide effective search results for images, video, sound and so on.

Bing's monetisation broadly follows the targeted advertising model. It uses its search abilities to feed advertisements related to the content of a search. Again, while advertising appears to be the primary economic practice, it is so only in terms of generating income, with the full economic practice relying on the reading of the WWW and its various commercial and community networks. Microsoft's early 2018 financial report established that Bing revenue rose by 15 per cent in 2017 to a total of $1.8 billion (Javed 2018). While a significant income, available figures make it hard to judge if Bing is profitable or a loss-leader that Microsoft is subsidising out of the profits made from commodities like its operating system and Office software.

Another major search engine is Baidu, which in 2017 had around 70 per cent of all searches in China, though only around 1 per cent of searches worldwide (CIW Team 2017). One of Baidu's founders, Robin Li, had a similar idea to Page and Brin's of basing search on an academic-citation-like search of WWW links. Li first worked on this idea with a few companies in the United States, but these efforts led nowhere. He returned to his native China to start a number of ventures, eventually setting up Baidu as a search engine (Levy 2011: 24–6). After an initial period of development, Baidu had to compete with Google in China during its establishment (later

Google withdrew from a China-based search engine, though access to it can still be gained through virtual private networks and other cloaking devices[2]). While the details remain secret, it is likely Baidu used a similar overall strategy to Google in reading the WWW through backlinks, though it also used its knowledge of China's languages to develop searches more useful to Chinese users (Fung 2008: 145–7).

To establish itself in competition with Google, Baidu had to ensure it generated enough traffic to achieve the secondary recursions of data needed to supplement the reading of the WWW. It also had to achieve sufficient traffic to gain enough advertising to gain enough income to, in turn, gain enough investment (and then profit) to grow. While this appeared uncertain for some time, Baidu adopted a tactic not available to Google by providing listings of mp3 music files, many of which were pirated. With some implicit protection both from China's then lax approach to protecting Western copyright claims, and from the Chinese government, who may well have been seeking a Chinese search engine, Baidu was able to build up a significant following in China (Fung 2008: 145–7; So and Westland 2010: 41–59). After Google withdrew from the country entirely, Baidu's dominance was secured.

Monetisation proceeds similarly on Baidu as it does on Google and Bing, through selling keywords that lead to targeted advertising driven by a reading of the WWW community and the records of searchers, but with a focus on China and South-East Asia. One notable difference is that at times Baidu has mixed paid-for advertising with 'normal' search results. This can lead to it being difficult to tell whether a search result is paid for or not. Similar issues have appeared on Google and other search engines, raising the key issue of trust. As we have seen, Google's strategy has been to mark and separate out paid-for search results, whereas Baidu has succeeded with a more obscure presentation; but within their practices each search engine has to manage the trust of its users in their search results (So and Westland 2010: 55).

There are a range of other search engines, some with specialist purposes. For example, DuckDuckGo aims to protect privacy. It does not follow users and their searches to record them and build a profile of use. To answer a search query it primarily acts as an aggregator, building on over 400 other existing forms of answering online queries. These 400 sites include many wikis and other collections of data (such as game Digimon's wiki, many 'cheatsheet' sites, and sports sites, for example using Sportsradar for some game scores). The major search engines Bing, Yahoo and Yandex are also mixed in among the 400 sources. Though little is known of how it works, DuckDuckGo states that it has its own web crawler that automatically searches the Web collecting links and information on which to base search results (DuckDuckGo 2018). Monetisation is achieved through perhaps the simplest form of targeting, as explained by DuckDuckGo founder and CEO Gabriel Weinberg: 'If you type in "car" you get a car ad, if you type in "mortgage" you get a mortgage ad ... We don't need to know about you or your search history to deliver a lucrative ad' (cited in Burgess and Woollaston 2017). These ads are drawn from the Bing and Yahoo Search Alliance.

DuckDuckGo represents a minimum in reading a community, but it still has to do some reading to generate its results, both through its own crawler and by relying on community-created resources in its 400 sources and on the readings Bing, Yahoo and Yandex make of the WWW. Stripping money to its barebones of connecting a search term to an advertisement makes clear the fundamental relationship: search first, ads second. DuckDuckGo does not involve the complexities of Google, Bing or Baidu, but strips search back to serve a specific ethical purpose, emphasising that along with community and trust, digital economic practices raise issues of privacy.

Community, Trust and Privacy

Search engine corporations have connected two distinct practices in search and advertising. Search existed before digital advertising practices (though, of course, not before advertising) and could exist without them; search was the magnet to be subsequently monetised. As we have seen throughout this chapter, search is based on automated readings of communities and collectives allied to further exploration of sociality among searchers once enough users have been attracted whose behaviour can be recorded. Advertising is then reliant on the search.

This also reflects a wider societal change that Turrow has called the transformation of the advertising industry into a surveillance industry (2011: 1–12). Other monetisation practices are possible, such as subscription sites, which we will return to when looking at other digital economic practices, whose difficulties Turrow tracks (2011: 41–2). But in the case of search we have seen that the overwhelmingly successful digital economic practice is to ally surveillance – in the sense of 'reading' the WWW and data on searchers – to the monetisation of targeted ads. Three terms are then pushing their way to the fore in these digital economic practices: community, trust and privacy. In conclusion, it is worth highlighting these more explicitly, as part of an abstract diagram of search as a digital economic practice to be further developed with other case studies.

A search engine has to create answers to questions and deliver them in micro-seconds. It has to have something to 'read' to inform its answers, and in the majority of cases this consists of two target populations. One is those who create the World Wide Web and particularly the chance this offers to explore the sub-groups within it; the other is consequent on the first and largely consists of those who search the Web, whose activities on their travels are recorded and correlated, using data analysis to 'read' these journeys. This reading then informs both the search results and who is targeted with which ads. 'Community' is often a hard to define and awkward to use word, implying much and delivering little, but in the context of search as a digital economic practice it can refer to these two sources that search engines rely on to generate information. The meaning of community in other digital economic practices will be further explored in subsequent case studies.

A search engine needs trust. The comparison of Baidu and Google on paying for search results to be integrated among the 'purer' results bring this issue to the fore. If a searcher does not trust a search engine to deliver at least reasonable results, then the use of the engine comes into question. This is exacerbated by the obscurity of search processes, particularly in relation to key algorithms remaining jealously guarded trade secrets. The existence of DuckDuckGo – along with Mojeek, which has a similar ethical stance on searching and privacy – points to a growing understanding of the importance of trust.

Privacy should perhaps be understood as 'privacy and surveillance', for the 'reading' of communities in their two dimensions creates detailed maps of individuals' preferences, all the better to deliver advertisements. Google has sometimes claimed that it is not in the advertising business but sees advertisements as knowledge and that it simply wishes to deliver better knowledge to its users, in line with its mission statement 'to organize the world's information and make it universally accessible and useful'. Yet its search results, like those of other search engines, come at a cost which threatens trust, not so much in terms of their accuracy, but by their breaching of privacy, which becomes obvious when ads are targeted at users who can hardly miss the way Mickey Mouse or beach holidays follow them around the WWW. To fuel search as a free service, communities have to give up information on their social relations, and to refine the search, individuals have to give up data about themselves in order to be profiled – to be identified as the same as or different from other individuals. All this raises issues of privacy and of how search engines manage to retain trust.

Following the digital economic practice of search through three different perspectives – users, advertisers and search engine companies – has offered a clear view of what is probably the greatest money-gushing land grab, oil boom and gold rush of the twenty-first century: reading communities to target ads. The billions of dollars in profit are evidence of this. Behind this practice lies the intersection of three dynamics – community, trust and privacy/surveillance – that together make up an abstract diagram of the digital economic practice of search. But this is only one such practice, and further examples will help complicate and extend our understanding of the digital economy.

3   Social Media: The Industry of Beauty, Wonder and Grief

> To experience beauty, wonder, or grief, we have to open ourselves to something happening to us ... This is ... how we become a self that can be open to the experience of the other. (McDonald 2006: 218)

Facebook, Instagram, Snapchat, Twitter, Weibo, Tumblr, Myspace, Google+, Orkut: the tags tumble out when naming social media. Yet across all these different platforms – and they have major differences in how they function and what can and cannot be done on them – what makes them a common phenomenon called social media? Further, is there an economic practice that they all share? In this chapter we will explore the digital economic practices of social media that have become both central to our social lives and, sometimes, the source of profit. There is already a considerable body of work on social media to draw on, which can be used to answer the first question. One early definition provides a useful frame for analysis:

> We define social network sites as web-based services that allow individuals to (1) construct a public or semi-public profile within a bounded system, (2) articulate a list of other users with whom they share a connection, and (3) view and traverse their list of connections and those made by others within the system. The nature and nomenclature of these connections may vary from site to site. (boyd and Ellison 2007)

Such a definition helps link different kinds of services, from Snapchat's time-limited photos to Instagram's curated photo collections, to random photos on Facebook and so on. This definition was developed by exploring what kind of selves and publics occur in such social network contexts. Papacharissi drew together considerable work on social media to argue that activities on social media 'expand the expressive equipment at hand, possibly allowing greater control of the distance between the front and backstage areas of the self; what is presented and that which is reserved' (2011: 307). In this account, complex versions of the self are immediately connected to publics that emerge in the same spaces; boyd calls these networked publics, and suggests they are characterised by invisible audiences, context collapse and the blurring of public and private (2011: 49). The audiences are invisible because on a social network it is never entirely clear who receives what messages. Context collapse occurs because audiences that might have been kept separate, such as family and work colleagues, can often see the same messages. And a blurring of public and private occurs in which it is unclear what particular divide of public and private is in operation, with what seem like private messages appearing more publicly, and vice versa.

If these are the practices of the self on social media, then the economies of such sites have also not gone unnoticed. While there is excellent work on sociality and social media, including that of boyd and Papacharissi, along with a significant number of others like Baym, Marwick and more, there have also been analyses of the political economies of social media by Dean (2012), Coté and Pybus (2007), Stark (2009) and Fuchs (2014) (see Jordan 2015: 120–39). The work on both the sociality and the political economy of social media suggests that social media are based on digital platforms through which the interactions between users can be pulled together as information, akin to how the data on searchers is correlated by search engine platforms. This information can then be used to target users for advertising purposes, or the lure of the platform can be used to create a subscription model where access has to be paid for. Pulling these threads together, I have previously argued that we should understand social media as a combination of, on the one hand, linked dynamics for creating public and private divides and, on the other, information enclosures that yield significant data about people's sociality to the owner of the platform which can then be used for monetisation (Jordan 2015: 120–39). While this summary suggests that much can be understood from existing work about what happens on social media and how it generates (or not) social relations, the economic aspects of social media have usually been analysed in relatively general terms. Here we will explore the digital economy of social media in more detail by analysing its economic practices.

Facebook

In analysing search I focused on Google because of its dominant role in creating a successful monetisation strategy by linking community, profiling and advertisement. In the early twenty-first century in social media, Facebook is a similarly dominant company in many parts of the world. In its full year report for 2017, Facebook reported 2.13 billion users were active worldwide at least once a month (up 14 per cent from the previous year) (Facebook 2018). For comparison, in the same year, YouTube (owned by Google parent company Alphabet Inc.) reported 1.5 billion logged-in users (Matney 2017), WhatsApp (the messaging service owned by Facebook) 1.5 billion users (Constine 2018), Twitter 330 million monthly active users (@twitterir 2018), and Snapchat 187 million daily active users (Snap 2018). Of course, these are not mutually exclusive results, as individual users might be active across all these different platforms. Yet, of them all, Facebook is the largest.

Facebook also follows Google in having worked out a form of monetisation that brings enormous profits. In 2017 its total net income was $15.9 billion, up 56 per cent from its 2016 mark of $10.2 billion (Facebook 2018[1]). Again similar to Google, Facebook gained the majority of its revenue from advertising. In 2017 it reported revenues of $39.9 billion from advertising and $0.7 billion from 'payments and other fees', meaning that an extraordinary 98 per cent of revenue came from advertising (Facebook 2018).

I will begin by looking at the digital economic practices of the dominant company (though the similarities between Facebook and Google in their monetisation strategies are similar enough that some of the earlier discussion of search can be relied on), before going on to examine other social media sites. Again, the economic practices involved will be split into three types: those of the user, the advertiser and the platform. Having noted how dependent Facebook is on a similar model of monetisation to Google, here I will start with the platform, then look at the advertiser, and finally consider the user, whose practices are quite distinct from those of Google users.

From Facebook's point of view, the data collected on users is marshalled to create a means of matching advertisements to users. Facebook collects a great deal of data on its users' age, location, gender and so on. With over 2 billion users, there is an enormous amount of data that Facebook can access to profile its users and match these profiles to appropriate ads. The algorithmic heart of Facebook's monetisation process lies in this relentless collection of ever more data and then the recursion of that data so that it grows into an ever more complex analytics of Facebook users. It is useful for Facebook to know one person well, but it is far more useful for it to know the interactions between people and their characteristics and what this indicates about their preferences, because that underpins profiling and targeting. Facebook's advertising policy was initially puzzling to many, enough so that a number of mocking websites grew up collecting screenshots of its failed ad targeting. But as the company developed it improved the data it used to match adverts to individuals, in the process establishing advertising as its main source of income. 'The Facebook advertising engine lets any buyer choose individuals by exact age (or age range), geographical location, gender, relationship (single, engaged, in a relationship, married), and education level (college graduate, college student, high school student)' (Turrow 2011: 145–6).

Facebook controls and has to decide how ads will appear. Some advertiser unhappiness has been articulated with advertisers arguing that the rather small boxlike ads on the side of a user's page are difficult to be creative with. However, Facebook also has to take the user experience into account, considering to what extent the placing of ads might alienate its users' sense of community or sociality. Rather like Google protecting the validity of its search results, Facebook has to protect the validity of its users' experiences, even if in doing so they have to deliver a different ad service than advertisers might want. Protecting that experience extends to curation of Facebook's content, which is done with significant amounts of human labour in addition to algorithmic labour. Gillespie (2018) tracks what he calls the difficult job of moderation and the affectively intense and often poorly paid labour that Facebook relies on to manage users' experiences. This will remain a fluid situation though with Facebook increasingly pressured to undermine their own feed of stories to a user's home page with more intrusive, particularly video, ads.

A second approach Facebook adopts is to encourage companies to set up their own Facebook page. This also allows actors, musicians and so on to present themselves to a public by creating a Facebook persona that is in itself a kind of advertisement. Similarly, companies can set up campaigns and create opportunities by curating their own Facebook image. All this provides valuable data; for example, knowing what kind of person might visit or friend a particular individual's or product's Facebook page starts to provide valuable evidence for who else should be sent ads related to that kind of individual or company. In this context, Facebook allows payments to boost posts so that they become more visible but are not ads that appear on the side of the user's home page. This provides an alternative ad revenue stream for Facebook and a way for businesses to build a profile by paying for greater attention.

Within these strategies Facebook has to make judgements not only about what kinds of ads it will allow and where, but also how to price them. Here is where Facebook's set of economic practices start to mesh with advertisers' practices. The options Facebook gives for ads must be attractive to advertisers, even if the platform holds the power as a place advertisers feel they have to come to. While Facebook determines ad sizes and placements it also, again like Google, offers extensive analytics about how ads are performing. These analytics face in two directions as they allow Facebook to adjust pricing to reflect effectiveness (itself measured in different ways, such as click per view and so on), as well as providing information for advertisers.

The complexities involved in such profiling and measuring are large, yet for the platform owner they reduce to the same economic practice of providing various forms of data back to the advertiser. This data may facilitate simple tracking of ads and clicks or may develop into support for broader campaigns to build a brand or boost a specific event or product launch. Facebook offers an interface called 'Ad Manager' which integrates both the choice of the audience for an ad and the keywords needed to trigger it, all the way through to feedback on how effective the ads have been, which in turn will feed into further iterations of the ad. These devices build on Facebook's ability to see and collect data not only on its users and ads but also on the relationship between advertisers and their ad campaigns. This puts Facebook in a strong position in relation to both its users and its paying advertisers as it can collect and analyse their behaviour. An important element in any platform owner's relationship to their users and anyone paying for their services is that the relationship is asymmetrical in information. There is no essential reason why platform owners cannot retain all the information on their platform, but, likewise, no reason why they cannot release that information to all users and service-payers. The asymmetry is about control and the choices a platform makes about what it does and does not share. A core economic practice of Facebook is the way it shares some information with advertisers about how their advertisements are performing, and some research about trends, but does not do this for users.

The final economic practice from the perspective of the platform concerns how advertising space is sold through Ad Manager. Facebook requests a 'bid' from an advertiser, which will define what their goal is, their audience, what placement is required, the timeline and what the advertiser is willing to pay. Through an algorithmically obfuscated process, these bids are then run through an auction to determine whose ad will be shown. Here Facebook is not just auctioning keywords but, through analysis of its data, working out which ad is most likely to succeed and which viewers are most likely to view the ad. Like Google, Facebook reassures advertisers because, in its own words, 'The amount you get charged is the minimum amount we would've needed to set your bid at to win the auction' (Facebook Business 2018).

Turning to advertisers' practices it is obvious that in general these mirror those of Google's advertisers, but in detail conform to Facebook's requirements. Here is something that extends the discussion of advertisers in relation to both Google and Facebook. In both cases, advertisers must seek to understand what the platform they are facing demands. The advertiser, and in Facebook's case also the client seeking promotion of their posts, must examine closely the requirements and workings of the platform they are using, but can only do so in two ways. The first is with the resources that the platform provides, while it is of mutual interest for client-advertiser and platform for there to be successful advertisements, the definition of success is different. For the advertiser success is selling more products, building the brand and so on, it is the interest of whoever is ultimately paying for the advertisement. For the platform it is to deliver success to the advertiser balanced with not undermining too much a sense of trust or authenticity of experience in the platform – be it social media or search – thereby balancing the long-term validity of the platform for users against successful advertising that satisfies advertisers and brings income. The balance of control in these differing but connected interests depends greatly on the health of the platform – health both in terms of the 'value' it delivers, be that search results, social relations or other, and the platform's financial health – as the stronger the platform is then the weaker the position of the client-advertiser becomes, because the platform controls what the client can do and how the client can measure its own success.

The second way a client-advertiser can manage its engagement is by seeking help from a range of 'experts' who work to manipulate the platform. This may or may not be successful and is a choice each paying advertiser-client has to make, including whether to develop in-house expertise or to hire in external help. Again, this is somewhat skewed as whatever expertise is used can in turn be manipulated by the platform as it seeks to maintain its own twin interests of generating income and maintaining the value of the platform to the user. These dynamics of control are shared between the practices of search and of Facebook so far explored, and so have been discussed in terms of such platforms more generally.

We can leave the client-advertiser here, struggling with an ad manager, trying to work out what a 'campaign' or 'brand building' is in Facebook's terms versus simply defining a demographic for their ads to be delivered to, and wondering, probably depending on the scale of the advertiser, whether to hire in staff to manage such things or to hire in some external help. The practices at their minutest level will be specific to each particular social media, yet they will pose eerily similar problems because, as is emerging, they are subject to similar economic practices that involve linking the value of the platform to the user to the ability of the platform to analyse the data it collects based on the activities of its users, while also providing a monetisation interface that mediates advertising value to various paying clients. This brings us to the user of Facebook, and here the everyday practices diverge significantly from those in search.

Facebook attempts to offer a platform on which people can express and develop their personal identity and community. Its mission statement for a long time was 'making the world more open and connected', although this was changed in 2017 to 'Give people the power to build community and bring the world closer together' (Constine 2017). The change is interesting because it revealed a prior assumption that connecting people would benefit communities. By 2018, however, the evidence suggested that this was not necessarily happening, as Facebook's role as a platform for trolling, alt-right politics and hate speech gained attention. Facebook CEO Mark Zuckerberg said of this change that:

> We have a responsibility to do more, not just to connect the world but to bring the world closer together ... We want to help 1 billion people join meaningful communities. If we can do this it will not only reverse the whole decline in community membership we've seen around the world ... but it will also strengthen our social fabric and bring the world closer together. (Cited in Constine 2017)

Explicitly discussed by Facebook senior staff in the context of this change was a recognition of the potentially alienating effects of liking, scrolling and posting on Facebook instead of engaging in 'real' and 'authentic' relationships. However well or poorly it is implemented, there is a conception of identity and community here that fuels Facebook's ambition, alongside other fuels such as avarice and competitiveness. To quote Zuckerberg again: 'You have one identity. The days of you having a different image for your work friends or co-workers and for the other people you know are probably coming to an end pretty quickly. Having two identities for yourself is an example of a lack of integrity' (Kirkpatrick 2010: 199; Kant 2015). Here Zuckerberg articulates a moral imperative behind context collapse: those moments on social media when the contexts – family, work, video-gaming friends, sports friends, etc. – come together, meaning that the various identities that people have cannot be presented sequentially to different groups but have to be viewed simultaneously (boyd and Marwick 2010: 122–3). How are these versions of community and identity practised by Facebook's users?

Facebook's attempt to create a platform that enables people to form communities and morally correct identities means users are confronted with a wide range of activities that they can pattern into practices. As of 2018, the Facebook user's home page, when viewed on a computer, consists of a horizontal top strip with three vertical panels below. The top strip allows users to switch to different types of interfaces and access drop-down menus for things like notifications, friend invites and settings management. The left vertical panel has a plethora of links to things like a news feed, Facebook's instant messenger, a marketplace for users to buy and sell items, as well as links to photos, videos and so on. The middle panel shows a series of posts, each consisting of text, images and replies to the original post, that appear at the top and move down; these can be ones the user has posted, ones that a friend of the user (and depending on settings a 'friend of a friend') posted or are 'suggested posts', which often seem indistinguishable from ads though they are presented as a post from a Facebook account. The right panel offers suggested pages and a number of ads (tagged as 'sponsored') in small boxes. On the far right is a panel for Facebook's instant messaging application, called Messenger, which allows sending of text messages to individuals or groups. If a user opens Facebook on a mobile phone pretty much the same things are accessible, though split up and having to move between each of the panels, and in the case of Messenger moving to a different app.

A user is then presented with all manner of things they can do in order to connect with others, and develop both their identity through what they 'do' and their community through the connections they make. Text, photos and videos can be posted. Comments can be made on one's own and on other people's posts. People can be sent requests to be 'friends', which results in users seeing each other's posts, unless one or other blocks posts or defriends someone. Groups may be formed which show posts to some people only. Facebook also integrates other ideas as they appear. For example, when Snapchat started to become popular, Facebook (after attempting to buy Snapchat) produced a rather similar application called Poke which allowed users to send time-limited photos or videos to people in their friends list (B. Gallagher 2018: 82–8). (This kind of poke confusingly crosses over with Facebook 'poking', which has varied at times but has usually meant sending a quick message to someone simply saying you have 'poked' them.) Practices within Facebook all build relations to other Facebook users, through these moments the user creates their own Facebook identity as well as the sense of community or sociality that they have on Facebook. The individual activities within Facebook, like friending, posting photos and poking, tend to coalesce into particular patterns. These patterns may also move across different social media. For example, 'friending' pre-existed Facebook on earlier platforms like Friendster, but, as boyd argues, it must be interpreted in relation both to each social media context and to how that context builds on and affects friendship outside of social media (boyd 2006; Papacharissi 2011).

The economic practices of Facebook users take the form of building a Facebook identity and Facebook social relations. They are 'Facebook identity and social relations' not because they are directed by Facebook but because they exist within its platform. Such identities and social relations then extend into other media, including other social media, and all other contexts in which identities and social relations are created. The ads, promoted posts and corporate identities that make the monetisation of Facebook possible are entirely intertwined with the establishment of Facebook identities and socialities. The value of this platform lies in its users' identities and socialities, and it is the reading of these that enables its monetisation through profiling and ads. This is a very similar moneti-sation strategy to that of Google and other search engines, even though the 'value', that is, the activities people come to Facebook to undertake, is very different.

Facebook is one way to experience an opening to the other, in a way that McDonald (2006) describes as not a subordination to the other but a subjectivation in an opening to the experience of the other. Facebook's monetisation is the monetisation of this fundamental experience of being-with and becoming-with others, in what Haraway calls the 'contact zones and unruly edges' (2008: 367–8, fn 28) through which all manner of encounters between humans, animals, machines and others take place. Facebook is truly an industry of beauty, wonder and grief.

The Industry of Beauty, Wonder and Grief

What of other social media? Do they too follow the same path as Facebook in extensively recording the activities of users, followed by a 'reading' of these activities as a basis for monetisation? I will look briefly at several other social media sites to see what we might find; how complex is the industry of beauty, wonder and grief?

The social media network WeChat had just over 1 billion monthly active users in 2018, making it the third or fourth largest such network worldwide. It had a major concentration in China; in 2016, 90 per cent of its accounts were based there, and in 2017 over 90 per cent of smartphones in China included the WeChat app (Hollander 2018; Beaver 2016). It is interesting to compare WeChat to Facebook particularly in three aspects of its practices that constitute it: growth of features, state support, and integration into finance.

WeChat users' practices contrast with those of Facebook users in that WeChat grew from being a messaging service, like WhatsApp or Facebook Messenger, into a more fully fledged social media network. The practices of its users have then changed and become more complicated in a different way to those on Facebook, which, while it has also extended its features, presented itself from the start as a social media site with multiple resources for users. WeChat started out with text messaging for individuals and groups; video clips were an early addition, and then, within its first two years, as mobile connectivity moved from 2G to 3G and so on increasing speed, video messaging and voice calls were added, all within the first two years. Emojis and stickers followed, and in a key connection to developing e-commerce WeChat added the ability to read QR codes (Milward 2018). 'Moments' was an important addition turning WeChat from a messaging service with features into being more like a fully fledged social media network, because 'Moments' allowed people who had friended each other to see a feed of updates from their friends using text, images, links and music recommendations and to post 'likes' on each other's feeds. Users reported that the primary content they liked to see on WeChat were 'personal life records' (Brennan 2017; WeChat 2015). Last, and perhaps most interesting, WeChat integrated mobile payments, allowing users to use WeChat to pay for pretty much anything by linking their bank account to the platform. Take up had become widespread in China by early 2017, with nearly half of all WeChat users stating that they carried no cash, though the platform was also in competition with Alibaba's version, Alipay (Brennan 2017).

Alongside all these developments allowing users to create their social life, a range of monetisation tactics involving both advertising and subscriptions were tried. Again, the practices of users and advertisers were mediated by the platform. For example, at times only two ads per day were allowed in a Moments feed, to ensure the ads did not undermine the user's social experience while also providing value for advertisers and income for the platform. WeChat also sells a range of things, primarily games, and offers businesses the ability to set up a presence. Finally, WeChat charges for money transfers between the WeChat app and a credit card or bank account, providing a further income source that is independent of advertisers. This monetary service was also behind the growth of WeChat when it linked this service to the custom in China of giving money in red envelopes (Hongbao) on special occasions, usually around Chinese New Year. WeChat introduced a way of sending money with a visual of a red envelope appearing on the receiver's screen, which proved highly popular (Shu 2015). The financial payment service had become a major practice in China that, as of 2018, remained in development in other parts of the world, where payment systems such as Google Pay and Apple Pay were still trying to establish their product. Western developers will in 2018 have been looking rather enviously at WeChat's prominence, along with Alipay, in this kind of financial practice. The monetisation strategies that providing a financial service offer are not particularly present in most non-Asian social media, but they offer an additional means of monetising communities, one that will be returned to in the next chapter.

While I have not tried to separate out too forcefully the different practices of user, advertiser and platform in examining WeChat, the previous discussions should allow an understanding of its economic practices. However, one aspect of WeChat that is important, and which has been neglected in the discussion of both search and social media so far, is the regulatory and governmental context within which digital platforms exist. For one of WeChat's advantages, similar to that of Baidu, is that it has had government support, as the Chinese authorities have sought to promote the digital economy in China during a period of fast economic growth. At times this has included not just support but also the elimination of rivals – not always just to benefit Chinese companies; Facebook like Google is banned in mainland China (Fung 2008).

China is important in understanding digital economic practices because both WeChat and Baidu make clear that the user/community, advertiser and platform triumvirate needs to be considered in relation to a fourth factor: the different ways in which governments intervene. Banning a competitor is perhaps the clearest and most radical kind of intervention. But Facebook has faced questions about privacy in Europe and the United States, and forms of regulation have come from bodies like the European Union. The Chinese government's relationship to WeChat and its parent company Tencent has, in general, provided a supportive environment. WeChat now has extensive records not only of people's social lives but also their financial lives, so that their likes, posts, pokes and friends can be correlated with where payments have been made. Some worry about this in relation to surveillance, and see a point at which WeChat might become a surrogate identity card system linked to China's attempts to begin directing individuals' behaviour through ranking systems like its social credit scoring system (Botsman 2017). Such an extension is possible because WeChat has become a record of communal life in China and so can be turned back toward the community not only to create sociality but also to create forms of control. The same possibility applies to all social media networks, not just those in China.

Following economic practices allows this analysis to connect these links in the social chain. Digital economic practices focus on the community that a platform has a particular way of reading, and they will have relations to government and other regulatory apparatuses. This is a theme that will be explored further when considering digital economic practices that are built on the disintermediation of regulation, such as car shares like Uber or accommodation sharing like Airbnb or CouchSurfing. For now, we can note how regulatory environments can play an important role, even if they do not seem, so far, to impinge on digital economic practices but connect rather to the way communities are formed, surveilled and manipulated through information platforms.

The case of WeChat shows how Facebook's economic practices, which are themselves similar to Google's, are not restricted to Facebook but involve ways of inter-relating the actions of users, advertisers, sellers and platform owners that are applicable to different kinds of social media networks. The way WeChat grew into being a social media network contrasts with Facebook, even if Facebook also at times added features. To finalise this analysis it is worth exploring one more such network in order to show that the success of these practices is not inevitable. The precarious fate of Snapchat in 2018 exemplifies this, as success and failure were both very much possible.

Snapchat initially offered users just one activity: sending a photograph which, after at most ten seconds, would be lost to both user and sender and was promised to be deleted from Snapchat's servers. Offering a service even simpler than WeChat's original messaging function, Snapchat found an audience for evaporating visual content based on the widespread use of smartphones. Users' practices revolved around the joys and possible provocations of taking quick photographs on a phone and sending them to one or more friends. Often called a sexting application – given the possibilities for sending nude or other erotic images safe in the knowledge that they would quickly disappear (and there is no doubt this was a lure) – the more fundamental attraction of Snapchat for its users seemed to be sending informal and possibly risky photos to friends, which might be sexual but also included taunting, humorous, or trivial moments (taking photos of friends asleep in class was one theme). A community, or series of communities, then coalesced around the enjoyment to be found on Snapchat, at a time when Facebook was expanding to the point of becoming, in a sense, normalised (B. Gallagher 2018: 50–68; Bayer et al. 2016).

Beginning in 2011, by the middle of 2017 Snapchat had 173 million daily active users, having seen a consistent growth rate from the start of 2014 when the figure was 46 million (Dogtiev 2018). The uses of Snapchat altered over time. For example, Snapchat offered various filters that would overlay a location and graphic on a photo or allow a user to alter their photo perhaps with dog ears or be shown vomiting a rainbow. Snapchat developed 'Stories' in which users could connect a series of photos and then share that, allowing a sequence of photos each of which is shown for up to ten seconds to be linked and sent as one 'story' to friends. For example, someone might go to an amusement park and take a photo at the entrance, several photos of rides, maybe some of eating, more rides, meeting a character, fireworks in the evening and then leaving. Stories developed from 'My Stories' into 'Our Stories' in which any user could add photographs (leading to Snapchat becoming a record of, or a way of reporting, breaking events as 'Live Stories'), and 'Custom Stories' in which only users who are friends can collaborate to add photos to a story. These stories modelled the development of 'Discover' channel, in which companies and individuals were offered the opportunity to create stories and ads on Snapchat (B. Gallagher 2018: 106–8, 156–62).

Snapchat floated on the stock market in March 2017, six years after its founding, with a share price that valued the company at $33 billion and which rose 44 per cent on the first day of trading. Since then Snapchat's market valuation has fallen from its first day high of $27.09 per share to a low in early May 2018 of $10.79; a drop of 60 per cent (Google Finance 2018). It reported losses for 2017 of $3.4 billion, up from losses in 2016 of $460 million. However, Snapchat also reported a 104 per cent increase in revenue between 2016 and 2017, from $404 million to $824 million (Snap 2018). Despite generating the users and community that seemed to go with successful monetisation in the other digital economic companies examined so far, Snapchat's financial health was precarious. How do we understand this failure to achieve profitability?

One indication of a difference lies in a statement by Snapchat's co-founder, CEO and all-round figurehead, Evan Spiegel, that while ads were coming to Snapchat he did not want them to be disturbing like those on other social media. In a 2015 interview he said: 'I got an ad this morning for something I was thinking about buying yesterday, and it's really annoying … We care about not being creepy. That's something that's really important to us' (O'Brien 2015). Initially Snapchat introduced such things as short movie trailers to try to generate revenue. It also kept much of its advertising to the 'Discover' channel, which users have to choose to go to, rather than integrating advertisements into their feeds. 'Stories' were also used to provide opportunities for companies to create self-promotional material and brands. Snapchat further explored the possibility of offering users direct purchases, for example of 'lenses' which allowed users to turn themselves into such things as a character in a film. However, as the income from lenses turned out to be significantly less than that from advertising, lenses were integrated into advertising, creating a more interactive kind of advertisement than simply showing pre-set material like a movie trailer, by allowing users new practices that advertisers saw value in – like turning themselves into a Charlie Brown character around the time a Charlie Brown film came out (B. Gallagher 2018: 215–17).

A further divergence was that the 'don't be creepy' approach meant that advertisers on Snapchat were often not given the kind of access to data that had become commonplace on Google and Facebook. Snapchat refused to provide extensive data, starting off with just 'a daily Excel spreadsheet showing metrics like how long users had spent in the publisher's edition and how many views each individual story had gotten' (B. Gallagher 2018: 182). Eventually, under pressure from advertisers but also from investors who wanted to see the company start turning a profit, more information was provided to allow advertisers to track their ads.

Snapchat's struggle to achieve successful monetisation continued into 2018. In March of that year it introduced the first compulsory ads, which ran for six seconds each and could not be refused by users. However, these did not run in the users' feeds and channels but in the 'Discover' section, which has to be chosen by the user. For example, when I tried this channel in early 2018, it presented me with a story made from a number of photographs and short videos that the UK TV personality Phillip Schofield had strung together, during which I received a six-second ad for women's clothing (Rutherford 2018). But I had to choose to go to this channel to see this compulsory ad; users of Snapchat are free to pass it by. Snapchat's monetisation efforts attempt to rework its existing model while protecting the sense of immediacy and humour its staff believe its community is built on. This bias toward protecting its community is such that Snapchat has begun to operate more like a series of small TV channels users may choose to view, rather than engaging in the personal targeting that has proven successful elsewhere. In direct contrast to Zuckerberg's 'one identity' claim, Spiegel has argued that

> Social media businesses represent an aggressive expansion of capitalism into our personal relationships. We are asked to perform for our friends, to create things they like, to work on a 'personal brand' – and brands teach us that authenticity is the result of consistency. We must honour our 'true self' and represent the same self to all of our friends or risk being discredited. But humanity cannot be true or false. We are full of contradictions and we change. That is the joy of human life. We are not brands; it is simply not in our nature. (Cited in B. Gallagher 2018: 203–4)

Spiegel is here both asserting what he thinks makes Snapchat successful and attractive to users and establishing a morality – don't be creepy – that has led Snapchat down a different route to monetisation than that taken by Facebook and WeChat. Even so, it has been pressured into providing some of the 'creepiness' of other platforms, and has yet to prove financially successful. In early 2019, as I write, the story of Snapchat's future success or failure remains uncertain.

Social Media Economic Practices

Snapchat, WeChat and Facebook offer us differences but all work within the practices that emerge between users, advertisers and digital platforms. WeChat further demonstrates that this triple set of interlocking practices must be seen as existing in a regulatory and government context. Both Snapchat and WeChat show that monetisation strategies can be extended to include different kinds of practices than just targeted advertising. There is the possibility of direct purchases, as in Snapchat's filters for photographs, while WeChat's integration of payment services offers another way to channel funds, as the platform can draw a percentage from such exchanges or charge a fee for them. Though I did not emphasise this in the discussion of Facebook, because of the dominance of advertising in its income streams, there are also instances of Facebook selling products, for example with games.

Across all three social media networks, following the practices of users leads quickly to social relations and some sense of a 'community' specific to that platform. As ever, the idea of 'community' is a vague one, indicating sets of interactions that are patterned and that offer a semi-stable social and cultural context. I will not extend the discussion into a theory of what community or social relations might mean in general, as it is more helpful to continue to explore case studies and turn to a more general understanding later. However, we can at this stage extend the idea of user practices into a fuller understanding that these are about the specific kinds of user activities that are part of each social media network. The ephemeral humour-based social relations typical of Snapchat contrast with Facebook's attempt to provide a platform for multiple aspects of social life through a range of activities. These in turn contrast with the way WeChat began as a messenger service and extended gradually into a community of many activities. Users and communities are linked in digital economic practices through activities.

Monetisation through advertising becomes a rather richer and more complex set of practices, particularly when thinking about the half of WeChat users who carry no cash as they rely on WeChat for purchases. In engaging with social media, whether to advertise to sell or to try to build the less concrete notion of a 'brand identity', these economic practitioners have to work with the user-community they find. If the attraction is the number of users – and we may be talking billions – and the ability to identify different kinds of users, then trying to profit from the economic practice of a platform means the advertiser has to conform to the requirements of that platform. It is possible that those bringing their money to a platform might be able to use that power to influence it, but all digital economic practices involve choices and actions that have to balance the interests of monetisation with the value that a platform's activities offer to its users. Even financially underperforming platforms, like Snapchat, are aware that any move that alienates users of a free platform too much may lead to the implosion of the platform. Platform owners are well aware that seriously compromising the experience of the user community could lead to an existential crisis for a digital economy practice.

Each social media network's practices remain broadly the same as those already discussed in relation to search. Offering free activities creates a community and leads to both a dependency on the activities of users and the capacity to capture information about those activities and users. The platform's inherent ability to capture this information can be articulated differently, as Snapchat's 'don't be creepy' ethos suggests. Yet it is this capture of a community that has so far proved existential for a successful digital economic practice in both search and social media: if there is no substantial community to draw on then the platform may as well not exist (as past users of Myspace, Friendster, Google+ or Diaspora may well attest). The network effect of more users creating exponentially more value in the activities on a platform is powerful and explains much of the success a social media network can have in retaining its users, but it is also a threat on a platform where nothing formally stops people from leaving. It also imposes a significant requirement for labour as the network must be managed and grow, and moderation proves difficult to automate. Managing this duality means that social media owners and managers have to maintain their community while also offering something to advertisers and others from whom the platform can draw revenue without fatally compromising its community.

WeChat powerfully demonstrates a further factor by highlighting the regulatory and government context, some form of which all digital economic practices will operate in. Laws, regulations and government agencies have appeared only relatively briefly in relation to the economic practices that have been examined so far. This needs extension and explication. Are governments and courts just a context that do not impinge directly on the economic practices of things like search and social media companies? Or is their relative absence (except in the cases of Baidu and WeChat) a demonstration that search and social media have in some way managed to avoid such agencies and have only had to deal with them after becoming successful? I am not suggesting that Google, Facebook and so on have not encountered governments or courts. Events such as the European Union regulating Google around privacy or the investigation into Facebook in the Cambridge Analytica controversy related to attempts to manipulate voters in the Trump presidential election or the Brexit referendum clearly indicate governments and courts are present. However, regulatory bodies have not been to the fore when the economic practices of users and communities, advertisers and finance and the platform owners and maintainers have been followed. To explore this further, the next chapter will examine a different group of digital economic practices whose very existence is predicated on altering regulatory contexts: those that rely on disintermediation and the removal of existing regulations, as Uber has attempted to do for taxis and Airbnb for hotels.

4   Taxis, Beds, Blockchains and Disintermediation

'Uber' has become, like 'Google', a word indicating not only a company but a whole activity. In Uber's case, that of ordering a paid car ride. 'Airbnb' has not quite made it as a verb, but is in many parts of the world now instantly recognisable as referring to a practice of renting rooms. After search and social media, these two companies offer a third kind of digital economic practice in the removal of previously existing intermediaries within services. This chapter will explore taxis, beds and the blockchain, as all three develop an economic practice of disintermediation.

Disintermediation refers to all the elements intervening in between the process of someone producing an item, like a phone, and the person who uses it. Often a phone is designed, then passed to another company to be manufactured, then passed to another to be sold wholesale (or in large amounts), then passed to another to be sold in individual shops and finally into the hands of someone who makes phone calls. Services like hotel rooms and taxi rides similarly have a series of intermediaries, though not necessarily in sequential order, that exist around the exchange between the hotelier or taxi driver and the customer: travel agent, fire regulations, registration of cab driver, membership of unions, taxes and so on. Disintermediation refers to removing at least some of these intermediaries so that a service is delivered with fewer, or different, outside parties to the service provider and customer.

This chapter will explore the digital economic practice of disintermediation through three cases. The first is Uber, which has attempted to replace or improve (depending on where you stand in the debate) taxi services and is now extending into other services like food delivery. The second is Airbnb, which offers anyone with a spare room the chance to rent it out without having to fulfil at least some of the obligations a hotel incurs. Finally, blockchain technology will be explored, as for some it offers the ability to disintermediate almost anything, including Uber and Airbnb, by offering a distributed form of trust. Examining the practices across these three case studies will allow for some general conclusions about what a digital economic practice of disintermediation consists in, and how it relates to the practices already explored in relation to search and social media.

Uber

A group of us needed to travel to a friend's house for dinner and, due to the effects of drinking on being a driver and the laws on drinking and driving, we were going to hire someone to drive us there. This was in California, involving a trip from Oakland to Berkeley and later in the evening back again. A taxi was called using Uber's smartphone app. It came at the appointed time and drove us smartly to our destination. During the trip one of us asked the driver a series of pointed questions about how Uber treated him, to which he gave generally vague answers. In the end the driver stopped the conversation by saying 'I just want to get my five stars', referring to the maximum possible rating passengers can give drivers, which they enter into an app on a smartphone, and which is then recorded by Uber to inform it, the driver and other passengers of the driver's performance.

Why was my friend and fellow passenger asking questions that suggested a suspicion of Uber? Talking to my friend and later thinking about the exchange, it seemed clear that the suspicion resulted from the feeling that Uber had somehow become the essential relationship through which we bought our taxi ride. We related directly to Uber and so did the driver, and this somehow put Uber in a powerful position, one my friend felt worthy of checking. What was fuelling my friend's suspicions was disintermediation. If we think for a moment about cab rides, there are intermediaries involved in the relationship of service user, or passenger, and service provider, or cab driver, even if we do not always know they are there. If I had been calling a black cab in London then we would have known the driver was regulated. For example, he or she would have had to pass a test, generally called 'the knowledge', to prove s/he knew enough London street geography to take us where we wanted to go. Our relationship to the black-cab driver would have been mediated by this regulation. A further way to understand inter-mediation is to recall one reason why we called an Uber in the first place – the Californian laws about drinking and driving. These regulations also reflect intermediaries – law, police, courts – that affected our behaviour. Uber is a company that relies on digital means and online communities to remove many (though not all) such intervening relationships and interme-diaries; it disintermediates to create its economic practices.

We can also see within the driver's response to my friend – when the driver said 'I just want to get my five stars' – that removing some interme-diaries may involve introducing new intermediaries. Each Uber driver is managed by their stars, which are reported to Uber by passengers, allowing Uber's platform to keep a score, with an average of less than 4.6 usually leading to a driver being deregistered (Cook 2014). Drivers are also able to rate passengers. Uber has in these ways become a new digital intermediary that relies on its community of passengers to manage its drivers, and on its community of drivers to deliver a service to passengers. The role of the intermediary now falls to the information platform run by Uber. My friend's suspicion was a suspicion of Uber as this new intermediary.

My anecdote introduces some of the core practices of Uber passengers and drivers in Uber and in the matching of driver to passengers and rating of both suggests some of Uber's platform practices. Requesting, being matched, and the driver providing transport are the obvious core practices. To avoid repetition of points made in relation to prior economic practices, I will focus here on the points of disintermediation that help us to best understand what is going on in Uber. Analysing disintermediation requires noticing what is no longer there, what has been removed.

For the passenger, paying for a journey in someone else's car is fundamentally a similar practice to hiring a cab or other service that provides a driver and vehicle. Uber, at the point we travelled anyway, had a policy of asking drivers to offer bottled water (at a price) to customers, which is not something I have ever experienced a London cab driver doing. Focusing on such details, however, distracts from the core of the practice. The differences between the black cab and Uber lie not in such details or in the journey but in the mediation of the process via an app. The Uber app offers not only matching and the ability to either book instantly and be told the waiting time or book in advance, but also a map on which the car's journey to pick up passengers and then its journey to their destination can both be tracked. The app offers the chance to rate the driver – an implicit threat or promise to the driver during the ride, as this is done once the journey is completed. Finally, the app offers an agreed fee which is not paid directly to the driver but via the app. The latter two contribute to a sense of 'control' in the use of the app by the passenger, in part by a visual representation in the app of where a summoned ride is, and a sense of speed or weightlessness, as a pause for payment is no longer part of ride. This also places Uber as a platform firmly in the middle of the exchange, with the money flow between passenger and driver flowing through Uber.

If for the passenger there is a fundamental similarity in hiring an Uber ride to prior practices of hiring a cab allied albeit to a sense, false or not, of greater information about the ride, control over the ride and less friction in the exchange, then for drivers a much greater change immediately opens up. You cannot explore the practices of drivers without asking what kind of driver. Uber offers both connections to existing professional drivers – though they may not technically be taxi cab drivers but limousine or other fleet drivers – and in UberX the idea of ride sharing. The latter is what Uber is more known for, though it was a later addition after services like Lyft seemed to be stealing an innovative march on Uber. In ride sharing on Uber anyone with a car and the required forms of identification can apply to become an Uber driver and share passenger seats in their car for a fee. For both kinds of drivers, the fundamental practice remains the same: preparing a car, picking up rides, the mechanics of driving and of routing to a destination to be paid. For existing professional drivers the new practices revolve primarily around registering on the Uber app. For 'ridesharing' drivers, however, the whole process may be entirely new. Though based on their (hopefully) existing skills in driving and navigating, the practices of preparing their car, allowing strangers into it and expecting payment for driving a route they would not otherwise have driven may well be unfamiliar. Both kinds of drivers are involved in very similar practices of being called by their app, offering a ride, and then being paid directly into an account by Uber rather than in cash by the passenger.

A core disintermediation for Uber arises here in employment. Uber has long claimed that it does not employ its drivers, arguing that they are independent contractors responsible for their own employment conditions. Uber is 'just' offering the service of a platform to facilitate connecting passengers and drivers. By considering their drivers to be contractors rather than employees, Uber removes the need to provide them with a number of cost-increasing and, for most of us, fundamental benefits of employment in things such as paid holidays, paid sick leave, and, in countries without national health schemes, some form of medical insurance. It also usually removes unions by treating each worker as self-employed. Whole swathes of regulations, negotiated agreements and legal requirements are thereby removed, to be replaced by new intermediations such as star ratings on the Uber platform. These disintermediation practices gave Uber a significant competitive advantage over other taxi services that had to abide by the regulations, and from the start Uber was controversial and contested.

For the driver this disintermediation may be obscured, and at first sight may offer benefits such as being able to work flexible hours, something Uber (and similar companies like Lyft) often publicise as a benefit to drivers. The not so well-publicised side of the practice is that all the costs of running a taxi fall on the driver: licensing, repairs, petrol and so on. Further, Uber sets the prices of rides and the percentage that it retains; in both cases, Uber can alter the driver's income in a way that is not obvious because it is mediated, ride by ride, by the platform. The actual numbers are contested, but a key analysis from 2018, which was adjusted in response to criticism from Uber, resulted in two methods for calculating the income of drivers in the United States. On one method, their profit amounted to $8.55 per hour, which meant 54 per cent of Uber drivers earned less than the minimum wage for their US state, and 8 per cent lost money being an Uber driver. On the second method (adjusted to take account of objections from Uber), their profit was $10 per hour, which meant 41 per cent of drivers earned less than the minimum wage for their state and 4 per cent lost money (Zoepf 2018). Drivers end up being responsible for all their costs, unable to control their income, and with an income that may lose them money and that for around half does not meet local minimum wage standards (Cherry 2015).

The process of disintermediation is not magical. For example, when Uber started to expand by opening in New York City, their then New York manager, Matthew Kochman, was initially instructed to ignore regulators on the basis that regulators were likely to defend an entrenched taxi industry. Kochman had prior experience of working with regulators and ignored the instruction, provoking the anger of Uber's CEO Travis Kalanick. As Kochman recalled, 'He was absolutely livid and said it was insubordination' (cited in Stone 2017: 175). Kalanick would later be questioned by officials about Uber moving into Washington DC and the stakes were made clearer. In response to Kalanick's claim that competition, that is allowing Uber to operate as it wished, would be good for the taxi industry, Councilman Jim Graham stated: 'You can't have competition where one party is unbridled and able to do whatever they please whenever they want to do it and the other party has their hands and feet tied' (cited in Stone 2017: 216; see also Cherry 2015). Numerous other examples show that regulation was often an issue wherever Uber opened and removing regulation was an advantage Uber explicitly sought.

By 2018 Uber's disintermediations were being challenged in many jurisdictions, even while ignoring regulations had given the company a major advantage. California's Supreme Court had defined three tests which could be used to decide if someone was an employee or an independent contractor, whatever the company or worker thought, and San Francisco's city attorney subpoenaed Uber (and Lyft) to demonstrate the nature of their relation to their drivers (Farivar 2018). Disintermediation is sometimes presented, particularly by those benefiting from it, as a smooth process that creates frictionless services where they did not previously exist, as seen in claims that an app would solve San Francisco's (and other cities') problems in providing enough taxis. However, disintermediation is often highly contested.

A tactic of Uber's has been to ignore regulation, sometimes not even to be fully aware of what it was ignoring, and by implementing its service become too big to be easily regulated. If the service is popular then its users can be mobilised to try to defend it when regulation finally catches up with it. Uber has several times called on its community – in the loose sense of those tied to its platform – to defend it from attempts to outlaw it in a particular city. Popular pressure on legislators is one way in which those who use or buy into Uber's economic and social relations become a visible group. In Europe in 2014 there was a cross-country protest by taxi drivers against Uber. Legislation in some places followed, with Berlin for example banning Uber based on a court ruling addressing a lack of safety for passengers being driven by unlicensed taxi drivers (Topping et al. 2014; Davies 2016). However, pressure could also come the other way. Following the 2014 rollout of Uber ridesharing in London, there were protests from conventional taxi drivers and intervention from the London Mayor and London transport authority, but by then Uber was running and in 2015 was able to produce a petition with over 200,000 signatures supporting its operation. The then London Mayor Boris Johnson oversaw the dropping of regulations to limit Uber, remarking that lawmakers were unable to 'disinvent the internet' (despite this being no kind of issue in relation to regulating Uber) (Stone 2017: 329–31). While each battle is important, to understand Uber's economic practices the general point is that all such battles are over whether it will gain some kind of advantage through the disintermediation of regulations relating to labour conditions, local taxes and other regulations.

The nature of Uber's service means it tends to be focused on cities and city regulations. It is not that wider regulations are irrelevant, but that local transport services often entail a focus at city level. This relates to a further disintermediation created through the app, which has varying effects across cities. The Uber app has used pre-existing maps such as Google Maps or Waze, leading to it eventually developing its own map, building not only on GPS systems but also previous mapping apps. No longer does a driver need to know the best way (or if trying to extend a cab ride, the worst way) around a city; it is enough to have the app navigate the route. This also gives passengers the security of knowing where they are and the assurance that the driver is taking a reasonable route. Specialist knowledge is here disintermediated. This may also amount to a regulatory disintermediation, as in the case of London where, as mentioned earlier, licensed black-cab drivers have to pass a test which requires them, without aid of maps, GPS or advice from a controller, to immediately decide the best route for a passenger's journey based on their comprehensive knowledge of London's street and landmarks. The extent of the training here is apparent from the fact that it usually takes three to five years to learn the routes and pass the test (Anthony 2001).

For Uber drivers then, the app becomes central to their practices; it brings them rides, navigates their routes, records their payments and shows them their ratings. The app presents itself to drivers and passengers as the centre of Uber, but the standard practices it enables are allied to the less obvious disintermediations of the regulatory and cultural conditions under which other cabs have to operate.

While the phone app is the key interface and connection for passengers and drivers, it is essentially a front end for the wider Uber platform. The platform's practice is to provide for passenger and driver but in a way that serves Uber's interests in monetising their relationship. The platform reintermediates: replacing the relations that have been removed by becoming the new go-between. While exploring the exact nature of the algorithms that Uber uses is impossible, as they are like so many algorithms secret, there are ways of seeing how this reintermediation reads its passengers and drivers to create a situation in which the payment between these two becomes a stream that Uber can take a proportion of to monetise its management of those relations (generally held to be 20–30 per cent of each fare). One example is surge pricing, which also points to the way Uber's reintermediation is not just about regulation and technologies but also about cultures.

Surge pricing refers to Uber's practice of initiating higher prices when there is increased demand for rides. The information Uber gained from running its platform allowed it to look at statistics on how often people were calling for an Uber before getting through. It found that on particular occasions, such as New Year or a major music festival, a user might be calling an Uber twenty times or more before getting confirmation of a ride (Stone 2017: 187). Uber has then at various times tried to implement a reading of its drivers that higher prices will bring out more drivers, assuming drivers are classic economic subjects, only to find that they had not reckoned with the culture of their passengers who expected the same prices as usual. As then CEO Kalanick noted after one early attempt led to a media storm against Uber: 'We tried to unwind decades of fixed pricing in personal transport in one night' (cited in Stone 2017: 189). The culture of passengers had not been read by Uber, who relied in this instance on a faith in demand and supply economic theory. In the examples surge pricing provides, we can see how, as the platform owner, Uber may manipulate its position to ensure passengers and drivers are matched so that fares are created from which it can draw an income, but that it also has to read and respond to the cultures and expectations of these two groups. The failure, in this case, to read its users clarifies that, even if Uber seems to be putting together disconnected economic agents, there are collective relations between users and drivers that Uber has to read through its control of data on user and driver behaviour. Surge pricing was subsequently implemented and has been closely monitored to ensure the data 'reading' and consequent understanding of users and drivers reflects the best fit, for Uber, of prices to situations of higher demand.

The reintermediation Uber implements is then that of a digital platform owner using their position to collect data and to read those using their platform through this data. Such a reintermediation can take such readings and implement changes while avoiding as much as possible taking on any of the regulatory practices that their business is based on removing. What in relation to previous practices has been called a 'community' – encompassing the wide range of 'social relations' read by a platform owner to create the value that attracts users – is in Uber's case something less than a full range of social relations, being limited to those needed to create a cab service. This is not, then, equivalent to the full range of human emotions that Facebook tries (successfully or not) to encompass, but a datafied set of particular social relations that only Uber has access to and which forms the basis for its business.

The final question is perhaps an obvious one: is Uber successful? And, in particular, is it financially successful? This is not as simple a question to answer as it is for some of the other companies examined in this book because, at the time of writing, Uber is not yet a publicly traded company and so is not required by law to disclose its finances. However, it was in the process of trying to float on the stock exchange, requiring some results be disclosed for the financial year 2017. These include two headline numbers which suggest Uber's financial position. The first is that the company's revenue for 2017 was $7.5 billion, making it around the 350th largest company in the United States. The second is that Uber made a loss of $4.5 billion in 2017. That is also a very large number and suggestive of a company failing to successfully monetise its disintermediation and reintermediation practices (Lashinsky 2018). On some analyses, the basis for any financial success Uber might achieve is highly questionable, because it is operating in a market where profit margins have always been thin, and it has grown primarily by subsidising the cost of rides to such an extent that it is hard to see how it can ever remove that subsidy. Horan goes as far as to argue that Uber uses predatory pricing to squeeze competitors using its $13 billion of investment to artificially lower prices in the hope of squeezing out its competitors. Furthermore, Uber has on several occasions raised the amount it takes from fares, thereby increasing its income but also squeezing its drivers, who in Lyft and others have alternative companies they can drive for. This obvious avenue for securing extra income has already been used significantly even while the company continues to lose large amounts (Horan 2017[1]).

While in 2017 Uber was a major global corporation generating significant revenue, it was also haemorrhaging large amounts of money. Moreover, during 2016–17, some aspects of its business that had been lauded as it grew were now being heavily criticised. Accusations of institutionalised misogyny were made against the company, based on what appeared to be a college-level male culture embodied in its first articulation of its values, one of which was to be 'superpumped'. Uber's predatory practices also became clearer with such things as its use of software to secretly bar inspectors from getting rides on Uber or the revelation that staff in Uber used its 'god' mode (in which some Uber staff can pinpoint where anyone using an Uber app is) to follow celebrities and opponents. Uber's co-founder and CEO Travis Kalanick, whose combative nature was held at least partly responsible for attracting this criticism, was eventually forced to resign in 2017. 'Superpumped' duly disappeared from the set of eight new values Uber proclaimed for itself. In relation to the company's financial model, however, some of this aggression made sense, as, on Horan's analysis, to eventually turn a profit Uber will have to dominate ridesharing to the extent that it can increase fares to close to double (Horan 2017). The financial story of Uber is, then, complicated, with success neither achieved nor guaranteed, despite the millions of rides and large revenues.

Uber demonstrates one version of a digital economic practice that disintermediates a range of existing regulations, cultures and practices in a particular service, followed by a reintermediation which introduces a digital platform as the core that connects users and providers of that service. Being positioned at this core allows the platform considerable scope to read its various users and establish its service, and then to draw revenue by taking a proportion of the money exchanged between the service users and providers. Before trying to work out how generalisable this practice is, and whether or not it relates to the economic practices of search and social media, it will be useful to look at further case studies.

Airbnb

A company often linked to Uber is Airbnb because what Uber was doing for taxis Airbnb might be doing for hotels. If we finished on Uber with that company's fundamental financial health, it seems appropriate to begin with Airbnb on similar ground. Like Uber, Airbnb in 2018 remained a private company so the required financial disclosure of a public company is not available. However, Airbnb is also providing some numbers to reassure investors and to position itself toward becoming a publicly traded company.

In 2017 Airbnb had an estimated revenue of over $3.5 billion, with profits of $100 million. The company seems to have turned the corner to profitability in late 2016, and maintained it through 2017 (Hook 2018). Its press office's 'fast facts' claimed that in 2017 Airbnb had 4 million accommodation listings in over 191 countries, and that since 2008 it had mediated over 200 million guests arriving at their accommodation (Airbnb 2017). Despite being publicity driven to present a positive view, these figures at least indicate the size and scope that Airbnb had attained by 2017.

When examining Airbnb it is superfluous to repeat many things already established when looking at Uber, I will then put away the technique of trying to follow practices from different standpoints and instead simply describe Airbnb's overall economic practice, interweaving the different points of view practices within the general framework. Airbnb's model is similar to Uber and Lyft's ridesharing concept, but applied to renting rooms rather than hiring cars. Airbnb claims it offers a way for anyone with a spare room (or empty flat or house) who wishes to rent it out to connect with someone who might want to pay to stay in that room (or flat, etc.). The company's self-propagated origin myth comes from the founders renting out space in their flat to make some money, and being impressed not only by the extra income but by the enjoyment they got from meeting new people (Stone 2017: 28–30). Belief in this story itself is not required, as its main function has always been to build Airbnb's claim that it is not just, or even primarily, a financial mechanism but a social one. Airbnb would often seem to prefer we believed that its aim is to create chances for people to meet rather than to generate income.

Airbnb's model, then, is to offer a platform on which people can advertise rental opportunities of various kinds, and by then matching visitors and landlords, Airbnb can create its own intermediations between the parties and take a proportion of the money subsequently exchanged. In 2018, the fees were 3 per cent for the 'host' (Airbnb-speak for the landlord) and 0–20 per cent for the 'guest' (these rates vary somewhat based on factors such as location and cancellation policies). In addition, the platform may take a percentage of fees for other things like Airbnb 'experiences' (Airbnb 2018). The guest's experience will often be similar to that of renting a hotel room or a holiday flat or house. The host may be doing something a bit different if they have not rented before, but their practices will still involve activities like cleaning up that are likely to be rather familiar. It is the intersection of these practices of entering and getting used to a new private space, and of letting others into that space, that the Airbnb platform mediates.

The disintermediation here is relatively clear. A series of regulations and checks that hoteliers and traditional landlords have to work with are eliminated. It is a model which presents the connection between renter and rentee as being much the same as if friends or family were coming to stay, even if the people involved are known only by the information they share on Airbnb's platform. The visitor gets what is possibly a cheaper room, or one closer to where they want to be, or in a style they want, while the owner gets some extra income and, if they are renting a room while staying in the property, they may get the experience of meeting new people. Airbnb collects increasingly large amounts of information, and receives more income as rentals increase, all the while avoiding regulations that a hotel or private landlord has to conform to, because Airbnb is 'just' a matching platform and is not responsible for the property, only for establishing the connection between visitors and owners. One obvious example is fire regulations, which in many parts of the world require that the furniture provided in rental properties must have an official fire resistance rating. Airbnb leaves it up to the renter/host to ensure that their property conforms to such requirements (including covering any expenses incurred). Another example is that in London up until 2015, planning permission from local government was required for a change of use if temporary sleeping accommodation was going to be provided in a property for the first time. This regulation changed such that since 2015 up to ninety days of temporary accommodation is allowed prior to planning permission being required from a local authority. The disintermediation can be seen in that prior to 2015 Airbnb was operating by facilitating renters in ignoring local regulation and since 2015 it has enforced a rule that no London property can offer more than 90 days rental through Airbnb, having had its disinter-mediation legislated into effect (Booth and Newling 2016b). Furthermore, while hotels have to pay their staff according to agreed wage rates and often have to engage with unions, the renter on Airbnb may not need to undertake such duties.

This process of disinter- and reintermediation can be further illustrated by the way in which Airbnb has sometimes taken on the responsibilities that regulation requires for rented accommodation. In an early incident, a renter returned to find their home had been trashed, with a hidden safe broken into and passports, credit cards and family heirlooms stolen. The renter posted a blog about the incident which was, after a few months, picked up in online discussion and from there became a major news story, particularly after Airbnb responded by saying it was in touch with the victim-host, although this latter claim was contested. At this point, Airbnb was making promises about the exceptional experiences to be had using its site, and controlling for behaviour primarily through its rating system in which hosts and guests each left a rating of their visit. After some confusion, the company responded to the media storm by apologising, working with the victim, and subsequently adding a number of reintermediations. These included a much expanded customer service team to take up and deal with such problems. They also created the Airbnb guarantee, which has at its heart an insurance scheme for hosts/renters promising coverage of up to $1 million, mainly for property damage – a version of the guarantees that hotels and travel agencies often provide (Stone 2017: 158–64). In 2014 in the United States, Airbnb began supplying hosts with carbon monoxide detectors, smoke detectors and advice on safety, again something that hotels would be familiar with. Even when Airbnb offered such devices their reintermediation did not extend to checking if such devices were installed or not, leaving Airbnb with a much simpler form of safety regulation than hotels have to work with (Stone 2017: 302).

Airbnb builds both finances and experience, reading and curating its users by drawing them through its platform. It gains an economic advantage by eliminating many regulatory and other requirements that hotels and private landlords are obliged to conform to, and then reintermediates the relations of guest to host, renter to rentee, through the platform. Over all this it casts a glamour that Airbnb is creating connections and ways of people inter-relating, with some income on the side. Questioned about regulatory issues in relation to growing an internet business like Airbnb, CEO and co-founder Brian Chesky stated: 'The first thing you need to do is grow really, really fast. You either want to be below the radar or big enough that you are an institution. The worst is being somewhere in between. All your opposition knows about you but you are not a big enough community that people will listen to you yet' (cited in Stone 2017: 311–12).

Community here seems to reduce to having enough users on the platform so that regulators who might react to its disintermediation practices have to negotiate with the company because it is offering a highly popular service. Like Uber, Airbnb often articulates itself as having a community at times when it needs that community to push back against regulations or inter-ventions that might harm its business. Again like Uber, Airbnb has been the subject of major controversy, particularly over whether its disintermedi-ation drives up accommodation prices, as it facilitates not only individuals renting out rooms, but also enables the owners of several properties to rent them out almost as if creating a hotel. Barcelona is a prominent example of this, with the city government looking to reduce unlicensed flat rentals, many of which are on Airbnb. Airbnb argues that it is actually helping the city, because it fuels the local tourism economy while also allowing residents to earn extra income. However, Barcelona's officials argue that this is false because many landlords using Airbnb have multiple properties that are being let solely to tourists, causing rents to be driven up and reducing the availability of property for local residents (Burgen 2017). A research group called DataHippo drew information from the Airbnb platform to claim that there was a concentration of Airbnb-enabled landlords in Barcelona in 2017.[2] One host had 204 properties and was receiving just over $43,000 in rent a day in peak season. The ten largest hosts had 996 lets, with 4,299 hosts having between two and five lets. Airbnb responded by claiming that 76 per cent of hosts in Barcelona only listed one property. Even so, it seems highly likely that a large proportion of Airbnb's income in Barcelona comes from a small number of hosts (Burgen 2018).

At the core of the argument is the question of whether Airbnb is creating a peer-to-peer sharing economy or a multiple-lettings hotel or landlord economy. The problem here, and the advantage for Airbnb, is that only it knows, because only it holds the relevant information, which it has been reluctant to provide, arguing that this would contravene its users' privacy. DataHippo drew information by mining (scraping) Airbnb's site for information, while the best available indicators come from 2014, when New York City regulators forced Airbnb to supply data on lettings over a five-year period. This data showed that while only about 6 per cent of hosts were operating large-scale businesses, these generated 36 per cent of all rents and 37 per cent of all income to Airbnb. In an indication of how its disintermediation of state regulations fuelled the company's profits, the report estimated that 72 per cent of lets were illegal, contravening New York City regulations on what kinds of properties are allowed to be let for less than thirty days. The report also pointed out that if its analysis was correct, then around $33 million in city taxes had been avoided. This provides an estimated quantification of some of the advantage that Airbnb as a platform creates, and of the losses that city governments may incur as a result[3] (Schneiderman 2014).

Putting Airbnb and Uber together suggests that a digital economy of disintermediation has potential power, even if it is not a guarantee of financial success. The similarity of disintermediation with search and social media is that owning, designing and controlling a platform on which the activities that make up practices are undertaken means that platform owners can create their own type of community, read that community, and then seek a means of drawing an income from it. Disintermediation communities diverge from those of social media because the latter attempt to supply a digital experience premised on deep emotional and personal relations, whereas disintermediation simply reads two already existing communities: those who pay for a service and those who provide it. The strength of disintermediation is that there is already a practice of financial exchange which the platform can draw revenue from, whereas for both search and social media a means of monetisation has to be developed, since financial exchange is not inherent in the main activities users come to the platform for. The idea of a 'community' that is read by a platform, and which forms the key component of a digital economic practice, is developed further in disintermediation. It seems clear that what is important are the activities which bring users to a platform and the consequent ability of the platform controllers to 'read' those activities through data in ways that can be monetised. Before turning to further case studies, it will be useful to examine one more disintermediating practice, because the emergence of blockchain technologies, most famously in the currency Bitcoin, works to disintermediate any exchange in which trust is required to be proven. In doing so, blockchain technologies explicitly hope to disintermediate all the things, including even Uber and Airbnb.

Blockchain Technologies

Blockchain technologies are most often associated with Bitcoin, which is an attempt to create a digital currency independent of government. However, it is important in understanding blockchain to recognise that Bitcoin is only one implementation of the general possibilities of blockchain technology. As a general and abstract practice, blockchain technology is a method for creating platforms that potentially disintermediate any relationship that requires an independent confirmation of trust.

A blockchain technology can be understood as a kind of distributed spreadsheet which is run peer-to-peer, meaning everyone on the network has a complete copy of the spreadsheet, in which each cell records one or more transaction of some sort. Each cell is usually called a block, and each new cell is added to all previous cells that have a transaction in them, thereby creating a chain: the blockchain. Each transaction is secured by cryptographic means that authorise the parties to the transaction, usually public and private key encryption systems. The block of transactions is then itself secured through a mathematical operation generally called 'hashing', which is a means of generating a unique identifier that is fast to create but extremely difficult to reverse. Each new 'block' added to the chain is hashed in this way to the whole chain. In theory, this creates an open distributed record of transactions that cannot be changed, thereby distributing trust. With a blockchain you do not need an external authority to guarantee a transaction, and you do not need to trust the other parties, because you can check the transaction in the blockchain, which is distributed and under no one's control (Gerard 2017; Casey and Vigna 2018; Popper 2015).

Each implementation of a specific blockchain has to solve two ongoing digital problems. The integrity of the elements in a transaction have to be maintained, and that means in digital contexts restricting copying of digital items which, if allowed, would mean being able to use same item (copied) in multiple transactions. It is worth noting here that the blockchain is a record of transactions, not necessarily the transaction itself, though with the right implementation digital transactions can be enacted in a block. The second implementation issue is how to decide which block is written to the definitive blockchain by a node on the network. If the network is peer-to-peer then potentially any node can record the new block to the blockchain leading to a proliferation of chains rather than one definitive record (Gerard 2017: 11–15; Casey and Vigna 2018: 12–13, 64–8; Popper 2015: 371–6). If implemented well and these two problems are overcome then a blockchain has the potential to be a distributed, cryptographically secured, peer-to-peer definitive record of transactions. As such, it has the potential, its proponents argue, to disintermediate any authority that guarantees trust; it is a disintermediation of trust.

As of 2018, there are many imagined blockchain disintermediations, though only a few operating implementations. Casey and Vigna argue that blockchain technology works and that it will transform trust. Here are some of the disintermediations they suggest blockchain technology could implement: property registries that record who owns land, houses, cars, etc.; personal identity records, which could be maintained by the individual rather than governments; supply chains in which companies can buy components directly; systems for allocating food and other necessities in refugee camps; and control of the information posted to the internet in forms such as music, images and so on (Casey and Vigna 2018: 8–9). One concrete example is a blockchain created by IBM, run by the US supermarket chain Walmart to record the lettuce and greens supplied to it; by 2019 Walmart will require all suppliers to participate. This is thought to have been precipitated by cases of infected lettuces, the idea being that the blockchain would ensure clear identification of which suppliers have infected stock in any future case (Nash 2018). The idea of establishing trust without intermediaries has significant attractions for libertarian thought, as libertarians tend to be distrustful of any government or institution, and argue that society would be best if there were no society but only sovereign individuals. As Golumbia documents, this means blockchain technology has a major fascination for right-wing commentators, though it is also attractive to some left-wing activists, for similar anti-government reasons, and particularly for those who are anti-banking; for example, Bitcoin advocates visited the Occupy Wall Street camp in Zuccotti Park, and one of the first businesses to take Bitcoin in payment was an anarchist bar in Berlin (Golumbia 2016; Popper 2015: 110–12). As, in 2019, Bitcoin is the most obvious and key implementation of blockchain technology, it is worth briefly discussing it as an example of a functioning blockchain.

Bitcoin solved the two implementation dilemmas mentioned earlier, to create a blockchain that also offered a peer-to-peer currency. It solved the problem of authorising who is involved in each transaction by requiring each participant to have a specific public and private encryption key. A participant signs their transaction with their public key, which is publicly distributed but can only be decrypted or encrypted properly with the private key. This creates a form of pseudonymity in which the Bitcoin encryption keys required to authorise an identity are public, but only the private key fully identifies who is behind a transaction. As this is a currency blockchain, it is essential that a participant can be identified for them to access, trade, buy or sell bitcoins (Popper 2015: 371–3; Casey and Vigna 2018: 66–8). Second, Bitcoin solves the problem of who will write the next block to the blockchain by implementing a kind of computational contest that requires a node on the blockchain network to find the answer to a mathematical question, and whoever answers it first gets to write the next block. While the question is entirely pointless, though requiring considerable computing resources to answer, the incentive is that whoever wins the race will receive bitcoins as a reward. This contest is run every ten minutes, at which point a winner receives bitcoins (in the terminology, they have 'mined' the coins), and the blockchain is extended by one block in which records are kept. The new block and chain is then broadcast to the all the nodes on the Bitcoin blockchain, over 50 per cent of which have to accept the new block as valid. Then the process begins again. There is a set number of bitcoins that will eventually all be mined, with the end-state being that of a fixed number of bitcoins in the world (Popper 2015: 373–5, Gerard 2017: 13–15).[4] Bitcoin is, then, a software program operating on a range of dispersed computers, which creates a shared, distributed ledger of transactions and at the same time produces a digital currency. It is the network that ensures Bitcoin can operate, and it is the community of the nodes of the network that creates and maintains Bitcoin.

The price of bitcoins – with several bubbles and busts in their value – has drawn a great deal of attention to blockchain technologies. The bubbles and busts, however, represent an economics of a rather old kind, though deeply ironic to those who see Bitcoin's political value as being that it would have a stable value akin to a return to the gold standard. Drawing on the previous discussions of Uber and Airbnb, the obvious question to ask of Bitcoin as a digital economic practice is: where is the reintermediation? If Bitcoin has disintermediated national central banks in favour of this technology, are there any reintermediations? Two immediately jump out.

One reintermediation is the power that flows to those with massive computing resources. As explained above, to win a bitcoin you have to win the race to add the next block to the blockchain by winning a computational race. As Gerard has most loudly pointed out, this process is an ecological disaster in which major amounts of electricity are required in the race to have the fastest hardware to win bitcoins through computations that are immediately discarded to start on the next set of computations, whose only point is to win bitcoins and write the blockchain. This led to a computer power race in which faster machinery required more electricity and generated a greater chance of bitcoins being won. As Bitcoin's value increased in relation to other currencies, and it gained fame as a currency disintermediated from government, more and more powerful machines were generated to win the race, resulting finally in processors manufactured specifically for Bitcoin mining. This finally put winning the race out of the reach of individuals, leaving it to groups with the resources to continue adding up-to-date machinery (Gerard 2017: 55–8). The disintermediation of central banks as printers of currency here led to a reintermediation of those with enough computing power connected to cheap enough electricity to win Bitcoin's competition to write the next block to the blockchain. In the first week of June 2018, five bitcoin miners won 93 per cent of the races to add the next block to the blockchain. One miner had 32.8 per cent and it only required this group to join with one other to account for over 50 per cent of the chain (Bitcoinchain 2018; Gerard 2017: 55–8; Schroeder 2018). As Bitcoin is designed to be pseudonymous it is possible that several of these large pools of miners could be run by the same group or related groups. This also raises the possibility that these groups could control over 50 per cent of the mining power, thus allowing them to rewrite the blockchain backwards and confirm it, opening up the possibility (which has happened in other attempts at blockchains) where someone gaining over 50 per cent can rewrite the blockchain to double count or change transactions (Schroeder 2018).

The second key reintermediation is linked to the Bitcoin software, which has to be updated and developed. The fact that it is open code is often used to argue that Bitcoin is safe as the code can be examined by anyone. While this is true, there are effectively two reintermediations here. First, only those who have the expertise and time to read the code can check whether it is safe and operating as it claims to. Real trust resides here in and is only available to programmers who can operate in this way and who have the time and inclination to do so. Second, even though it is open as free software, only a few programmers have the right to actually make changes to it, or 'commits' as they are known. Those with the relevant expertise in programming can examine the code and offer new code to add to the program, but only a small number can implement changes, a right that passed from the original coder Satoshi Nakamoto to a small group. This group grew to five individuals at one point, though later shrunk to four (Popper 2015: 46; Bustillos 2015). In short, those with both the coding expertise and the authority to commit changes to the code are the new intermediaries.

In addition, being open source, anyone with the will and expertise can take the whole codebase and develop a different version implementing different ideas, in what is called a fork. This happened with Bitcoin when, due to its increasing popularity, it became slow to register transactions as the block was itself too small to include all the transactions being undertaken. At this point, after a complicated and lengthy struggle to come to a collective decision, the Bitcoin software split, or forked, into two versions (one of which only had two programmers able to implement changes) (Bustillos 2015; Popper 2015: 366–9; Casey and Vigna 2018: 72–8). This reveals an ongoing vulnerability inherent in Bitcoin's reliance on a small group of programmers who can change the program, because the Bitcoin software, like any blockchain technology, will only be as good as its implementation, and while cryptography makes some elements of a blockchain difficult to manipulate, this will only be so if the programmers have done a good job.

Bitcoin's implementation of blockchain technology demonstrates both disintermediation, with no central bank issuing currency, and reintermediation, with the platform offering new intermediaries, which we can expect to be the case with any blockchain and any disintermediating platform. The hoped-for creation of peer-to-peer trust with no intermediary runs straight into the same problem facing anyone discussing a network who does not take account of the protocols defining who or what can be a node on a network and what a node can do (Jordan 2015: 64–81). The community, in this case the network of computers making up a blockchain, will have to be intermediated by programs which are open to manipulation and require updates. This does not mean blockchain technologies will necessarily fail to implement distributed relations of trust, but for present purposes it makes clear that for every disintermediation there is a reintermediation and, as a digital economic practice, the nature of these mediations is to generate economic value by creating some form of networked community or networked relations.

Conclusion

Disintermediation as an economic practice relies on digital technologies to remove a range of regulations and existing institutions and then reintermediate a digital platform. The reintermediated platform creates relations between individuals or groups who are either seeking or offering a service, be it hotel rooms, cab rides or trust. Revenue can then be drawn by taking a portion of the payment for the service. A disintermediation digital economic practice creates two of the central components already identified in search and social media: activities that can only be conducted through the digital platform, and the grouping of these activities into some kind of collective that can be 'read' or datafied by the platform. Having a financial transaction within this relationship between different users of a service offers a different form of monetisation to targeted advertising or selling data, by allowing the platform to take a proportion of the financial exchanges occurring within the activities on the platform.

The removal of the middle layers from a transaction and their replacement with new layers can now be seen to be a possibility of digital economic practices. An example is the rise of Twitch.tv, which offers anyone with a reasonable computer and internet connection the possibility of creating their own TV channel by streaming live whatever they are doing on their computer. This is like a live-action version of YouTube's creation of TV channels through content that is uploaded; on YouTube these are rather like finished TV episodes whereas on Twitch the content is usually live and ongoing. Created largely by gamers streaming their game play and inter-acting with their audience, Twitch has thousands of channels, with the most successful drawing millions of subscribers and creating the possibility of professional gamers subsisting on the revenue they receive from donations, subscriptions and advertising. Though Twitch began with gamers, it hosts any streaming content and has seen the rise of conversation or flirting channels, often provided by young women streaming themselves. Anecdotal evidence suggests that the Chinese version of Twitch, Huya, is split roughly evenly between such flirting channels and video game playing. Across Twitch the creation of a connection between the streamer and their audience remains the key to creating a successful channel (Johnson and Woodcock 2019; Anderson 2017; Gandolfi 2016). Television has in this sense been disintermediated from its expensive studios and then reintermediated in a number of ways through YouTube, Twitch, Huya, Vimeo and other sites.

Disintermediation helps to push forward what might be meant both by users of platforms and the collectives, communities or groups that are read by the platform as the basis on which monetisation can be built. Users are defined by the activities they undertake, and this is made clearer by disintermediation generally having two kinds of user on either side of a service. This is unlike in search where the search engine is the service users relate to, and also unlike in social media where all the likes, posts and so on are created between users relating to each other in the generation of sociality and their moments of beauty, wonder and grief. Users or individuals in digital economic practices begin to resolve into their activities on a digital platform.

In disintermediation, the idea that has been termed 'community' or 'social relations' is further articulated. It is generally easy to see what these terms refer to in social media. Facebook, Snapchat and so on all generate digitally mediated social and emotional relations between people. Grouping people according to different kinds of activities or services – calling a cab, providing a ride, renting a room, etc. – creates what seems like a more attenuated idea of community. Disintermediation takes a step away from ideas of full sociality as it is not central to disintermediation that those who rent a service form a community in its fuller sense, and similarly for those who provide the service. All the disintermediations examined above do in fact have a sense of community and try to promote one, but the core economic practice does not necessarily need users of the service to form peer-to-peer relations with each other in anything but an attenuated sense, such as giving star ratings. However, just as search reads its community 'second hand' from web links and data to personalise search, disintermediation reads the collective relations on its platform back into its reintermediations. Groups, communities, sociality and other terms used so far resolve down to something less like full emotional and cultural sociality and more like the ability of a platform to read the collective data of those undertaking activities on the platform. In this understanding, 'community' is required for a digital economic practice but will be specific to each type of practice and to each instantiation of a particular platform.

As is clear from all the case studies discussed so far, monetisation follows activities. The activities which create a successful platform present opportunities for monetisation in different ways: through renting attention with advertising, 'taxing' monetary exchanges on a platform, selling data services and so on. Bitcoin is interesting because in this case there was no attempt at direct monetisation when creating the currency – the Bitcoin platform was in a sense a not-for-profit disintermediation. The financial drama around Bitcoin and other blockchain currencies comes from their participation in Ponzi-like schemes or in currency inflation and deflation. Services have also been built up around Bitcoin, for example in exchanges that offer opportunities to trade bitcoins for other currencies. This may seem odd, but the riches some have gained from mining bitcoins were often accidental riches coming from a project that had no monetisation strategy but set out to change financial systems and the idea of money itself.

This confused disconnect in Bitcoin between the income people may generate from activities using Bitcoin and the lack of an attempt to monetise the platform itself points to a further question that needs attention in considering digital economic practices: What is the relationship between activities, users, the platform's services and reading of collective activities, and monetisation? Is monetisation essential in digital economic practices? Bitcoin and other blockchain technologies point away from the obvious financial statistics for digital economic practices, which I have liberally strewn throughout these case studies, and toward practices that have a confused place in discussions of the digital economy and profit. Free software, Wikipedia and the World Wide Web Consortium all represent practices that do not seek monetisation but which have similarities to digital economic practices. Exploring these not-for-profit digital economic practices in the next chapter will offer a way of clarifying what monetisation means in the context of users, activities and platforms.

5   Free Stuff: Economic
Practices Without Profit

Profit or Not?

Blockchain technology poses many questions, and a less obvious one about the digital economy appeared at the end of the previous chapter: is monetisation necessary to a digital economic practice? While many have made, lost and tried to make money out of Bitcoin and blockchain technology, its fundamental workings do not necessarily include monetisation, which is rather a by-product of how that blockchain was implemented. There is a parallel here with the way Facebook, Google, Baidu, WeChat, Snapchat and many others have implemented a free service enabling particular activities and once they achieved success then sought ways of gaining revenue. Success in these cases has come primarily from some kind of network effect that begins to make the platform exponentially more likely to be the place anyone goes to for the activities offered there.

How different is this from other economic activities? While no economic practice can be said to be successful if no one is enacting it, is it possible to be successful if the practice is functioning but there is no revenue or profit? A bookshop that sells no books is perhaps not a retail economic practice but a library. A mine that does not sell what it has extracted will not last long as an economic practice of extraction. Social media and search can provide their full range of activities with no concern for making money, and even the disintermediators need not extract income from the exchanges between service users and providers – as the dreams of blockchain suggest. Is it possible that the creation and capturing of certain activities through a digital platform, that can then read them as a collective practice, can continue with no thought to the extraction of revenue?

One way of exploring this proposition is to relate it to a question asked by many – and in particular economists – who are puzzled when they encounter activities such as free software, Wikipedia or the World Wide Web: why do people work on these projects without being paid? Perhaps digital economic practices cannot be fully understood from a viewpoint that assumes the economic must be centred on monetary profit and loss. Do such non-financial economic practices open up different ways of organising exchange and economic activity? There have been many discussions of the 'commons' provoked by digital platforms, and it is worth exploring whether some forms of information commons are similar to not-for-profit digital economic practices.

This chapter will pursue these questions both to extend the parameters of digital economic practices and to ensure the visibility of alternative economic possibilities, as an integral part of digital economic practices, to the gargantuan profits and losses of the Googles and Facebooks of the world. The case studies of free software (and open source) and the World Wide Web Consortium will be explored, followed by a briefer examination of Wikis and Wikipedia.

Free Software

Free software, and the related but distinct open source software,[1] was articulated in the period when software began to be traded and have a monetary value. Previously, software had mainly been bundled with hardware and usually not been considered a separate product, often because it was closely associated with a specific piece of standalone hardware. As a result of software becoming a commodity, access to its code was denied through digital obfuscation, making it impossible to read the fundamental instructions that made up the code while allowing use of the results of those instructions (just as I type this text and can change it without seeing the underlying code that makes those changes possible). This technical closure was allied to a legal closure that secured intellectual property rights to the code, making it illegal to copy it whether you could see the underlying software instructions or not.[2] The canonical story of free software's origins derives from this change, as what had often been a community of coders freely sharing and improving code now fractured under the pressure of competitive practices of selling code as a product (Williams 2002: 10–20).

A response came particularly from one coder, Richard Stallman (though it was not an uncommon reaction among coders), that code should be improved openly for the sake of the better use of computers, and that this was best achieved through a community of coders who freely shared their code to develop it. Stallman and others then set about writing code that was freely released – free both in terms of access to changing the code and free of cost. To many operating explicitly or implicitly on the model that human beings are selfish and seek financial gain from whatever they do, this approach seemed (and seems) paradoxical. How on earth can quality software be produced, and who will do it, if it is done for nothing? In 1976, Bill Gates, having decided that early computer hobbyists must be copying (stealing in his view) software his company (then called Micro-Soft) had written, wrote a letter arguing that this was hurting computer development. He claimed: 'Who can afford to do professional work for nothing? What hobbyist can put 3-man years into programming, finding all the bugs, documenting his product and distribute for free?' (Gates 1976). Gates's letter was written before free software was really formed as a movement, and is an easy (and often used) target, but it starkly encapsulates the perceived problem as being one of practices and income. Gates's letter is also often cited because his claim was repeatedly proven wrong over the next forty years, with major programs being written for free and distributed with the code available to change and give back to others. These include operating systems like Linux (which Google primarily runs on); the Apache software that runs the majority of servers providing content for the World Wide Web; LibreOffice, a fully-fledged office suite with word processor, spreadsheet, database and so on; a browser in Firefox; and a number of email clients of which Thunderbird is arguably the most notable. This development of free software occurred simultaneously as Gates oversaw Microsoft's creation of a hugely profitable software-based empire, alongside many other companies who have thrived by keeping software private and proprietary to enable selling it.

Free software is created in programs whose fundamental code is open to being changed by anyone who can access it (usually over the internet) and has the skills to work in that code. Those taking the code and altering it are then obliged to contribute their improvements back to the original codebase. Programmers can then pick and choose which projects they want to get involved in, knowing that whatever they contribute will be returned to other coders. In this way the activity of coding is distributed, voluntary and collective, at least it is in the more idealised accounts of free software (Weber 2004; Jordan 2008; Williams 2002; Raymond 2001).

The practices of free software split strongly between users of the software and those who contribute to its functioning. For example, I can download and use LibreOffice to write these words but I do not have the skills required to open up the code and change elements of its functionality, nor do I have the time to help write documentation explaining how to use a program. If my contribution to LibreOffice is restricted to using it, and sometimes making a financial donation, then I am a different kind of user to those who created the possibility that I type into a word processing document using LibreOffice. These two sets of intersecting practices will be distinguished as those of users and makers.

The practices of users can in turn be split between individual users of free software like myself, and collective users such as businesses, governments and so on. The former type of user's practices will be familiar to any computer user who downloads, installs and uses software programs. Here the variations are relatively minor between individuals using a free software word processor or a proprietary one, as is also the case even with more complex programs such as an operating system. Access to technical support may seem like it will have different emphases but for both free software and proprietary programs the primary means of support in the early twenty-first century is online, particularly through either FAQs or forums (and the ability to search to see if someone has already answered a question). While the individual user is also engaging a practice of freedom in coding, simply by using free software, they are relying on and using that freedom rather than it affecting their daily practices when creating documents, keeping an operating system running, serving up websites and so on.

Collective users are institutions that adopt a somewhat different approach in their take up of free software. While they may use the software as given, they also have the ability to customise it to their liking because the source code is open. Collective users are thus situated in between users and makers. There is both an element of use like any program, akin to how individual experience free software, and a key element of opening up the program's existing actions to create new actions. For example, the desktop software used by Google was for many years adapted from the version of Linux called Ubuntu, leading to it being called Goobuntu. In 2017 there was a shift to using the flavour of Linux called Debian (of which Ubuntu is itself a derivative), which after internal testing and adjustment emerged as GLinux (Vaughan-Nichols 2018). While the use of a desktop minute to minute might be similar – clicking, typing, etc. – there is here an added set of activities around customisation and adaptation. Such activities may also save money, and given the size of some groups using free software this may be considerable, even if any savings have to be balanced against the costs of customisation and contributions back to the code.

IBM is an interesting example, with its turnaround from being a major loss-making company in 1993 (for many it was headed to oblivion) to a company with a profit of $5.8 billion (IBM 2017). While this shift had to do with many factors, particularly the transformation of the company from a primarily mainframe hardware company to a focus on computer services, one factor has been the use of free software and particularly Linux. This use does not simply reduce IBM's costs, as the company contributes to the development of the software, which in turn makes for a better Linux that IBM can build its services around. In 2006 it was estimated that IBM was contributing around $100 million a year in development to Linux – even though the software is cost free, it is the 'cultural' free that is vital:

the freedom to inspect and adjust the code. Moreover, because this is a collective endeavour, with any contributions back to the code being then available to the codebase, anyone contributing may benefit IBM or Google or any other user. In the same year as IBM's contribution to development was estimated, it was calculated that the total commercial investment in Linux had passed $1 billion a year (Samuelson 2006: 24).

Discussing IBM also makes the point, so far perhaps too often implicit, that digital economic practices may be taken up and developed by companies and organisations that existed prior to the spread of digital and internet technologies. While many of the practices I am examining are in companies that arose alongside the spread of the internet and the digital, there are also existing companies that take up digital economic practices. It is worth noting, in passing, that such practices are not restricted to entirely new companies, just as it will be intuitively clear that not all new companies in the twenty-first century have to be based on digital economic practices.

These are then the economic practices of free software seen from the point of view of users, entailing free access to the code, the ability to manipulate the code and the requirement to contribute back improvements to the code. Collective users, such as IBM or Google, then straddle the types of users being both those who take the programs and use them much as I use LibreOffice to write these words and the users who manipulate and change the code, the makers. To fully grasp the economic practice of free software it is then important to examine the ways in which corporations have become free software makers, alongside other makers, and explore what making free software means. 'The open source process is a bet on the idea that just as important as the code itself and probably more fundamental is the *process* by which the code is built' (Weber 2004: 14). The process of writing code involves people sitting at computers typing in sets of instructions using computer languages which are saved and shared by being integrated into a program's codebase. In this sense, coding is the obvious day-to-day practice of making free software. However, as Coleman's ethnographic work shows, though this is true, writing code must be set in the context of a range of other practices that together create software that is free (Coleman 2012). Weber has argued that the three key dimensions of free software are property, community and politics, and I have built on this work to articulate them as collaboration, objects and property (Weber 2004; Jordan 2008). Building further on these bases, particularly in light of the work of Kelty (2008) and Coleman (2012), the practices of those actively making free software programs can be understood across the three dimensions of those who code, decision-making about code, and how the changed code contributes back to the first two dimensions.

Free software emerged to create software projects that were coded by groups of voluntary coders; by definition then, participants had to be some kind of programmer. A 2002 survey of contributors to such projects found that 58.1 per cent were professionals in the industry while 35.4 per cent were university-based, either academics, students or in other IT roles, making a total of 93.5 per cent (FLOSS Project 2002: Part 4, 12). There are some opportunities for writing documentation and for working on legal issues, but the core activity is the production of software by a community of those with sufficient expertise in the practice of coding. Linux, especially in its early years, is often taken as the benchmark for this kind of interaction, given the speed and responsiveness with which its creator, Linus Torvalds, checked through suggested changes to the code before committing them to an updated codebase – an often-used example of how to motivate people to become part of a voluntary project[3] (Jordan 2008: 48–50). The vision of an open community is in fact limited to people with certain types of expertise. The openness is further limited in practice because the people involved in free software overwhelmingly work on only a few projects, with 71.9 per cent involved in between one and five projects over their time as a free software programmer, and 55.3 per cent involved in only one or two projects (FLOSS Project 2002: Part 4, 31–2). In many projects only a small number of volunteers contribute significant amounts of code. For example, the number of contributors who have had changes included in the Linux kernel has gradually increased to a high of 1,821 individuals for version 4.12, but the top thirty contributors made 16 per cent of all changes in 2017 (Corbet and Kroah-Hartman 2018: 11).

A significant change in the vision of an open community of coders has followed from some free software projects becoming integrated into large institutions, both corporate and government. Programs of major significance for corporations, such as Linux or Apache, have begun to be primarily coded by employees of those corporations, while other programs remain more within the open community of coders. For example, the contributions to Linux made by programmers who were not being paid by a company to do Linux work fell from 14.6 per cent in 2012 to 8.2 per cent in 2017. The top nine contributors from companies provided 45.5 per cent of all changes, and out of 80 per cent of all changes only 8.2 per cent were done by volunteers. Linux is, as already noted, integral to a number of large companies and it is no surprise to see IBM making 4.1 per cent and Google 3 per cent of all changes in 2017 (Corbet and Kroah-Hartman 2018: 14–15). Apache's server software notes that all contributions to it are voluntary, as is the case with Linux, but it has not tracked who is paid by another company to contribute changes, nor does the development report for the LibreOffice suite state where changes to it come from (ASF 2017; TDF 2016). Coders offer voluntary contributions, but Linux's evidence is that the coding for programs used by major corporations is increasingly being done by employees of those companies. This does not necessarily undermine the ambitions of free software, but it suggests a further split within the notional open community of makers depending on whether a project is attracting institutional support or not.

This raises the second major component in free software's creation and development, because in an environment where over 90 per cent of the participants can alter the program, and in which all can access the means of changing the program, the question arises as to how decisions about changes to the code can be made. Who chooses what is committed to the program? What stops many different programs from proliferating? This component consists of an ethic and a range of organisational forms.

The range of organisational forms refers to how each free software project is structured. If a project stays very small, it may have minimal organisation; only a few people could mean the project stays entirely open among those people. However, even in small projects it will be relatively quickly realised that there is a need to control the code so that everyone knows what the latest version is that should be worked on. Among volunteers, and perhaps particularly at the start of projects, many realise there is a need not to disperse what energy and commitment there is on competing versions. As the code is open and can be altered by anyone with the skill, there is always a chance someone will work on an out of date version or on something that others are already doing. This has led to the emergence of code repositories like GitHub or SourceForge that track which version of a program is to be worked on. Such technical solutions also exist in wider organisations, as a repository on its own cannot decide which changes should be committed to and when to adjust code. For example, Apache runs a committee structure in which votes go to those who are elected onto a committee, with that same committee voting people onto the committee. Linux runs on a 'benevolent dictatorship' (or not so benevolent as noted earlier) model in which, when Linux was smaller, Linus Torvalds decided what code went in, and then, as Linux grew, a number of others were given responsibility for deciding on aspects of the code, with Torvalds having the final say (Weber 2004: 89–93).

The second way of coordinating coding practices involves a general cultural commitment to using working code. Often stated as the 'does it run' principle, it mirrors one half of the slogan used to describe early internet governance: 'rough consensus and running code'. If organisational forms correspond to 'rough consensus', then 'running code' is the process of using software as it is developed to see if it works (Jordan 2008: 52–9). This appears to be a technological solution in which a project executes the code it has and developments follow wherever the code appears to work most successfully. However, it is more an externalisation of cultural choices about the nature of code than a matter of letting the technology decide. Factors such as elegance of code, sometimes interpreted in terms of how few lines of code are required, or usability, judged by whether the code is easy for people other than the original writer to alter, are all engaged. At the same time, if a function of a program is considered important enough, a development project may persist even if it never runs. As Weber notes, 'Technical rationality always is embedded in a cultural frame, which for open source generally means Unix culture' (2004: 88; Jordan 2008: 52–9).

The practices of writing software are integrated with ways of organising and making decisions. The last key element is also one of the most famous characteristics of free software – its commitment to a distributive definition of property. For free software to remain free in the sense of allowing anyone to access and alter the code, it had to find a way to exist in the context of laws about intellectual property. It had to prevent someone taking freely available code and applying a restrictive licence to it that excluded others from working on it. The answer was an inversion in which particular licences, most famously the Gnu Public License (GPL), require anyone using that code to keep it open to others and to return any fixes to the codebase, in return for which they can take, copy, distribute and charge for the code. Licences often go through wide consultations, for example version three of GPL received a total of 2,636 comments. Licences are a key moment at which expertise other than coding becomes important to free software. This is then a practice of arguing about the nature of licences that are then applied to the activities of coding software (Weber 2004: 16).

Free software, and to an extent open source, is reliant on a community taking up voluntary activities. This is not a fully fledged 'community' in the common sense way we might think of it, but a community of activities. It channels its work through platforms like code repositories, email lists, online fora, conferences and so on, all specific to each project. The complication here is that the code repository and other elements of free software projects create a more open platform, partly because the moment of monetisation is refused. While the activities and the platforms exist in free software, the drive for financial gain is not present.

As with blockchain technology, this raises questions about the relationship between such practices and economic practices, especially monetisation. While there is no question that free software has found its way into a range of economic practices – IBM and Google have been highlighted here – the point is that an economic practice need not be reduced to the function of profit or revenue. If economics is not reducible to profit and revenue, however important they are, then in relation to digital economic practices it is important to see how the practices of free software have similarities and differences to those of search, social media and disintermediation. Without the need to record and monetise, the platform itself may be more open, consisting of the principles of a community of experts, means of resolving disputes, and information as a distributed property, all of which are instantiated in various places such as code repositories, fora, email lists and so on, which are not necessarily homogenised into one digital platform. It is tempting to think this is how not-for-profit digital economic practices work, but it could simply be a result of the fact that free software is a differently productive activity, in which something is made, whereas search, social media and disintermediation are all activities which result in fun or the provision of services for users, but in which there is nothing like the drive to create a specific product (Cullen 2016; Core 2018).

It is not yet clear how to relate free software to digital economic practices. Exploring free software uncovers the intersection of activities, platforms and collectives similar to that seen in the previous case studies, but shifted into a somewhat different form with the absence of monetisation. It is then useful to continue this exploration with a look at the World Wide Web and then at Wikis and Wikipedia.

The World Wide Web and the World Wide Web Consortium

The World Wide Web (WWW) emerged in the early 1990s to become a core way of presenting and organising information across the internet. The WWW relies on the construction of websites put up by many different individuals and institutions, who then choose to make links between some of those sites. In the two years prior to June 2018 there were around 45 billion webpages on the WWW (De Kunder 2018). If practices on the Web involve surfing from site to site, on the one hand, and building and maintaining websites on the other, then what holds these practices together? What makes the WWW a 'space'? A key part of the answer is the standards that define what a website builder must do in order for their site to become part of the WWW network.

One example of these standards at work is the early introduction of the 'blink' tag. In constructing a website a small piece of code 'tags' what is being written to appear a certain way; for example, the size or type of font, whether it is in bold and so on. Early in the emergence of the Web a tag was implemented which made text blink on and off; the designer of the tag, Lou Montoulli, did not discuss or even announce the change but just implemented it in one browser, Netscape. 'It was kind of an Easter egg in the product ... everybody just found it, right?' (Montoulli cited in Gillies and Cailliau 2000: 260). While it became popular, it also became routine to note that many writers used it and every reader hated it. The broader issue 'blink' pointed to was that if multiple products or people implemented all kinds of tags then the WWW could fragment into a range of spaces with information only accessible if you happened to have or knew you had to have a certain browser or server implementation. The response was to set up the World Wide Web Consortium (W3C), which oversees the standards of the Web. If everyone writing for the WWW uses their standards it should ensure a consistent space in which everyone can connect. The W3C's role is to discuss and publish such standards. This does not prevent institutions or individuals diverging, or the standards being controversial, but W3C aims to ensure a set of standards which, if adhered to by most, will create an information space that is consistent and accessible (Gillies and Cailliau 2000: 273–305; Berners-Lee 2000: 36–41 and 91–102).

Of course, this does not end disagreements about what should be part of the WWW. For example, a difficult issue emerged around 2013, and was still not fully resolved in 2018, when the W3C explored the creation of a standard for an encryptable media extension (eme). Widely understood as the implementation of digital rights management on the Web, eme would standardise how browsers interpret content that is secured by digital rights encryption of various sorts. Eme was already in play on many browsers as an anti-piracy mechanism, and W3C explored how to standardise it. Opponents raised two key issues. First, that it provided 'weapons' for rights holders, such as music or film companies, to reduce freedom of information on the Web. Second, that it created a security vulnerability as the implementations of eme on each browser would not be open to scrutiny by researchers (Reynolds 2017; Doctorow 2016). The point for the present discussion is not the particular nature of this dispute but that the WWW as a platform is maintained by such arguments and the resulting standards.

The WWW is then both the content and activities of websites interconnecting, and a set of standards, with the latter constituting the Web as a platform. Google, Facebook, WeChat, Uber and so on all require users to come to their integrated digital platform, which connects to a coherent back end of servers ensuring the centralisation of data about users, and often does so over the Web. The WWW as a platform is a set of standards that allows other sites, sometimes themselves linked to an integrated platform, to be accessible to users and to be able to be linked. The Web does not then assert ownership over the data that flows around it, nor does it possess any particular ability as a platform to monitor its users and turn them into data. W3C attempts to maintain and develop the Web through standards, and it refused both centralisation and trying to make itself into a for-profit entity.

Different routes involving monetisation were possible, however. Very early in the development of the WWW, its main inventor and coder Tim Berners-Lee thought of setting up a company to create a browser, a path taken successfully soon after by the makers of the Netscape browser (Berners-Lee 2000: 83). The financial possibilities here can be underlined by noting that when Netscape floated on the stock exchange in 1995 it was valued at $2.9 billion on its first day (Lashinsky 2015). A further monetisation opportunity would have been to charge for the use of W3C standards. (Some might see this as having been at least partially implemented through the membership fees that W3C charges, but these fees support the work of W3C and there is no charge per use for any of the standards.) This second opportunity was not taken because Berners-Lee and others were consistently more concerned with creating the WWW as an open information space than with monetising it.

Like free software, W3C creates a community and platform, a range of users and opportunities for monetisation, which it refuses. This refusal, again not unlike free software, allows W3C's platform to be a distributed set of cultures and standards. It also means that ownership is not claimed of the information that flows around the WWW, while ownership and control is formally maintained over the standards that keep such information flows going. As with free software, this looks like an inverted version of the digital economic practices in relation to information that were examined in previous chapters. The difference between for-profit and not-for-profit practices stems from the status of information as property, because search, social media and disintermediating platforms all privatise the information that flows through them, whereas the W3C's non-monetised digital economic practices control (both formally and culturally) the standards by which people use their platform and not what flows through the platform. A second difference is that instead of monetary values, a sense of the value of a commons is central to non-monetised digital economic practices. There is a strong commitment to the broad benefits of software that is open to inspection, updating and returning to its users and coders, just as there is a powerful commitment to the general benefit of an open and consistent information sphere through the WWW. This should not be read as suggesting a platform entirely free of either property relations, forms of cultural and community valuation, power dynamics and forms of income, but it is not marked by the drive to private profit. Finally, very much like monetised digital economic practices, the practices of free software and W3C rely on voluntarily given time and the collective activities of many users. To create the WWW, and so for the W3C standards to be relevant, many people must implement websites; likewise many must contribute code to make free software programs happen. As with free software, many websites are now produced by people paid to design and implement them, but the connection of a site to the WWW, and each site's implementation of standards, can be and often is a voluntary contribution, and just as there are well-funded sites that draw large amounts of traffic there also remain sites created for an individual's or group's activities. Work, labour and leisure activities are part of all these practices in ways that seem to evade our given definitions of work, leisure, labour and play. To draw these conclusions out further, an examination of one other not-for-profit project will be helpful.

Wikis and Wikipedia: Economic Practices Without Economy

The internet is famous for a range of reasons, one of which is the creation of sets of practices, based on freely given time, that lead to high-quality products that are often given away for free. We have seen this in the cases of free software and the WWW. One suggestion arising from this review is that the nature of the 'platform' shifts once the claim to ownership of information derived from the activities of users is not made. To finish this examination of the causal links that make up digital economic practices, it will be useful to look briefly at another similar platform, that associated with Wikipedia and Wikis.

Wikis are light and speedy content management systems that allow many people to add to and alter the information they contain. They are not meant to have a pre-set structure, instead the structure emerges as the contributions are made. Wikis then encourage many people to contribute on whatever the topic of the wiki. For example, there are many game wikis on which players add details about a game and can edit each other's entries. There are a number of software programs available to implement a wiki, such as the original WikiWikiWeb or the now widely used MediaWiki. Each wiki software program generally manages a server, on which content is stored and served out, and a front end which any user sees and which enables them not only to read the wiki but to add to it or edit existing content. Who can contribute can also be controlled, creating variations between wikis from the totally open, where anyone can make changes, to the partially closed, where editing is restricted to authorised users. The leading wiki software programs are free software, ensuring they can develop through free collaboration (Lih 2009: 3–9).

Wikis offer a mechanism by which a generalisable platform can be implemented in specific ways. It sets up a digital centrality through the server–client relationship, which ensures the knowledge on the wiki is updated for each user to reflect one version. Users can be managed in different ways, from a totally open and anonymous system through to users having to register with whatever proofs of identity the platform might require. There is both an essential element of collaborative information sharing and a commitment to an ethics of openness, which, as authors like Tkacz (2014) and Birchall (2014) have pointed out, has a meaning additional to the obvious and well-publicised one of a trust benefit through transparency. The ideas behind transparency construct a particular kind of public who are constantly examining those who are being open; in wikis this means examining the changes or additions to whatever the wiki is about. As Birchall notes, 'The data public, therefore, is understood to be constituted by vigilant auditors and "inno-vative" entrepreneurs. It is not simply a matter of monitoring information and data but of making it productive' (2014: 83–4). In short, this is a good subjectivity for a particular kind of economic formation that places responsibility for both creativity and accountability onto its users.

Clearly, as an economic form, there are similarities between wikis and other free platforms that individuals contribute to, social media for example. The possibility of monetisation is also present in wikis through advertising, and many game wikis are awash with advertisements. A monetisation strategy based on subscriptions may run into a common difficulty for user-created information resources, in that there will be resistance to providing free contributions if those contributions are not themselves available freely.

The most famous wiki of all is Wikipedia, the online collaborative not-for-profit encyclopaedia, which became one of the leading stories in the rise of user-created and -maintained free platforms on the internet (Bruns 2008: 101–67; O'Neill 2009: 147–60). After an abortive attempt to create a traditional encyclopaedia online (Nupedia), with entries commissioned from experts, a group of people, most prominently Jimmy Wales and Larry Sanger, began using a wiki platform to create an online encyclopaedia (O'Neill 2009: 147–50). Launched in 2001 it initially allowed anyone to write and edit articles, and was (and remains at the time of writing) free to read, with no advertisements. It has grown hugely to become a likely destination for anyone seeking information, even if it has also become a byword in humour for false statements. I will not cite the current number of pages and articles, since that will be even larger by the time you read this from the time I write, but it can be taken for granted that Wikipedia represents a huge store of knowledge. What is interesting is its accuracy, who contributes to it and controls it, and its sustainability.

Unlike prior professionally written encyclopaedias, Wikipedia's articles are more likely to be accurate the longer ago they were written, simply because they can be updated and there are potentially many eyes to check them. Bruns notes that a large part of the control over the entries on Wikipedia comes from community oversight based on three principles: writing from a neutral point of view, writing verifiable statements, and not basing entries on original research. These norms are supported by certain high-target pages, such as those for US presidents, being restricted to authorised groups of editors; by automated means of checking on unusual patterns of making changes; and by bans for contributors who persistently disrupt or post false information. O'Neill traces the way in which what seems like a fully open community has its own institutional norms and decision-making protocols (much as free software projects often have clear, if sometimes informal, decision-making mechanisms offering different levels of power to different programmers) (O'Neill 2009: 166–8; Bruns 2008: 113–18). In terms of accuracy, a non-peer-reviewed 2005 study in *Nature* found that Wikipedia was broadly as accurate as the *Encyclopaedia Britannica* (Giles 2005). A 2004 study of a sample of articles on difficult or controversial topics found that most had been vandalised at some point (for example, by deleting content), but that corrections arrived in a short space of time (Viega et al. 2004). None of this prevents the kinds of difficulties affecting an encyclopaedia that updates only when a volunteer takes on the responsibility of doing so, with biographies of living people an example of entries that need to be treated with caution.

Despite these issues, Wikipedia continues to produce a vast wealth of openly accessible information. It relies on a large number of authors to do so. In 2014, on the English-language version, there were a total of 4.4 million article creators and 674 billion edits that had been made. On both these counts there is a broad pattern of fewer people contributing many times and many people contributing a little. Fourteen per cent of all edits were made by the top 1,000 editors, with 33 per cent made by the top 10,000. For article creation, 42 per cent were made by the top 1,000 creators and 60 per cent by the top 5,000 (Wikipedia 2014).

Wikipedia is paid for by the Wikimedia Foundation, which solicits donations and states that the average donation is $15. In 2016–17, the Foundation received $87 million in 'donations and contributions', which represented 96 per cent of its total revenue of $91 million. With expenses of $69 million and assets of $120 million, this put Wikipedia in a reasonable financial position, though one dependent on continuing to gain donations

(Wikimedia Foundation 2018a, 2018b). While $91 million in revenue and a solid balance sheet supporting a freely given away and extensive information resource is a remarkable achievement, it is also not the billions that Google, Facebook and others make. This is not lost on many who wonder what Jimmy Wales, the primary public face of Wikipedia, thinks about not being a billionaire while also being a 'tech visionary', many of whom have made billions (Cadwalladr 2014).

No doubt Wales and others in charge of the platform could have tried to make a profit. Wales has pointed out that if they had tried to do so, then Wikipedia would have been very different as it might well have been structured to attract ads and views in rich countries (Cadwalladr 2014). In addition, would those providing the articles and edits have continued to do so if they found out that their activity was generating privately held profits? Similar controversies have emerged in other areas, and it is not always clear that an open and freely available platform based on the input of volunteers can transition to a profit model, even just with advertisements, without the volunteers seeing their activities turn into work they feel should be remunerated. That said, there are many wikis, particularly game wikis, which do feature advertising and to which people continue to contribute. This is more complex than it might look, however, as many game wikis are created independently of the company running the game, and advertising may supply the income a volunteer gamer needs to keep the site running, sometimes to the extent of appealing for ad blockers to be turned off when visiting the wiki. Further complexity may arise if a gamer-run wiki uses a more commercial platform because it automates or makes the process of creating a wiki easier, and participants then accept ads as the cost of that functionality. The issue of what labour, payment and freely given activity mean in relation to each other here shifts depending on the context of the activity rather than the activity itself. Further, Wikipedia and wikis generally offer the possibility of free and openly editable information sources that are united in a single platform. This is not the distributed platform of W3C or the distributed cultural practices of free software; all the tracking and recording of who looks at which page and so on that fuels much advertising is present or potentially present on wikis.

Again, here we have practices that are patterned and organised through sets of activities, a digital platform and a particular conception of the ownership of information. This makes up the recognisably digital economic practice of Wikipedia, which could be formed differently in other wikis, but which in Wikipedia returns collectively created information to a wide, open set of users and offers the chance to contribute to potentially many people. This represents a different vision of a commons to those of free software or

W3C, in the form of a commons that is run through a centralised platform but which refuses the typical ascription of exclusive and private property to the information on the platform and information about users that can be derived from the platform. Though it may seem a bit odd or ungainly to refer to Wikipedia as a digital economic practice, it shares most of the characteristics of other such practices so far examined, except for its refusal to monetise. The latter it shares with free software and W3C, opening up the possibility of other ways in which digital economies may operate.

Conclusion: Economies and Commons

Exploring digital economic practices that do not monetise reveals some things familiar from previous chapters and some things that are new and strange. While the idea of an economy without a profit motive may seem odd, it is an essential aspect of some of the major phenomena of the digital age. This allows us to do two things in concluding this chapter: to discover in the resemblances what we might need to abstract in order to theorise a digital economy of practices; and to see in the differences how more commons-like and publicly minded practices may come with the digital economy.

The similarities are clear in the continued confusion of categories, of the words that no longer work, especially those such as labour, play, activity, leisure, paid, voluntary and so on. This concatenation of meanings shifts depending on the contexts in which activities are undertaken. Not only can the same activity undertaken in a different context at a different time have a different economic meaning – as in the case of a coder who works for a company and contributes in their spare time to free software projects – but the same activity undertaken at the same time can mean different things in different contexts – such as the social media post that is monetised which remains a familial, emotional post to the poster and another opportunity to refine advertising to the platform owner.

But there are differences as well, particularly in the way a lack of centralised control does not eliminate the presence of a platform through which activities come to gain their meaning as economic practices, but produces a different version in the form of a distributed platform. Such a distribution produces further complexity as it foregrounds the cultural and ethical elements of a platform that are intertwined and co-constitutive with its technological elements. Free software may need repositories like GitHub, but such technological elements hardly define the platform, and in their functions they are an expression of the cultures and ethics of free software. Whereas privatised platforms may present the user with a technological face, often only foregrounding their cultures when controversies like privacy emerge, non-monetised platforms may foreground their dispersion and reliance on the ethics and cultures of those who use them. This should not, however, be seen through rose-tinted glasses as a fully flat peer-to-peer system, since there are protocols that control access and community-generated norms – you can be banned from Wikipedia, and you can be ostracised from a free software project with all your code rejected. Yet, in refusing a simple good versus bad opposition, we should not fail to see that the idea of a 'commons' has emerged as an integral possibility of digital economic practices. The information commons has a basis when information is distributed rather than exclusively owned, as will be discussed further in Chapter 9.

Not-for-profit digital economic practices both affirm some of the elements of such practices, particularly their reliance on collective activities and their relation to information and digital platforms, and introduce further complexity, especially by separating monetisation from the other elements of digital economic practices. The final case study will focus on the digital economic practices of gaming, which bring together the different elements explored so far.

6 Warhammer, Warcraft, Just Plain War: Online Games and Digital Economic Practices

Gaming as a Digital Economy

The idea of an information commons is threaded through digital economic practices that ignore or refuse monetisation. The idea recurs that certain practices on a platform whose content is open to viewing and changing could form an information resource held in common by platform users, rather than being privatised to the platform controller. An inverse of this idea emerged early in the monetisation of the internet when one of the more obvious strategies was to charge a subscription for access to a platform. It seemed (and seems) obvious to many that if someone controls a platform with a valuable resource then one way to profit from it would be to make access conditional on payment. This chapter will move from the previous chapter's concerns with non-monetised practices back to monetisation, yet it is worth noting that there are common ideas emerging about the nature of digital economic practices, whether these are for profit or not. Subscriptions are a useful place to start because they reflect a common set of practices.

While the subscription model has been touched on in previous chapters it has not yet been brought to the fore, though there are many examples. The financial newspaper the *Wall Street Journal* is one, along with the UK's *Times Higher Education*, which offers a number of articles free per month, after which payment is required. The music streaming service Spotify offers a hybrid model with a choice between a free service that includes advertising and a paid service with no advertisements and extra features. Finally, there are sites that offer what can be called 'voluntary' subscription models, such as the UK *Guardian* and *Observer* newspaper group, which offers a fully free online service with ads but asks for voluntary subscriptions to support its journalism (Turrow 2011: 41–2). These strategies have proven variably successful, with several paywalls having to be removed as readers simply migrated to free services, but also with some successes. In an environment dominated by free access to services, which much of the internet offers, subscriptions are possible but can be difficult to make stick.

Of all the attempts to implement a subscription model, online video or computer games are one of the most successful. Games also bring together many of the different practices that have been discussed so far. In online games, we will find straight paywalls, free access but with added services and/or without advertising if you pay a subscription, free access with purchases of items that exist only on the platform, as well as varying levels of player involvement in forming and changing games. Kerr's work is important here as it offers a comprehensive account of games as an industry, building on the work of cultural and creative industry and games scholars. Work on games as an industry is allied to a range of work that, as Taylor notes, comes from the belief that 'it is only in trying to understand the interrelation between components that we actually get to the heart of the lived experience of play. From software to institutions to informal practices to meaning systems, gaming on the ground is constituted not through one vector but the intersection of many' (Taylor 2012: 249; see also Taylor 2009; Kerr 2016; Kline et al. 2003; Juul 2013).

To begin with, it is worth noting the overall size of the games industry. However, an immediate caveat has to be offered, because playing games often requires specialist hardware as well as the game software. Console games, such as Xbox and PlayStation, require hardware to be bought (and usually then connected to a screen such as a television) before the games made for these consoles can be played. For games on computers there are often bits of hardware needed to play some games, particularly graphics cards. Restricting the overall numbers to purchases of game software, one calculation put the global games industry at $109 billion in 2017, with China the largest national market at $38 billion and the United States the second at $30.4 billion. In a different calculation, the US games industry representative body put income in the United States at $29.1 billion over the same period (McDonald 2017; ESA 2018). An estimate of hardware revenue in 2016 claimed that specialist gaming computers, upgrades and accessories brought in a total of just over $30 billion,[1] and another in 2017 that there were 47 million console units sold worldwide with an estimated value of $4.71 billion (Orland 2017; Statista 2018b; Grubb 2018). The chart figures for software sales in 2017 recorded that 300 million games were bought worldwide (VGChartz 2018). In comparison with other entertainment industries: the global music industry income for 2017 was claimed to be $17.3 billion, and global movie box office revenues $40.6 billion (not including TV and video revenue), with 2017 seeing $11 billion income in the United States (IFPI 2018; Statista 2018a; TN 2018).

A rough comparison of film and games sales in the United States[2] in 2017 sees games software and hardware adding up to $64 billion, with film box office and the top 100 DVD/Blu-Ray sales adding up to $13 billion; the US music industry for the same year totalled $5.9 billion. Even if we remove the $30 billion estimate for PC hardware revenue (which seems high), then games are larger as an industry than movies, and certainly larger than music. Another way to view figures is that many estimates claim that 80 per cent of film industry revenue comes from secondary markets and only 20 per cent from box office receipts. If this is so, then an estimate of US film revenue would be around $55 billion, which would make it either larger or smaller than games depending on the accuracy of the estimate for PC hardware (Kerr 2016: 33). Close to the movie industry in size, the games industry is now unquestionably a significant component of the entertainment, cultural and creative industries, the digital economy and the global economy.

Something to note early on is that the terms 'online', 'video' or 'computer' twinned with 'games' cover a huge range of different kinds of play, from solitaire to mass online combat. Kerr notes a segmentation of the global games industry into console/handheld games, PC games, online client/ server games, online applications and mobile applications (Kerr 2016: 39–40). As she has fully established and explored these types I will not repeat her work here, but instead will follow the practices of certain types of games in order to see how they are or are not constructed as economic practices. As with previous chapters, I will not attempt a comprehensive survey but will focus on one of the clearest examples of an essentially digital gaming practice – massive multiplayer online games (MMOGs) – followed by an examination of several other kinds of games. MMOGs are a useful place to start because they are inconceivable without the internet and digital technologies. This is not to presume that MMOGs are the chief gaming form globally, though they do have a significant presence in gaming markets worldwide (Kerr 2016: 37).

MMOGs

The nature of massively multiplayer online games can be introduced through some key characteristics, before turning to the economic practices of such games. MMOGs are online environments that are logged into and present themselves as a three-dimensional world in which the player, seated at their computer, can move a character around the virtual world. There will be many other characters, some human controlled and some software scripted, in the environment, which will usually have a theme, such as space, *Star Wars*, Tolkien-like fantasy and so on. Activities of various sorts will be presented to the user, sometimes highly restrictive and scripted – such as quests to reach a specific location in the world or to collect a certain number of game items – all the way to very open – such as building whatever a player can with the means and materials provided. These are also persistent environments, meaning that the 'world' they present remains there whether the player is logged in or not (Taylor 2009). Three broad areas of practice can be traced in such games or gaming environments: players, platform builders and maintainers, and the interaction of players and platforms.

An MMOG player downloads and installs some software and opens an account. In the vast majority of such games, once logged in they will be presented with choices. Some of these choices will be to do with appearance and some with the abilities their avatar will have in the game. For example, in *World of Warcraft* (WoW) a player can choose to be a gnome or orc as race and male or female as gender. Neither of these choices will have a significant effect on anything but the avatar's looks, but the player will also have to choose a class, such as warrior, rogue and so on, and this will have a major impact as it will define the ways in which they can act (for example, using a sword and shield rather than being able to fire magic fireballs). Not all games flatten race and gender completely but the tendency is for them to split in this way, making race and gender both essential – in that they cannot be modified within the game environment – and inconsequential – as they have little effect on gameplay. As Higgin (2009) has noted, even this structure can lead to the invisibility of race, with 'black' being a difficult skin colour to find in most MMOGs (though this may be changing with more recent battle royale games). Overly sexualised body types are common in many MMOGs, offering choices for gender stereotyping through appearance (Jordan 2015: 170–2; Taylor 2009: 93–124; Park 2005). A name can be chosen, and perhaps some adjustment of the gameplay characteristics of an avatar can be made, and then entry to the game world is possible.

Once in the gaming environment the gamer will (usually) be represented on their screen by an avatar over whose back or shoulders they can see. Sometimes MMOGs are first-person perspective, or can be set to be so, this being when the gamer does not see the back of their character but only hands or what is held in front of the body, but MMOGs are more usually in camera mode peering over a gnome's (or troll or orc and so on) shoulder. Using the keyboard and mouse the avatar will be moved by the gamer, becoming their doubled body, and actions such as hitting or walking will be initiated by using keys or the mouse. Similar environments on consoles such as PlayStation and Xbox will be navigated with a controller specific to each console (though MMOGs have traditionally been dominated by PCs). Once the gamer is in the game they can talk to other players, fight with them and with other software-controlled characters, join guilds or in-game clubs and work cooperatively, perhaps be able to build or buy their own house and customise it, and engage in various ways to level up a character, with each advancement often offering some extra abilities to their avatar. The gamer may engage in fighting scripted encounters with avatars, such as a dragon, driven by an artificial intelligence (usually called PVE for player versus environment), or in battles against avatars controlled by other players in spaces that range from fully open, with hundreds of players in combat, to spaces that limit the number of avatars to produce evenly sided small-scale contests (usually called PVP for player versus player). Death comes often in such environments, such that they can be characterised as being not so much about death as about resurrection, with the penalty for dying and coming back to life defined differently in each environment (with, for example, such things as lost time, or some in-game monetary penalty or similar) (Jordan 2015: 165–7; Juul 2013).

All these activities will be tied together by a particular theme to the environment, which often sets up some kind of conflict that the player becomes enrolled in, something that has been theorised as a form of 'militarised masculinity' that has dominated game design (Kline et al. 2003). Themes are often a kind of Tolkienesque 'swords and sorcery' fantasy world, with elves, orcs and dwarves common (and there is a *Lord of the Rings* MMOG), but they can also be space-based, such as *Eve Online,* which focuses on flying, trade and combat, or based on a well-known franchise like *Star Wars.* While fantasy and space are the most common themes, there have been superhero, children's and other themes. A player may progress as an orc in *World of Warcraft* defending the Horde against the Alliance, or be a stone-skinned troll of Midgard invading Albion and Hibernia in the older *Dark Age of Camelot,* or try to become a Jedi in *Star Wars Galaxies* or *Star Wars: The Old Republic.* Whatever the theme, the gamer's actions will consist of manipulating an avatar in all kinds of complex ways via an interface, and increasing the avatar's abilities and connections to other avatars in order to engage in group projects. For the player, there is the fun of flinging fireballs at a dragon, or trying to become the most advanced character, or meeting a group of friends who venture into deep dark virtual places together. Many hours of activities may be spent in these environments, and some of the actions may be repetitive (the 'grind' as gamers call it); but all are in service of the gameplay experience in terms of both performing well and progressing the narrative that the game's theme presents (Chen 2012).

Practices are different for players and platform workers. Whereas the player uses computers, keyboards, networks and connections to be free of them in the course of gameplay, the platform's workers must write, correct and develop the software, create and connect a series of servers, manage accounts complaints, and give advice, and do so within financial restrictions that will be an essential measure of survival or failure for the virtual world. If the players are looking for the weightless magic of living an extraordinary life, then the platform's workers deal with wires, electricity, computers and code (Jordan 2015: 90–3). Each MMOG is structured in its own way, but they broadly share a basic architecture in which each user has a 'client' or piece of software on their computer that communicates across the internet with a centrally maintained cluster of computers. Each player's computer stores a set of files that create the visual and aural details of the virtual world, for example the sound of a sword swing or the texture of stone in a castle wall, or the particular pointiness of an elf's ears. The centrally maintained server keeps a constantly updated record of where every client is reporting their player's avatar to be and what they are doing, and constantly rebroadcasts to all the players updates on each player. If I fire a firebolt at a gnome, then all those around should see me do that, and whatever effects the firing a bolt has should be updated to all: the graphics and sound of the firebolt will be called up from the local store of files on my computer at nearly the same time as they are called up on everyone else's, because the server has received information from my software-client that the bolt has gone and has rebroadcast this information to all players. The consequences of the bolt – say the gnome is killed – are then rebroadcast and recorded in the game's databases. All this happens in milliseconds across thousands of different gamer accounts (if not more), and the process goes on and on. Maintaining this 24 hours a day, seven days a week is a practice of relentless materiality.

A further aspect concerns changes to the gaming environment. All the distributed game files on each individual computer have to be the same, or the game develops contradictions that are likely to cause it to crash, meaning any changes have to be broadcast to all players during or prior to playing. It is possible for players to build houses or spaceships, for example, as long as the building work can be rebroadcast, just as a sword swing can, but this can pose difficulties if different game worlds emerge between players. Changes are often made incrementally, correcting bugs or altering gameplay, and there will likely also be major updates every one or two years that make significant alterations to the game. Alongside this materiality of the game world is the range of services required to identify gamers and their accounts, secure income through these accounts, and provide support to players. These are the practices of coders and network engineers, of institution organisers and of the artists and designers who draw and plan how the game environment and avatars will look.

Once we reach the relentless materiality involved in servicing a player base then the practices which come when the player and platform intersect and cannot be separated can be seen. For example, providing a forum in which players can communicate with each other is a common practice. Here players can post threads on a topic that others can contribute to, and the game owner can provide responses. But players often post more than just polite enquiries or praise of the game, conforming to the longstanding pattern of online textual communication that more people contribute, disagreements are difficult to end and people are considerably ruder than when face to face (Sproull and Keisler 1993). Criticisms of the game are posted and discussed in great depth, and the game owner has to respond since, from one point of view, it is now running an online space for criticisms of the game it is trying to promote. Early on some games closed down their official forum but this only led to one or more unofficial forums becoming a home for players. Some game owners hire staff to deal with community management in the hope of encouraging a degree of co-production between the game designers and its players and maintaining some leverage over criticism (Kerr 2016: 94–103). The general point is that a practice like a game employing community managers whose role is to foster a community and to mediate between that community and the game designers and maintainers, is a practice that inextricably mixes the player with the game owner, game employees and their technology. The game is not only community dependent, a similarity to previous case studies of digital economic practices, but here we see a set of practices that are crucial to the success of a game that are between the player and the platform.

In 2012, the president of Electronic Arts – in 2017 the eighth largest game company in the world by revenue (Newzoo 2018) – claimed he had never agreed to proceed with a game that was stand alone, requiring all EA games to be open to players being networked in some way. Such a move was claimed to follow his consumers' wishes, while others have noted that a constant internet connection allows for active digital rights management, and that it indicates the integration of gamer relations within the game into game design (Humphries 2012). Other examples of such interconnection in MMOGs are player events that may or may not be supported by the platform. I once presided, as the priest (using my troll avatar), over an in-game wedding between two players, and the game provided me with a unique cassock and removed some monsters from the area the couple wanted to be wed in. Perhaps a small gesture, but it is an example of the active intersection of game platform and gamer. Players may also campaign for changes or be enrolled in testing, and, depending on the openness of the game, may themselves be able to make changes to it. Banks has explored this kind of interaction, terming it 'co-production' (2013: 90–5). While such an intervention in the game is easier in standalone games, because a change in an MMOG usually has to be distributed to all players, it also marks the line between what players can do through creative use of the game and what the game platform controls. There are points where player and game will be inextricable and other points where their practices are separate (Banks 2013: 19–20).

Another example of practices intersecting concerns the question of who owns what a gamer produces. Most MMOGs have an in-game economy with a currency that can be earned in different ways, such as by killing monsters and looting them, or by making in-game items and selling them, and so on. Who owns the results of such activities? The game provides the possibility but the gold in a player's virtual pocket is only there because of the player's activities. When gamers have tried to sell their in-game currency for out-of-game currency many games have banned this, often with the support of other players, who do not want someone to have more gold in-game just because they have out-of-game resources. Companies have been set up to generate in-game currency and sell it to players, an aspect which became racialised with the presumption that those just mining gold and not fully playing the game were often from China or South-East Asia (Dyer-Witheford and De Peuter 2009: 137–51; Castranova 2005; Jordan 2005). Here the controversy produces responses which mark out a community for each game. It also highlights a cross-game issue, as gamers and platforms find similar problems arising over gold-selling across different games.

This inter-space between players and game platforms is, then, primarily one of the community and the possibilities for action in a game that facilitate the creation of a mass player base, who have to cooperate to play the game and who, largely because of this cooperation, become an active force in the creation of the game. While the platform claims ownership and limits creative possibilities through control of software and hardware, this is balanced by the fact that the game requires groups of cooperating players and player ingenuity. Steinkuehler argues in relation to both *Lineage* and WoW that 'in-game communal norms amplify, enhance, negate, accom-modate, complement, and at times even ignore hard-coded game rules' (2006: 200). This inter-space is one in which the community of gamers for each MMOG is made visible in their interactions with the platform at several levels, to the point of in-game protests (Corneliussen and Rettberg 2008). Further, the conflicts, discussions and controversies that make the game community visible often also make visible issues of the ownership of information, which the platform asserts but which gamers may counter in their collective play, not always in ways either side appreciates. MMOGs include practices that revolve around issues of information ownership and communities of users, with the boundaries of both fluid at points, and at others enforced absolutely in code: be banned from a game and you will not be able to play, try to do something not allowed in a game and you will be stopped (for example, in WoW, if you swim too far from some islands you move out of the game world and your avatar will be automatically killed; you will never swim between some places in Azeroth).

Such are the main practices of MMOGs in relation to gamers, the game platform and the way their interaction creates a third 'in between' domain in which community becomes central. I have so far deliberately kept financial issues to one side – they have barely crept in when mentioning account management or gold-selling, and a more determinedly ethnographic account would by now have had plenty to say about MMOGs and money. It is then time to explore how these practices of MMOGs are monetised.

The first MMOG-like games were free, text-based environments called MUDs or MOOs. As the gaming industry took off alongside the growth of the personal computer market, the practice of paying for a standalone game emerged, which allowed a gamer to possess and play the game much as if they had bought a book and could take it home to read. Some non-3D MMOG games were a kind of interim between text-based MUDs and fully fledged 3D environments, but MMOGs are usually held to have emerged fully with *Ultima Online* in 1997, *Lineage* in 1998 and *Everquest* in 1999. As *Ultima* had been a pioneering and successful franchise of standalone computer games (with nine releases starting in 1979), there was an obvious continuity in a monetisation strategy of income from game purchases, to which was added a monthly subscription. *Lineage* became highly successful in South Korea and South-East Asia and was the largest MMOG for many years (Park 2005; Steinkuehler 2006). By the early 2000s the player numbers for these games were beginning to entice games companies, with *Lineage* having close to 3 million active subscribers in 2001, *Everquest* half a million, *Ultima Online* around a quarter of a million and new entrant *Dark Age of Camelot* also at a quarter of a million by 2002 (MmogChart 2005). With a market in Asia of around 3 million and in Anglo-America and Europe of around 1 million, there seemed to be potential for profit.

The possibility of profit was underlined by the financial model with its two elements of an initial purchase of the game at a price comparable to buying a standalone game, and then a monthly subscription. Further, the initial lump purchase could be repeated at intervals by releasing substantial upgrades with new gameplay facets – such as extra lands to explore, different types of characters, special items, raised levels of characters, etc. From around 2010 onward this model was felt by many to be in decline, with the common wisdom in the gaming blogosphere being that transition from it is inevitable; but it is impossible to understand the attraction of MMOGs to for-profit companies without examining this point in their history when, in the West, there was hope that after *Dark Age of Camelot* and *Everquest* a game might top 1 million subscriptions, and *Star Wars Galaxies* with its major franchise connection was watched closely. A million purchases and a million subscriptions were an attractive financial proposition. *Star Wars Galaxies* was to disappoint, not substantially increasing the market beyond *Dark Age* and *Everquest* (MmogChart 2005), and a Western-centred view usually failed to recognise that the possibility of millions of subscribers had already been realised in South Korea and South-East Asia. It was with *World of Warcraft*, launched in 2004, that MMOGs blew past preconceptions of their market, with the game reaching 5 million subscribers within a year and gaining a peak subscription of 12.5 million after four years with the release of its third expansion (*Wrath of the Lich King*) (Knight 2015). By 2018 this had fallen to around 5 million, but WoW had also established a rhythm in which the release of an expansion pack brings a rise in subscriptions which tails off after players have explored the new material, until another expansion is launched.

What does this mean in terms of income? In July 2018 a one-month subscription to WoW cost $12.99.[3] The next expansion (*Battle for Azeroth*), introduced in August the same year, cost $49.99. However, this expansion will not work if a player does not already have the basic game and some prior expansions, which cost $59.99 if bought from scratch. The attraction should be clear: at least 5 million monthly payments of $12.99 (around $65 million per month), plus a one-off income of between $250 million (just for the expansion) and $300 million (for the expansion and previous games). The subscription income continues to come in month by month and can be considerably higher around the time expansions are released, which is every two years (seven expansions over fourteen years). In addition to subscriptions, WoW offers various in-game purchases, including pets (a small kitten called Mischief will follow you around in-game and costs $10), particular mounts (like a dragon for flying or a lion for riding on the ground, that cost $25, though other mounts can be earned in-game without paying), as well as services such as changing your race from dwarf to night elf, which costs $25, or changing your name ($10) or appearance ($15), and so on.

WoW is run by a company called Blizzard that is in turn owned by Activision; figures are not available in their annual report for WoW specifically, as Blizzard runs a number of games, including the popular non-MMOG *Overwatch* (launched in 2016) and the video-card game *Hearthstone*, linked to WoW. In 2015, with no expansion in WoW, Blizzard had a net revenue of $1.5 billion, in 2016 (which saw the launch of a WoW expansion and *Overwatch*) $2.4 billion, and in 2017 (no WoW expansion) $2.1 billion (Activision 2018). Even with a subscriber base at less than half its peak, WoW was bringing in substantial income.

These revenues come at some cost, as an MMOG must maintain its infrastructure, service its customers, pay for new expansion development, and acquire a passionate community that it must enter into a relationship with. The relentless materiality of adding (or subtracting) computers and maintaining a service in which millions of players send in information that has to be handled and sent back out to those same millions creates major resource demands. How much does this cost in the case of WoW? Such figures are difficult to find, but in a call to financial analysts Blizzard claimed that between 2004 and 2008 it spent $200 million in total on staff salaries, hardware and everything else. The game in its first year (it was launched in November 2004) gained 5 million subscribers each paying $12 a month, meaning that by the end of its first year its income was $60 million a month or $720 million a year; by 2008, with the number of subscribers climbing to over 10 million, it was receiving an income from these of $1,440 million a year. Assuming the $200 million figure for expenses in 2004–8 is accurate, it seems safe to say that WoW has been highly profitable (Modine 2008).

Despite WoW's success, the dual model of game purchase and monthly subscription has begun to be seen as outdated, with a new model rising under the banner of 'free-to-play'. In 2012 the Chief Operating Officer of EA, Peter Moore, argued that what he called 'mainstream games' would all become free-to-play:

> I think, ultimately, … microtransactions will be in every game, but the game itself or the access to the game will be free. I think there's an inevitability that happens five years from now, 10 years from now, that, let's call it the client, to use the term [is free.] It is no different than … it's free to me to walk into The Gap in my local shopping mall. They don't charge me to walk in there. I can walk into The Gap, enjoy the music, look at the jeans and what have you, but if I want to buy something I have to pay for it. (Moore cited in Karmali 2012)

The new monetisation strategy is to give away for free the software or client that players need to access the platform and play the game. Once a group of players is created then monetisation may proceed relying entirely on in-game and other transactions. Although, as mentioned, WoW offers various purchases in addition to subscription, it is perhaps not surprising that, given its subscriber numbers, it has not pursued this model. One example of an MMOG game that has done so is *Rift*, which started using the purchase-plus-subscription model but shifted to a free-to-play monetisation strategy.

Rift is very similar to WoW in its structure and first emerged as one of a series of expected 'WoW-killers', none of which ever achieved WoW's level of success.[4] It was again set in a broad swords and sorcery world, with PVP and PVE divided and the latter based on complex encounters with AI-run monsters (similar to WoW). The game launched in March 2011 and claimed to have gained 1 million users by August that year and to have generated $100 million in revenue in its first year. It also admitted to having spent just over $50 million to develop the game, and a year after launch claimed to have raised $85 million to invest in further development (Makuch 2012; Graft 2011). Unfortunately, as a private company, it is difficult to find information on subscriber numbers or profitability for *Rift* or the company that owns it, TrionWorlds. What happened next is that after what seemed a strong start in 2011, the company moved *Rift* to a free-to-play model in 2013, allowing the whole game to be played for free but with in-game purchases for some gameplay items and for various pets and cosmetic items. It also developed a 'patron' model, which offered various gameplay benefits – such as faster movement, quicker gaining of gold and the like – if players took out a subscription. *Rift* publicity was always clear that if you played for free you would be able to experience all of the game, though completing it might take longer if no payments were ever made. Coming full circle in 2018, it was announced that *Rift* would offer a separate subscription-only server, returning part of its world to the original subscriber model, and sparking much debate over whether the free-to-play model was itself failing. *Rift*'s decision to offer both a free-to-play and a subscription model was partly driven by player demand for the latter, often articulated by players as being a better way to play because subscriptions put all players on an even footing (Machekovech 2018).

Free-to-play is thought to offer potential profitability because it can generate larger numbers of players who are happy to pay for various benefits in a game even if benefits are only cosmetic, such as a distinctive hat. Free-to-play relies on micro-transactions, which involves keeping individual sales relatively low cost so that players do not feel they are paying too much each time they decide to pay for an item, such as a hat, or not. One of free-to-play's central dynamics is maintaining players' belief that other players are not able to pay to win the game, or at least are not able to do so in any substantial way. *Rift*'s answer to complaints that the game is 'pay to win' stresses that all items in the game, particularly the most valuable, are available for free-to-play gamers. Other games have had to carefully manage such perceptions and the realities of gameplay to ensure their community is maintained. It is true both that, in the world of free-to-play games, players always have another option, and that games can require a major investment from players both in the time it takes to create a well-equipped high-level character and in sociality if one becomes part of a guild based on many friendships. Leaving may look easy as there are plenty of other games, but it is not always so simple. For regular players, leaving a game may be the same as leaving a social circle, not unlike a sporting club, and may be easiest to do when a guild as a whole moves, as mine did when we formed a WoW guild based on friendships created in *Dark Age of Camelot*, moved to WoW together, then to *Warhammer Online*, then back to WoW and finally to *Rift*. Game platforms will then have commitments like these from players and will have to ensure their free-to-play strategies do not undermine the commitment of players by undermining their sense of fair play and of being members of a gaming community rather than just sources of income for the game. As Lin and Sun (2011) have argued, a central issue with maintaining players in such games is whether free-to-play models start to shift players' perceptions of themselves from being members of a gaming community to being consumers.

Free-to-play relies on revenue from a number of sources. The two primary ones are income from buying items or services for the game and targeted advertising based on data mining (Kerr 2016: 74–8; Nieborg 2015: 7–8; Evans 2016). Kerr calls the latter a 'platform logic' and notes that 'The general characteristics of freemium games that rely on indirect revenue streams, including advertising, product placement and user data, have much in common with social media and search services more generally' (2016: 74). Given the discussions in previous chapters, little needs to be said about the strategy of targeted advertising in this context. In-game purchases split broadly into buying cosmetic items, such as clothes, and buying aids in playing the game. Cosmetic items need little explanation and will consist of anything the game controllers can create that they think players will buy – I have already mentioned the pets and specialist mounts that can be bought in WoW. (It is important to note that these mounts are entirely visual, they do not move faster or in different areas to mounts that can be earned in-game; they just look different.) The second kind of purchase might include access to weapons that are difficult to earn in-game, or the ability to level up a character faster; as Evans argues, this is essentially about 'monetizing player impatience' (2016: 565, 574–7). Another stream, which has been criticised by regulatory authorities, is something akin to gambling, in which a player buys something, a box for example, which contains some items but the player does not know which items. Opening the box then reveals a randomly allocated piece of loot which may be of little value or very rare. This dynamic is familiar to MMOG players, since if they kill another character in the game then the reward will often be a randomly dropped item, and players sometimes go back over complicated encounters multiple times in an attempt to gain a rare item. In addition to other streams of income, then, randomly generated rewards are a familiar feature in games which can be monetised in addition to other streams of income (Orland 2018).

There is a difficulty here for the game platform as there is the possibility of alienating players who feel others are gaining too much advantage and that the game has become unfairly tipped in favour of those with real-world money to spend. A broad perception of this among players can push them to move on to other games. As mentioned above, this was partly what lay behind *Rift*'s decision to come full circle and offer a subscription version alongside their free-to-play model. Kerr argues that, after a few games began offering purchases that effectively created 'pay to win' game environments, 'Companies have increasingly realised that developing "cosmetic" additions to their games which players could purchase but which had no impact upon the balance of the game were often most successful' (2016: 74). Since the gaming community has to accept that any ability to buy things that affect gameplay is 'fair', this effectively limits what the gaming company can create. As Kerr notes, this also leads to further requirements on companies to monitor and work with gamers, both through data and through community managers, in order to adjust what the game offers (2016: 119–24).

What can we make of these economic practices? First, they are mixtures of already existing or pre-digital economic practices, particularly manufacturing and retail, and of digital economic practices. On the one hand, practices of monetisation that rely on buying something – remembering that even in 2018 games are still often bought as physical items with a disc inside a branded case – conform to existing economic practices (much as Apple and Microsoft do), even if the bought item may be downloaded rather than provided in a box. On the other hand, a system of constantly updating what has been bought, with bug fixes or changes to gameplay, allied to repeated purchases of expansions and to other strategies like advertising and in-game purchases, ensure a reliance on very digital economic practices (Nieborg 2014). MMOG economic practices are thus a hybrid, as Kerr points out when arguing that many games have multiple production logics, and as Fung notes in examining different strategies for the monetisation of games in China (Kerr 2016: 183–9; Fung 2018: 59–61). MMOGs rely on digital economic practices as they have to ensure a collective practice which creates something akin to a community or multiple groups with common interests in the gaming environment, while at the same time employing non-digital economic practices like commodity purchasing. It is now worth exploring this hybrid economic logic in relation to other digital gaming forms.

All the Other Games

Online, networked, video and computer games cover a wide range of different types of games and game platforms. I will briefly look at three broad types: non-persistent worlds, consoles, and app and mobile games. Even these three broad areas do not cover all of gaming; augmented reality games, for example, received a major boost with the release of *Pokémon Go* in 2016, and virtual reality is being commercialised as I write in 2019. Casual games like solitaire are often bundled with operating systems and are played particularly by older players. However, rather than trying to be comprehensive, it will be enough here to expand the discussion of MMOGs as digital economic practices by looking briefly at several other types of games.

Non-persistent virtual worlds are often first-person shooter games which present as a 3D environment but offer only a slice of the open environments MMOGs rely on. These slices tend to be repeated 'maps', restricted in size, on which smaller groups of players are dropped for a battle, the end of which leads to all characters being removed from the map. Any persistence is created across such battles by factors external to the virtual environment in things like leader boards, rankings and so on. Such time-limited battles also exist inside many MMOGs, often called scenarios or battlegrounds, in which players can move from their open virtual environment to repeated small-scale maps with limited player numbers. Emblematic non-MMOG games of this type include *Counter-Strike*, in which a group of terrorists is faced by a group of counter-terrorists, and *Team Fortress*, which pits groups of nine players against each other. Such games have become more popular since 2016 with 'battle royale' versions in the emergence of PlayerUnknown's *Battleground*, *Apex Legends* and *Fortnite*. These games put a number of players, up to 100, in an environment in a battle, during which the area being played on reduces over time and is won when only one player is left. These games have expanded the popularity of non-persistent first-person shooter games and have connected multiple platforms, in particular extending from PCs and consoles to mobile devices.

These games employ all the monetisation strategies already discussed, from subscriptions and one-off purchases through to free-to-play strategies of customisation and in-game boosts. While the in-game practices are distinct from MMOGs in terms of playing in limited environments repeatedly in small teams, these games develop persistence outside the game environment to repeatedly draw players to the game, allowing monetisation strategies though the creation of player communities. The 'fun' of such games is drawn across a repetitive environment to keep players engaged, though a central attraction is always the testing of skills by players against each other. Further engagement comes from acquiring in-game skills, upgrades, and intermittent gameplay and virtual environment changes, as well as extra-game resources such as forums, rating systems, and, finally, connections to e-sports (the latter offering the 'ultimate' in team competition, tantalising players with the possibility of becoming a professional gamer) (Taylor 2012; Phillips 2015).

Console games are moving closer to becoming cross-platform, particularly when *Fortnite* connected PC games, console and mobile devices in 2018. Yet from the 1970s, when consoles first emerged with the game *Pong*, consoles have been associated with a particular type of game linked to a blockbuster franchise (Nieborg 2014; Kerr 2016: 70–8). Console gameplay is different primarily due not to the game but to its controllers, which diverge between consoles and are different to PC or mobile controls. The content of games, however, largely continues the theme of competitive and often violent contest. What evolved over time was a particular form of gaming digital economic practice based on major franchises such as *Halo, Grand Theft Auto, Call of Duty* and more, each of which created a set of gaming fans who were fed downloadable content for each game and then new versions of the game at intervals (not unlike the MMOG path successfully pursued by WoW in updates and expansions or non-gaming software releases such as MS Office). 'The Call of Duty series shows that the Triple-A game has transformed from a stand alone, singular artifact into a perpetually extended, more open-ended commodity type that corresponds with a particular "system of control," combining the franchising publishing strategy with digitally distributed game extensions' (Nieborg 2014: 49).

This strategy proved successful not only with obviously violent games like *Call of Duty* (essentially fighting wars of various sorts) or *Grand Theft Auto* (essentially perpetrating violent crime) but also with such games as *Legend of Zelda* (a mixture of puzzles, interactions and fighting) and the *Super Mario* universe (which includes racing games, fighting and puzzle jump games). Nieborg argues that console games are strongly marked by this strategy, which integrates technology, gameplay and monetisation, to the extent that other kinds of strategies and games have been squeezed out by the cost to a game studio of repeating the blockbuster.

App games have arisen as smartphones and tablets have increased in power, becoming essentially mini-computers with screens, colours and processing speeds advanced enough to run games. These are games that have been dubbed the 'casual revolution' in gaming as they are often designed to be played in short five- to ten-minute bursts, fitting into commutes and brief periods during a day when a player has a few moments. They are a mobile innovation, being playable wherever the player happens to be, even sometimes without connectivity if the game has an 'offline' mode. This is gaming in what Hjorth and Richardson call the 'interstices of everyday life' (2011: 121), and it can earn its creators a high income. For example, King Digital Entertainment grew from $63 million in revenue with a $1 million loss in 2011 to $1.8 billion revenue with a $567 million profit in 2013, eventually being bought by Activision Blizzard in 2016 for $5.9 billion (Nieborg 2015: 1; Lunden 2016). King make *Candy Crush*, and took over from game maker Zynga (who made the game *Farmville*) as the largest app game maker after Zynga's successes with Facebook games had demonstrated the potential of the market.

App games are the exemplars of free-to-play. Out of an over 300 million person player base, only 3 per cent pay any form of subscription or direct fee to be able to play. Instead, pretty much everyone plays for free on apps. This leads to a distillation of the essentials of free-to-play as already described for MMOGs: payment for cosmetic items and for items which improve or extend gameplay, and targeted advertising based on mining player data often allied to a payment to remove ads. Funding through ads is, as Nieborg argues, buttressed by a third pillar that he calls 'virality', which consists of ways the game insinuates and promotes itself leading to further incentives to purchase in-game items. For example, in *Candy Crush* you can send a life you have earned or bought to another player as a gift; similarly all kinds of items earned or bought in *Farmville* – horseshoes, nails, etc., in general the items needed to develop a farm – can be sent to other *Farmville* players as gifts. This leads both to community development along the lines of the likes, pokes, etc., familiar from social media, and to incentives to purchase more items to send as gifts (Nieborg 2015: 8).

The above are three different kinds of gaming practices that are quite distinct from MMOG gaming but which essentially share the same moneti-sation strategies, and in some cases operate monetisation in ways similar to search and social media. There are also a number of other practices that are worth noting which emphasise not only the hybridity of gaming economic practices within games and their gameplay but also their wider connections. For example, the gameplaying streaming service Twitch.tv, already mentioned when discussing disintermediation, is a platform on which gamers can create their own channels and draw revenue through donations from viewers, advertising and subscribers. These are live-action channels with streamers often playing games for five or more hours a day, during which viewers can hear and see both the gamer, what the gamer is doing in a game (that is, what is on the game player's screen), and sometimes have someone visibly commenting on what is happening in-game, while at the same time being able to write in a stream of comments or interact in real time in other ways (Johnson and Woodcock 2019; Anderson 2017). On Twitch (and its Chinese equivalent Huya) it is watching game players and the lure to some players of becoming a professional based on Twitch revenue that has grown the platform into become a major content provider with, in early 2018, 15 million daily active users, 140 million monthly users and, perhaps most telling of its success as a new platform for video content, 2.2 million monthly broadcasters (Smith 2019). In August 2014, Twitch.tv was bought by Amazon for $970 million (Gittleson 2014). The creation by each broadcaster of a relation to their viewers and their successful embedding of that relation within broader game communities – such as websites, conferences, events and so on – again mark this supplementary economic practice to game playing as one dependent in a digital context on the creation of collective relations. Similarly Steam, an online platform for selling games created by gaming company Valve, may look immediately like a game shop that happens to be online, but it also strives to generate a 'Steam community' based on friends lists, comments and other means of drawing income not only from selling games but by becoming a home for gaming communities.

While supplementary practices such as streaming look aside from individual gamers, they are worth briefly mentioning to emphasise how online games allow us to see the intersection of different kinds of economic practices. Games continue and develop monetisation models seen in case studies, emphasising both the potential hybridity of communities and monetisation within digital economic practices and their connections to other kinds of economic practices.

Conclusion

If these are the monetisation models operating in the gaming sector, to what extent should we draw attention to their similarity with other such models, for instance to subscriber models that have been around for a long time in relation to magazines or newspapers? In relation to economic practices, sectoral analysis is an abstraction from everyday actions. The value of a sectoral analysis is not to suggest there is operating in the everyday world a 'pure' kind of digital economic practice but to isolate and identify some specifically sectoral economic practices that exist in constant interaction with other practices. As 'digitally native' as Google is – with targeted advertising its predominant source of revenue, connected to a free service and the mining of communities – it still likes to sell stuff like the Pixel phone (which of course allows greater integration with the world of Google). Similarly, as focused as Apple is on the design and sale of items of combined hardware and software, it still offers some significant digital economic practices with things such as iTunes. By exemplifying hybrid economic practices, games support the argument that creating a sectoral analysis is not to claim there are separate practices in the everyday but to abstract out the dynamics of a digital economic sector in order to identify that sector.

One important aspect of games is that they not only bring together a range of digital economic practices (including in some cases having success-fully disintermediated game retail stores) but also integrate non-digital economic practices. The exemplar here is the Steam platform, which could be seen as simply an old-fashioned retail outlet for the digital product of computer games, and which certainly offers that service, but which also tries to integrate gamer communities. Steam offers groups of gamers ways of interacting, for example through friends lists that allow a gamer to see if their friends are online and what they are playing as well as what their friends have recently bought or played. What differentiates Steam from a simple storefront is the creation of such collective activities among gamers that underpin friendships and communities. This is based on not only buying the game through Steam but on playing it through the Steam platform; that is, if you buy for example *Total War Napoleon* in order to either beat or to be Napoleon then you start that game by first starting Steam, or when you directly start the game it invokes the Steam platform. With gamers returning to Steam to play their games, the platform is then able to offer activities that create communities and to begin to draw revenue from them. Steam has had a peak of 18 million concurrent users online and, offering just one day as an example, on 9 February 2019 had a minimum of 10 million and a maximum of 16 million users logged on to its platform (Steam 2019; Joseph 2018).

A significant step here is that games bring to the fore the shift a number of scholars have traced when arguing that digital economies often substitute renting a commodity for owning it, even if they appear to be offering that commodity for sale:

> digital retailers insist that ownership depends on the terms of an end user license agreement ('EULA') – that incomprehensible slew of legalese you reflexively click 'I agree' to dismiss. Those terms – negotiated by lawyers working for retailers and publishers – determine your rights, not the default entitlements of personal property. And buried within those thousands of words that we all ignore is one consistent message: you don't own the books you bought; you merely license them. That is to say, you have permission to read them. Until one day, you don't. (Perzanowski and Schultz 2016: 2)

If you have bought a game that requires an online connection, and nearly all games now do, then this means you can be banished from the game anytime the owner of the platform feels that is necessary. Sometimes banning is a mechanism for securing community, for example when banning cheats or those using unauthorised hacks to gain gameplay advantage (Consalvo 2007: 83–105). In short, however many boxes of games a gamer has bought, if a game requires plugging into a network then they have in effect only rented it. Many digital services operate in a similar way, whether Amazon's Kindle for books or the way companies can turn mobile phones off remotely; in many cases, what appears to be bought turns out to be rented (Perzanowski and Schultz 2016). Similarly, the music service Spotify allows tracks to be downloaded and listened to without a network connection, if you have a premium subscription, but if you then cancel that subscription you lose access to downloaded tracks; what seemed downloaded and available is revealed as rented. Of course, this is not the case with all digital commodities, and there are still games with single-player modes that in ownership terms are more akin to the book you hold in your hand than the book you store on a Kindle. Nevertheless, articulated in different ways in different practices, the scholarship that Perzanowski and Schultz bring together identifies one consequence of digital economic practices to be a shift from owning a commodity to renting it. This dynamic is one I will return to when modelling digital economic practices in the abstract and general.

This leads to the final point of this chapter because, for all their connections to a range of digital and non-digital economic practices, games draw on a broadly similar structure to the other digital economic practices so far surveyed. There are in gaming players who take up activities for leisure or fun that begin to look oddly like labour when repetition is required (and some games include activities that are more obviously like labour, such as digging with pickaxes in *Minecraft* or mining in WoW). These activities are mediated through complex platforms whose core compo-nents are maintained by, both owned and controlled, an institution that attempts to define and guide how these activities will create and spread group or collective actions, actions that in themselves are essential to the success of the game. For example, in WoW you cannot defeat Ragnaros the Firelord by yourself, you will need a raid of forty gamers; without those thirty-nine others Ragnaros will languish in a cavern with the game diminished (Chen 2012). This mediation of the platform includes both obvious things such as the game environments and clients controlled by the platform owner, as well as a range of spaces for discussion and devel-opment by gamers which may or may not be under the control of the gaming company, which has to grapple with its 'community of action'. Grappling with the community involves defining what is and is not the property of gamers or game, what changes may or may not be made to the game, what responsibilities the game platform has to correct bugs and to provide new content, and so on. Monetisation is consequent and dependent on these inter-relations and particularly on how property and access are defined in the interactions between gamers, game platform and game controllers. Non-monetisation is also possible, and there are a range of free games (some of them pirated and some not) that maintain even MMOG environments with free access. Pirate examples include the launch of WoW, *Warhammer Online* and *Dark Age of Camelot* servers, some of which offer an earlier version of the game (and for a nostalgic gamer often a better-loved version of each game) or, in *Warhammer*'s case, revive a cancelled game (Orland 2016).

The broad, repeated conclusion from looking at economic practices in digital contexts as diverse as determinedly free Free Software to determinedly mining your emotional life for profit Facebook is that there are activities – often provided for free, and sometimes by subscription or for a one-off payment – that can only be undertaken by engaging with complex digital and internet-dependent platforms. These activities create a wide range of collective actions, but each set of such actions is specific to its platform and underpins a complex sense of groups of collective actions or a 'community of action'. The platform controller controls access to, and many aspects of, the activities but is also itself dependent on the community of action; without the activities – of gamers, searchers, cab riders, etc. – the platform exists for no purpose. The platform controller may then, if their platform is successful, seek ownership over the data flowing across it, turning freely undertaken activities into corporately owned data points. They may then also seek to monetise this conglomerate of practices through all the techniques discussed in this and previous chapters. As in any economic venture, profit is not guaranteed, but it can undoubtedly be gained by some of these techniques.

Analysing games has allowed a further exploration of how digital economic practices have developed in one of the most significant entertainment and leisure industries of our time. Analysing games has ensured that the point is not lost that digital economic practices necessarily intersect with other economic practices. Analysing games has brought to the fore the dynamics of subscription as a potentially successful digital economic practice when tied to an exclusive digital platform, and suggested that this is itself connected to a broader social shift from owning to renting. Finally, at the end of this chapter, analysing gaming has allowed for the identification of certain elements that may underpin the digital economy as an industrial sector. The time has then come to turn away from following concrete practices in the everyday and articulate a theory of the digital economy.

Already concepts have begun to appear within the analysis of digital economic practices, and these are often concepts already formed through significant debate. The obvious example is the recurrence of the word 'free', particularly while puzzling over its relation to the ability of some practices to monetise freely given time in activities. As noted briefly in the introduction, the examination of practices involves concepts without which it would be impossible to articulate what is going on; for example, I have at times had to indicate how ideas like collective activities and community or working for free have had to be interpreted to understand the examples of digital economic practices being examined. There is now an important shift in this book's argument toward focusing exactly on such concepts to try to model the digital economy across the different cases that have been explored and theorise how such an economy works. Such a shift is marked by a change of subject towards concepts, starting first with existing theories and then moving to a formulation of a model of the digital economy that reflects the digital economic practices already discussed. This will also necessitate a change of tone as more abstract ideas and more authors are discussed, instead of trying to follow how a particular practice plays out.

7   What We Think We Know About the Digital Economy: Profit, Labour, Production and Consumption

Digital economic practices are the repeated, everyday actions or habits that construct a set of exchanges that constitute an economic sector. Trying to see practices meant following them through case studies exploring different points of view within complex sets of actions and activities. This method was prompted by identifying conceptual difficulties in existing ways of identifying the digital economy and recognising an ongoing confusion between examining the effect the digital and the internet have had on the economy generally and analysing whether there are specific effects of the digital that create new economic patterns that may then affect the wider economy. The path of identifying specific digital economic effects has been taken, leading to a primarily qualitative analysis of practices. Having progressed this through case studies it is now possible to begin conceptualising the dynamics that have been identified in the case studies. To help with this there are a number of particular areas of existing work on the digital economy that are now clearly relevant to analysing the elements of digital economic practices that have been suggested by the preceding qualitative analysis.

There are three broad existing conceptual problematics or debates that will help build an understanding of the digital economy in light of the previous case studies. First, profit taking and exploitation have been analysed in terms of surplus value and rent. The focus of a range of thinkers here has been on explaining where both profit and value creation come from in digital economic activities. Second, it has been argued for some time that free labour is an important issue in digital contexts. This has proven a long-lived and empirically rich but also conceptually complicated debate involving issues such as when activities freely undertaken for enjoyment can be considered labour and vice versa. Third, there has been considerable debate about the collapse of the producer/consumer divide with the rise of terms like prosumer, playbour and so on. The debate here focuses on activities in which production and consumption occur simultaneously and encompasses issues conceptualising merging production and consumption. The three conceptual complexes of exploitation, free labour and producer/consumer will be examined in turn; in each case it will become clear that such concepts address central issues of the digital economy and that there remain important conceptual problems that will be addressed to theorise the digital economy.

These three areas are focused on for two related reasons. First, all three have been recurring themes in the case studies: What is profit and how does it happen? What are leisure, labour, production and consumption and how do they relate to 'communities of action'? The case studies have offered repeated examples of these issues coming to the fore that cry out for conceptualisation. Second, these are the three key areas of discussion among those who qualitatively examine the digital economy. While qualitative and practice-based research are not exactly the same thing, they are closely related in trying to provide a fundamental causal analysis on the basis of which more quantitative and more focused qualitative research might proceed. As explored in the introduction, without an understanding of what the digital economy means it is impossible to statistically describe or quantitatively analyse the digital economy. The three issues of exploitation, free labour and producer/consumer are the concepts from the last twenty years of scholarship that can help to form such an understanding of the digital economy. All three existing debates will turn out to be similar in identifying a key and important issue in understanding the digital economy, in contributing insight and concepts to help understanding, but doing so with sometimes confused and problematic conceptual frames.

Profit, Rent, Debt, Exploitation, Value

Of all things about digital industries it is money that can be guaranteed to attract attention. The massive profits made by some of the companies charted in previous chapters, and the remarkable valuations of new companies, often hit the headlines. For example, Snapchat hit a valuation of $28 billion on its stock market launch and in 2019 Uber valued itself at £100 billion while never having made a profit. 'Burn-rates' – the rate at which a company is losing money – seem sometimes to be offered up with pride, with Snapchat and Uber again being examples, the former losing just over half a billion dollars in 2016 and the latter $1.85 billion in 2017 (Helmore 2017; Feiner 2019). Where the digital economy is concerned, money in large amounts often goes hand in hand with a large number of users, claims about 'disruptive technologies' (Facebook's original slogan was 'move fast and break things'), and plain old-fashioned soap-selling hype. But what is the nature of profit-making, when it happens? A number of monetisation strategies have been identified in the case studies; is there a conceptual understanding that draws them together? Work in this area has been largely, though not entirely, developed by those inspired by Marxist thinking, which will allow us to take advantage of where Marxism and post-Marxism are most powerful, on value and exploitation, while acknowledging where they are vulnerable, on profit. On the subject of profit, value and exploitation in relation to the digital economy Marxism has interesting things to say that will help the argument progress from case studies to a conceptual foundation.

If identifying where profit is made is the starting point, then in Marxist terms this will be close to where exploitation occurs in an economic system. Broadly speaking, two theoretical accounts have been offered of the conditions that have led to massive profits for some digital companies. The first revolves around rent and implies a larger discussion about the place of debt in twenty-first-century capitalism. The second refers to a more classic Marxist analysis of surplus value, noting that the very stuff of internal emotional life has become directly commodified and subject to value extraction – an account particularly associated with social media analysis and echoed by some non-Marxist analysis. Looking at these in turn will set out some ideas for understanding profit in the digital economy.

The argument for rent as the source of exploitation and profit in the digital economy was put by Pasquinelli, in an analysis of Google in which he borrows a slogan coined by Vercellone: 'rent is the new profit' (Pasquinelli 2008: 91–3). The argument drawn on by Pasquinelli relates to Marx's concept of the general intellect. Marx claimed that knowledge is embodied in the machines of industrial capitalism, meaning that scientific, organisational, technological and other forms of knowledge have become a general force in production. Following Vercellone and other theorists, Pasquinelli argues that in cognitive capitalism the productive force of the general intellect has been generalised in the brains and activities of many individuals enmeshed in digital and internet technologies. This distributed productive force is then rented out and controlled through intellectual property rights. The way Google 'reads' the WWW and draws rent from that reading through advertising is one example. In this way, rent becomes the source of profit in cognitive capitalism (Pasquinelli 2008: 92–7; Vercellone 2005, 2006; Huws 2014: 159–63). Huws similarly uses Marx's theory of value and, while deflecting some of what she calls the 'convoluted' nature of the argument around the general intellect and rent, she also argues that 'most of the profit' of typical digital and internet companies 'comes from some combination of charging usage or commission fees to service providers and/ or service users and/or advertisers – in other words, rent' (2014: 163).

It might be thought that this analysis reflects the way the control of intellectual property means we no longer buy to possess but pay to rent, as seen in the prior discussion of 'rent not buy' as a monetisation strategy. But Pasquinelli and Vercellone are articulating a different argument that is as applicable to Google and Facebook as to any tendency in what Vercellone calls cognitive capitalism. However, this collapse of different kinds of monetisation into one kind of profit-making elides some of the complexity uncovered in our case studies and equates what have so far seemed quite distinct kinds of practices. With this cautionary note in mind, it is worth taking a look at the other relevant arguments, for this attention to rent as profit shifts Marxist thought considerably because such thought had for a long time seen rent as a parasite on the truly productive force of surplus value.[1] Much Marxist ink has been spent on this argument that rent does not produce value, meaning that over economic cycles rent may be the source of transitory profit but does not reflect the huge increase in value created by industrial capitalism, which was the fundamental source of profit. A different interpretation than Pasquinelli's and Huws's applies a more classic Marxist approach focusing on surplus value in the analysis of cognitive capitalism. This can be initially approached by way of Dean's work.

Dean takes from Marx the argument that value 'derives from the social character of labour'. Cognitive capitalism's distinction is that it 'seizes, privatizes, and attempts to monetise the social substance. It doesn't depend on the commodity-thing. It directly exploits the social relation at the heart of value' (2012: 129). What we do online, every photo or status update or post, opens up our social relations to direct exploitation by companies farming the surplus of all our interactions on the various services or platforms we use. This argument is not entirely different to those like Pasquinelli's on rent. Value is derived from something like the social character of knowledge, in Pasquinelli's case the general intellect and in Dean's the social character inherent to labour. However, Dean's focus on value and surplus suggests a direct relationship between the labour involved in using social media and the value produced there, whereas Pasquinelli's focuses on the way rents can be derived from owning the social knowledge produced on information platforms (Dean 2012: 131–3).

Andrejevic's work is also useful here, as he begins with a strong argument that exploitation exists in the way individuals' information is taken from them and then aggregated to target ads that, in turn, produce profits. Though many see this as a privacy issue, Andrejevic argues that framing it around privacy has shortcomings that an approach based on exploitation does not (2013: 150). From here his path is: 'To what extent analytic definitions of exploitation can be applied to unwaged forms of partici-pation that generate value appropriated by those who control the platforms upon which this participation relies?' (2013: 153). Yet the more Andrejevic specifies how the process of privatisation of personal information on digital platforms is a form of exploitation, the further he moves from the technical definition of exploitation as the extraction of surplus value. Instead, he reasserts the importance of the moment of alienation in exploitation – that is, the moment when a worker's labour is taken from them and presented back to them as the property of the owner of the production process – applying this to the appropriation of information: 'we might level the charge of exploitation to highlight the way in which the capture of personal information turns our own activity against ourselves' (2013: 157). The charge of exploitation has here become more one of alienation that is prior to exploitation understood as the extraction of surplus value. This is a valuable point; as Andrejevic argues: 'The potential usefulness of an exploitation-based critique of online monitoring is that it invites us to reframe questions of individual choice and personal pleasure in terms of social relations' (2013: 161). But it also becomes confused in so far as it requires assuming that freely given leisure activities, such as gaming, searching, posting and so on, are alienated labour. Others from different though related theoretical frames have argued for a similar relationship between the users and the owners of information platforms like Facebook or WeChat. Stark argued that:

> As hyperentrepreneurial capitalism looks for new spaces to mobilise the creative energies of 'members', social networking represents an effort to capitalise not only user content but the users' personal contacts as well. Commercial social networking is an expression of the centuries-long dynamic of capitalism: the ever-greater socialization of production combined with the privatization of profits. Social networking sites then become sites of contention over this latest effort at commodification and the intensification of the search for value. (2009: 209)

Though differently framed conceptually, the substance of this claim of an information surplus is similar to Zuboff's (2019) idea of a behavioural surplus. I have argued that information platform owners and controllers gain an information surplus as only they can correlate the individual information presented to them by their users (Jordan 2015: 200–7). The value of the approaches here lies in their analysis of the nature of any surplus in relation to value, profit, exploitation and their social conditions, and this analysis, like that of rent, seems applicable to many of the monetisation strategies previously explored. Yet there is a curious flattening where the analysis, particularly of social media, might be presumed to be a basis for defining a general form of cognitive capitalism or, for Zuboff, a surveillance capitalism. This is a difficulty that lurks within such analyses – a sense that they presume in their starting conditions the exploitation that they will find in their results.

In short, the arguments of Dean, Andrejevic and Pasquinelli briefly outlined above, and of Fuchs that will be touched on in a moment, presume that the activities conducted on social media or online are labour. Dean states: 'Facebook and Amazon, like many internet companies, claim ownership of information placed on their sites. They claim as their own property the products of unremunerated creative, communicative labour' (2012: 127). The issue here is the assumption that what is done on internet sites is labour. Fuchs similarly argues that 'Users of commercial social media platforms have no wages (v = 0). Therefore the rate of surplus value converges towards infinity. Internet prosumer labour is infinitely exploited by capital' (2014: 111). There are important theoretical objections to such a model,[2] but the more relevant issue based on what the case studies of digital economic practices have shown is not so much the relationship of activities to value, profit and surplus, but that the analysis proceeds because all user activities are assumed to be labour. This is despite the evidence that people supposedly providing free labour do not consider it labour, and that they fully understand that the companies may reuse their data. This is both acknowledged but not integrated into analysis by several Marxist theorists. Further, it is not often acknowledged that such companies make new information out of that drawn from users and that this information would not exist without the company's work (Fuchs 2014: 107; Neff 2012; Jordan 2015). This leads back to one of Marxism's most vexed ideas – 'false consciousness' – with the argument that individuals do not know that what they are doing leads to their exploitation:

> Networked information technologies have been the means through which people have been subjected to the competitive intensity of neoliberal capitalism. Enthusiastically participating in personal and social media – I have broadband at home! My new tablet lets me work anywhere! With my smartphone, I always know what is going on! – we build the trap that captures us. (Dean 2012: 124)

The faults of Marxism in analysing the digital economy remain the faults of Marxism. False consciousness is a deeply problematic concept which cannot be deployed, as it implicitly is in much of the foregoing analyses, without significant concern for what is being claimed. Presuming that participants in digital economic practices do not understand their exploitation reduces them to dupes who need to be led to the fuller understanding required to change society. Such ideas have proven deeply problematic in both Marxist theory and practice for a long time (Scholz 2017: 109–10; Hall

1986). This is not to say that all Marxist or Marx-inspired analysis suffers exactly these faults or fails to use the powers of Marxist analysis to gain insight into the digital economy. I have noted the power of the concept of exploitation used by a number of analysts to drive home critique and to see who is benefiting, often to obscene levels of financial profit, from digital economy practices. The work of those like Jarrett (2016), Qiu (2016) or Dyer-Witheford (2015) are essential to understanding relations of power in the digital economy. Yet there remain a number of conceptual problems that have been part of Marxist thinking for longer than the digital economy has existed, which recur in some Marxist analyses of the digital economy, and which need to be criticised.

Further issues could be raised here, such as the complexities of the 'transformation problem' which, put crudely, points out that even if Marxism correctly identifies the source of capitalism's dynamism in the exploitation of surplus value, this does not explain profit. One can produce great amounts of value and still be unable to sell any of it. This theoretical problem is held to be solved by some and to be fatal to Marxist theory by others (Mason 2015: 151–6). The fundamental problem with the detail of these arguments is, however, that presuming all activities to be labour, while adopting a Marxist understanding of labour, imports the basis of the argument's conclusion into its premises. Refusing this conceptual move does not entail ignoring the insight that whoever controls a platform can reap extra information from it. But it is problematic to assume that labour is a given in digital economic practices. Unsettling this presumption, while taking forward ideas about value, surplus and rent, requires looking into what labour means in digital economic practices. This points us to a second set of concepts that need to be explored in relation to ideas about free labour.

Free Labour

All the likes, tweets, blogs, photos, snapchats, meme links and private messages are what make digital platforms come alive. If no one is there being active then there may as well be no platform. It is all this activity that forms the basis of the bargain in which people's information about themselves is correlated with their activity thereby offering the platform owner a path to information they can try to monetise. This relationship between freely given time in activities and profit was recognised early on in critical analyses of the internet's effects on society and the economy. The debate was initiated and largely formed conceptually by Terranova's 2000 article 'Free Labour', although many important related ideas had already been formed in feminist discussions of domestic work as free labour (Ross 2013: 30, fn 1; Duffy 2017: 7–8). Terranova's own formulation of the problem is worth quoting at length:

> This essay describes the digital economy as a specific mechanism of internal 'capture' of larger pools of social and cultural knowledge. The digital economy is an important area of experimentation with value and free cultural/affective labour. It is about specific forms of production (Web design, multimedia production, digital services, and so on), but is also about forms of labour we do not immediately recognise as such: chat, real-life stories, mailing lists, amateur newsletters and so on. These types of cultural and technical labour are not produced by capitalism in any direct, cause-and-effect fashion; that is, they have not developed simply as an answer to the economic needs of capital. However, they have developed in relation to the expansion of the cultural industries and are part of a process of economic experimentation with the creation of monetary value out of knowledge/culture/affect. (2000: 38)

Writing before the success of Google (whose first profitable year was 2001) and not long after the bursting of the dot.com bubble, Terranova identified a range of different activities taking place on the World Wide Web – discussion lists, chat groups and so on – that, she argued, constitute the digital economy. This economy, then, is built out of activities that Terranova identifies as labour that is unpaid. She also embeds several complex, if not contradictory, positions in this conceptualisation, including that labour is not called for by capital but is a response to cultural industries and the monetisation of knowledge; and that it is not simply labour and is not usually recognised as labour. These issues recur in two key claims made both within Terranova's analysis and in many later discussions of free labour in the digital economy.

First, 'Labour is not equivalent to waged labour' (Terranova 2000: 46). Activities on the internet are labour, whether they are waged or not. Labour is presumed to be the right concept for the myriad activities that were undertaken even on the 2000 internet, let alone those explored in the previous case studies of digital economic practices. As argued in relation to exploitation, such a claim forecloses an understanding of what is done by many on the internet as being anything other than labour. Second, 'Free labour … is not necessarily exploited labour. Within the early virtual communities, we are told, labour was really free' (Terranova 2000: 48). Terranova notes that exploitation was not necessarily present because many gave their time knowing they would be rewarded with a collective product such as a thriving forum or a good website. Her scepticism is signalled by the phrase 'we are told' and by her subsequent arguments, which do not explore how labour can be labour if it is non-exploited and given freely, such that the activity involved should perhaps be called something other than labour. Further, these claims do not directly grasp the issues that arise in calling freely given activity in digital contexts 'labour' and connecting it to monetisation, in particular the problem of false consciousness according to which all those creating the Web or simply an email list are implicitly conceptualised as dupes of a capitalist profit-making system. There is a duality in the word 'labour' as it is able to reference labour as 'activity' as well as labour as 'work in an industry', and this creates a lack of clarity in its conceptualisation.

These dilemmas are repeated in subsequent accounts of free labour and digital labour, and are sometimes present in the debates around immaterial labour. Scholz's 2013 edited collection of essays, which built on a well-known conference series, stands as a monument to these intellectual dilemmas, and anyone who reads it may end up both angered by exploitation and confused about what free, labour, and digital mean. Ross's essay in this volume acknowledges the foundational importance of Terranova's work and argues that 'In most corners of the information landscape, working for nothing has become normative, and largely because it is not experienced as exploitation' (2013: 17). Wark identifies the same problem in relation to computer games: 'In a game like the popular World of Warcraft, you pay for the privilege of labouring to acquire objects and status that are only artificially scarce' (2013: 70) – here the equation of game-playing with labour is unproblematically asserted. De Kosnik's contribution is entitled 'Fandom as Free Labor' and argues both that 'fans' profuse contributions to the Internet can be regarded ... as labor', and that 'Fans ... do not regard their own activities as work that adds or creates exchange-value (rather, they think of their efforts as adding personal use value) and do not seek compensation for their activities' (2013: 99, 105). In the same volume, Andrejevic, Dean and others similarly draw on Terranova's landmark work but in doing so often reproduce the dilemmas of reconciling the concepts of free, paid, labour, pleasure, activity and so on, having already made the presumption that activity on the internet is labour. The same dilemmas are repeated in other work on labour in the digital economy (Dyer-Witheford 2015: 91–3; Scholz 2017: 101–6; Massanari 2015: Ch 1).

This view of labour has been contested. Hesmondhalgh notes the intellectual and moral strain involved in equating physical sweatshop labour with social media activities, arguing that some accounts of free labour are 'crude, reductionist and functionalist, totally underestimating contradiction and struggle in capitalism. The underlying but underdeveloped normative position is that all the time we spend under capitalism contributes to a vast negative machine called capitalism; nothing escapes this system' (2010: 280). The core issue Hesmondhalgh identifies is the lack of empirical differentiation between different kinds of labour, play and activities within different contexts in cultural industries: if everything has become exploited labour then this implies the triumph of an all-encompassing digital capitalism with no outside, as everything we do is labour for capital. Neff builds on empirical work in which she examined the practices of information workers in Silicon Alley in New York. A complex view emerges as she finds the workers to be fully aware of the financial and health risks they are taking, and to be attracted by working on specific kinds of projects, on teams of like-minded and skilled others and with the possibility of reward offered by the small chance of achieving a major success (Neff 2012: 153–6). She argues for the idea of 'venture labour' to claim that workers are risking their labour time as a speculative investment, instead of an investor risking their venture capital. With venture labour the risk involved in creating and maintaining a company is transferred from the company to the workers. The point is not to praise such a shift, but to note that it presents a different and complex perspective on what is occurring instead of a blanket view premised on the exploitation of free labour (Neff 2012: 160–2). Both Hesmondhalgh and Neff offer complex accounts of what is going on in contexts where activities and labour are not always matched by payment.

Scholz develops these concepts with a shift of focus from free labour, to embedding ideas of free labour into a concept of digital labour. He terms digital labour 'a set of human activities that is predicated on global supply chains of material labour; it is about human activities that have economic value and are performed through a range of devices on highly monopolized platforms in real time on a truly novel and unprecedented scale' (2017: 6) What is possible here is an argument that there is an outside to labour and that there are other kinds of activities than labour or work (Scholz 2017: 101–6). Yet within this complex account of digital labour, there remain issues with understanding activities that are not labour that contribute to digital platforms. Scholz offers the example of poorly paid workers who create gold within online games but who also sometimes take time to play the game as a game in their own time. He argues that 'Working for amusement, gaming, and scamming virtual worlds all hides labor in games, wrapped in the ideology of play' (2017: 40), adding later that 'Sheer life has become the source of profit … The most significant participation in today's digital economy is not primarily intellectual; it is life itself' (2017: 144). In the former passage Scholz erases the division between work and play, all becomes work, and in the latter he erases the distinction between life and exploitation. While the latter is another articulation of the theme of mining sociality for profit, the dilemmas surrounding the distinctions between labour and other activities, between paid and unpaid labour, and between exploitation and non-exploitation remain confused even within this complex account. Moreover, accounts in which everything becomes labour present us with a capitalist dream in action – everything that is done is done for capitalism, suggesting that struggle and conflict have been foreclosed.

Coté and Pybus (2007) offered one of the earliest analyses of social media and labour, arguing that a new form of immaterial labour was being developed in the early social media network Myspace, which they saw as being in conflict with affective social relations. They stress the affective dimensions of the activities of Myspace users and do not lose sight of the social relations being built there. Yet they also recode this as being encompassed by and developing into a new kind of labour which is in conflict with affective relations. For example, they stress that there are often 'refuges' in which affective relations not valorised by capital can exist, and argue that these are potential sites of conflict with and contestation of capital: 'there is always something within MySpace that remains a refuge, albeit one always being surveyed by capital for enclosure' (2007: 103). The reduction of social relations to labour is refused by arguing for a new form of conflict around what Coté and Pybus call immaterial labour 2.0. Making such distinctions is also important for other reasons. For example, Qiu's (2016) compelling analysis of what he calls iSlavery – referring to the conditions of workers producing many of the technological devices through which the digital economy is maintained – requires that we do not collapse all life into labour. If we have no distinction between life and labour, how can slavery in the factories be understood conceptually? And Qiu's work makes abundantly clear that conditions of slavery exist among workers. Dyer-Witheford also makes powerful use of a distinction between labour and proletariat, offering an account conceptually complex enough to be able to recognise economies in which 'a large proportion of the working class is workless' (2015: 13). However, it is Jarrett (2016) who makes the most sustained intervention here, hoping to provide a solid foundation both for Marxist concepts of exploitation in digital media and for refusing the notion of false consciousness.

Jarrett takes Fortunati's theory of domestic labour as a model, arguing that we should understand social media interaction as involving something like an, at least, two-stage process, somewhat like Coté and Pybus. In the first stage, the affective dimensions of liking, posting and so on are built up from the use values consumed by the poster or liker prior to the posting or liking. Anyone can engage in these affects, the moments of beauty, wonder and grief, by building on existing relations. 'Contrary to the logics of the alienation thesis, "liking" a friend's status update continues to manifest an inalienable and affectively powerful social relationship' (Jarrett 2016: 124). Yet, at the same time, Jarrett argues, once this genuine affective connection has been made it can be transformed into a value for the platform, which exploits it as free labour for the purposes of generating targeted advertising. Though Jarrett is pointing to two moments, they both derive from one set of actions – the like or the post – which is subsequently either directed back to the poster as a form of affect or privatised by the platform as a bit of information useful to creating advertisements in search of profit (2016: 105–24). This duality obviates any notion of false consciousness – as it is entirely consistent for someone to be conscious of their affective relationship and of the exploitative use being made of it – and suggests a complex way of understanding the contexts in which an action may be understood as leisure or as labour.

Jarrett opens up a conceptualisation of labour and activities on digital platforms in which two interpretations of the same act are possible. The idea that one action may have multiple contexts will be important in guarding against the kind of reduction I have identified in some theorists, which reaches its apogee in despairing and accusatory claims such as 'life is profit' and 'infinite exploitation' and derives its purchase through the internal contradictions embedded within many concepts of free labour. Stated this way, I have emphasised the contradictions and complexities within the concept of free labour. Reading such literature often gives the impression of a set of ideas struggling to escape a pre-existing vocabulary which does not grasp what authors like Terranova are trying to identify. This is partly because the free labour debate identifies something important about digital contexts, in that many people do freely contribute time and activities that create the digital world and sometimes massive profit for others. If the conceptualisation of free labour is problematic, then its fundamental insight is valid in that many digital places, objects and practices are created and maintained through collective and unremunerated actions.

As with the discussion of exploitation and profit-making in digital contexts, ideas of free labour identify something undeniably important while at the same time are complex to the point of contradiction and confusion. While I am not suggesting we simply take forward the concepts of free labour or exploitation so far examined, there is value in the debates surrounding them that raise issues such as the uncertainty over whether an action is leisure or work. I will return to these ideas later, but for now there is one further complexity that needs to be explored, concerning the nature of the products being produced and consumed within the digital economy. As Lazzarato stated: 'The consumer is no longer limited to consuming commodities (destroying them in the act of consumption). On the contrary, his or her consumption should be productive in accordance to the necessary conditions and the new products' (Lazzarato 1996). Lazzarato provides a link to the third set of key concepts that need introducing as tools for theorising digital economic practices, in relation to the collapse of the divide between production and consumption.

Produsage, Playbour, Prosumerism, Co-evolving Co-creation

The phenomenon identified and conceptualised through a range of neologisms like prosumer and playbour is of a collapse between the producer and consumer of products. It is often closely related to ideas about free labour because someone doing something they consider leisure or fun for free that is also used by a company as part of a product both breaches consumer/producer divisions and may be considered free labour. However, prosumer or produser is also something conceptually distinct from the issue of users not being paid when monetary value is made from their activities because free labour need not breach the consumer/producer divide.

Many of the phenomena behind the idea of this collapse have been seen in non-monetised digital economic practices, particularly in the case of free software. As outlined earlier, free software is a movement based on collaborative computer programming, done freely and shared via the internet usually within a grown (rather than planned) and often semi-formal organisational structure. Anyone with the skills can contribute. It should be clear that the programmers who create the code do so in order to use it, and often use it while creating the code. Similarly, it is now common for gamers to be able to create their own modifications to games that are then shared with the community of gamers; the activity of production here is also an activity of consumption, since creating the modification is often just as much a part of the gameplay as it is of game production. Wikipedia editing, blog writing and citizen journalism are all activities facilitated by the internet that have also been identified as exemplifying the collapse of consumer and producer.

This collapse was first conceptualised by Toffler, who introduced the idea of the prosumer as part of a new system involving 'the willing seduction of the consumer into production' (1970: 275; Bruns 2008: 12). While Toffler argues that the prosumer is a fusion of consumer and producer, Bruns traces the way that Toffler glues together these two different figures rather than working out what is new in the posited fusion. In effect, Toffler envisages 'merely the development of even more advanced consumption skills by consumers' (Bruns 2008: 11). It is worth looking more closely at Bruns's influential work developing the concept of produsers and produsage because he is among the most determined in arguing that welding together two contradictory ideas – production and consumption – is not an answer to identifying what is 'new' in the collapse of the boundary between them. Bruns explains what his concept of produsage is trying to capture by describing where it came from. Industrial production, he argues, separated out the producer and consumer, with the product being created by the former and then used up by the latter (2008: 9–17). He then specifies that produsage involves informational products and that a particular network infrastructure was required to create the possibility of produsage.

Bruns outlines four principles that follow from the implementation of what he calls the 'technosocial affordances' of produsage, which are a shift to processes of products derived from probabilistic rather than directed problem solving; equipotentiality rather than hierarchy; granular rather than composite tasks; and shared rather than owned content (2008: 19–21). With such an infrastructure in place the four principles of produsage may emerge. The first principle is 'open participation, communal evolution' (2008: 24–5). The assumption here is that in produsage the evaluation and improvement of products will be most successful when more people participate in that process, meaning that involvement should be open. The second principle is 'fluid hierarchy, *ad hoc* meritocracy' (2008: 25–6). This assumes that everyone involved can contribute, even if not necessarily in the same way or with the same quality of work. Organisation then emerges in a way that ensures it remains both changeable and based primarily on the participants' ability to contribute. Third is 'unfinished artefacts, continuing processes' (2008: 27–8). Here it is recognised that produsage's products are always changing and developing. On the model of software, produsage creates artefacts that can both be used and continually updated and developed. The fourth and final principle of produsage is 'common property, individual rewards' (2008: 28–30). Produsage's products are shared between produsers – think of Wikipedia being available to all – while in the production process different degrees of expertise and commitment differentiate produsers, offering them opportunities for reward often through some sort of community recognition.

This picture of product creation and use is far from that of an industrial factory manufacturing a commodity which will be sent to a shopping mall to be purchased. Produsage, in contrast, creates such things as Wikipedia, the vast interconnected sites of the World Wide Web, interlinked blog sites and major free and open source software projects. It is not that production and consumption in the industrial sense disappear, rather that this novel form emerges in new relations to the old. It is worth noting two specific issues with this conceptualisation, which will lead to a final general point about attempts to explore the breakdown between producer and consumer. One is a theoretical complication having to do with the relationship between the infrastructure and the principles of produsage; the second is an empirical argument about the extent of produsage's spread.

Theoretically Bruns's definition of the necessary infrastructure for produsage assumes much of what he finds in his concept of produsage. No doubt we would expect the two to be closely related, but the structure of his argument posits the infrastructure as a precondition of produsage, and then finds that produsage mirrors the infrastructure. There is also no doubt that, like many other authors, Bruns is identifying innovative forms of product development and use, but his specific conception of produsage folds back into a less well empirically established positing of certain infrastructural changes. In particular, his conception of the network is similar to many that have been challenged for their over-emphasis on flattened hierarchies and peer-to-peer communication and their failure to articulate accompanying forms of hierarchical exclusion and control. As Galloway has argued, no network exists without protocols that define who can access the network to become a peer on it and what a peer can do on it. Networks are never simply fully open peer-to-peer interaction, they are always defined by the protocols that determine what a peer is and what a peer can do. Further, protocols are often defined hierarchically, leading to many apparently flattened peer-to-peer communication and distribution systems only existing if there is also hierarchical and strictly controlled means of deciding who can be part of the network (Galloway 2004; Jordan 2015: 64–83). By assuming a lop-sided version of the network as a key infrastructure for produsage, Bruns then finds this version mirrored within produsage as a concept.

The empirical argument is developed by Banks in his ethnographies of computer gaming and player contributions. In relation to Bruns, Banks asks whether, 'in the effort to foreground the productive agency of media users and consumers ... Bruns perhaps too quickly overlook[s] that much of this activity still predominantly occurs through commercially owned and produced platforms and tools' (2013: 20). Banks's work in contrast emphasises that when he researches what Bruns might call produsage in action, this is nearly always in the context of 'old-style' industrial companies aiming to sell a product to a consumer. Banks's point is not that Bruns ignores industrial production techniques, but that companies are evolving and integrating co-creation techniques in the context of both commercial and more produsage-like principles, and that Bruns tends to separate the two.

At this point, it is worth recalling the implication of Jarrett's argument that one action may be articulated in different contexts with different meanings. An implicit assumption in most produser debates is that actions form a unity that has to be understood with one consistent explanation. The challenge set by the collapse of the producer/consumer divide is that certain individual actions can be seen to be doing two contradictory things, both producing and consuming. However, if this presumption of a unitary action is put aside, and the possibility that one moment or action can be articulated differently in different contexts is introduced, then perhaps a way of understanding production and consumption is to step back from both concepts and examine the contexts in which an action may be productive or consumptive. There will be further discussion of this conception of action in the next chapter, but it is useful here to see it emerging from a number of key theoretical debates.

As with free labour and exploitation, the collapse of the consumer/producer divide foregrounds key economic factors that have arisen since the late 1970s, as the internet and computer revolutions emerged and took hold. This has been clear in a number of ways, and most obviously in relation to non-monetised digital economic practices. Yet the current conceptualisations of this breakdown of the divide remain questionable. Bruns is the most committed theorist attempting to define something new, but his concepts, while powerful, remain problematic, whereas committed empirical researchers like Banks tend to fall back on combining two contradictory concepts in ideas like 'co-evolution'. Other research might have been analysed here, including Dyer-Witheford and de Peuter (2009) on playbour, Jenkins (2006) on convergence, and Benkler (2006) on network wealth, but all of these throw up similar problems. Banks and Jarrett perhaps point in the right direction: the context in which production and consumption collapse or are superseded by something new is the key element, and one which will need to be understood when theorising digital economic practices.

Conclusion: Important Faulty Concepts

In conclusion, it will be helpful to discuss one concrete example that will bring together the ideas introduced in this chapter, as a basis for theorising the digital economy in the next. The best example I know of is Banks's (2013) work on the development of the train simulation game *Trainz*.

Trainz is a railway simulator that runs on computers, allowing users to design and build their own railway tracks and drive trains down them (that is, to view this all on their computer monitor). It began simply enough as a software program produced to be sold for others to consume. However, as Banks explains, early on, pre-existing communities of enthusiasts looking for some kind of train simulation computer program began taking an interest. The company engaged with this community, offering it tools to work with the pre-packaged software. This was not a simple relationship, however, involving both creativity and conflict, with the community's wish to see the company's promises to give them further information and tools to work with the software fulfilled, and its frustration when those promises were not fully kept. Emblematic of this relationship was the fact that when the first game shipped without steam locomotives, the volunteer and fan community managed to produce working steam trains before the paid company employees did, even though the latter were already working on it. Amid all this activity, the company began paying some members of the community for their productions (Banks 2013: Ch 3).

I will highlight three sets of relations here: First, there are fans who make content which is integrated into commercial releases of the *Trainz* software, and who are offered and accept payment for their activities. These fans were already creating for *Trainz* but then shifted to work on particular projects that may be suggested either by themselves, by other members of the fan community, or by the company. Second, there are fans who make products which are integrated into commercial releases but who refuse to accept payment. As one fan creator stated to Banks: 'even if you take only a dime you take the responsibility for a flawed product … and concern about customer satisfaction might convert a hobby into a burden' (2013: 106). The third set of relations stems from the fact that the game was on the verge of being cancelled on several occasions as it failed to bring in expected revenue, and was only kept alive due to the highly engaged fan and fan creator community. At one of these crisis points the company decided to rely almost entirely on the fan creator community for new art content, and sacked many of its in-house content producers (Banks 2013: Ch 3 and 102–11).

These three sets of relations all involve forms of labour and leisure, paid and unpaid, forms of what has been theorised as exploitation (such as taking free fan content and including it in commercially produced game packages), and shifting relations between production and consumption that cannot be easily contained or captured within these terms. The example of *Trainz* is notable because of the varied relations all present within the one economic activity, ultimately that of making a profit by selling software and maintaining a community. Contained within this single economic practice is an array of different actions which may also be the same actions – for example, researching, designing and then implementing a new train model – which may be undertaken for leisure, play or employment or a combination of all these. The three conceptual problematics this chapter has outlined – free labour, exploitation, and the breakdown of the producer/consumer divide – are all represented within this example, even as the conceptual problems remain.

All three conceptual problematics are clearly of importance to understanding the newly emerging form of economic activity associated with the digital, while also being both confused and confusing. What seems to be needed to understand what 'free labour' or 'produsage' mean is to shift from the presumption that these are issues of work, labour, leisure, and instead start with the activities undertaken in the digital economy and then examine how such activities are formed in ways that may produce what we think of as work, labour and leisure that may or may not be remunerated. The concept of exploitation needs to be detached from the presumption that value is extracted in order to explore how the undeniably enormous profits made by some digital companies relate to the activities of those who use the products of these companies, and how both users and platform workers contribute to making such products. In all three cases, new phenomena and processes are identified whose theorisations advance our understanding and yet remain uncertain. The next step is to combine this range of conceptual problematics with the evidence gathered from the case studies in order to develop a general theory of the digital economy.

8   The Digital Economy

Models and Modelling

The hybridity and complexity of digital economic activities have been followed from different points of view. Some elements have emerged repeatedly, suggesting elements of digital economic practice. Remaining entirely with the points of view within specific practices obviates any chance of seeing across points of view and, by implication, across their associated monetisation strategies and economic moments. This seeing across is needed to identify the repetitions and habituations that characterise a practice. To move from the specific points of view and activities of users and platforms to a general understanding of an economic practice requires abstraction and theorising. To help this process, the previous chapter articulated concepts relevant to a qualitative analysis of the digital economy. In moving from activities to practices, from the ephemeral to the habituated and repeated, the next step will be to model causation. In this chapter I will first briefly recount the conclusions of the preceding case studies. Following this, I will outline two broad causal forces, building on and re-conceptualising the ideas examined in the problematics of exploitation, free labour and produsage in light of the evidence from the case studies. The third section will then model digital economic practices, providing a schematic or abstract map that figures the digital economy.

When examining search, we saw that digital economic practices resolved into a community that could be 'read' through data, the trust needed to use a search engine, and the surveillance by the search engine that enables it to read the inter-relations of those who search. Monetisation through advertising was consequent on the success of this trio and integrated them through the use of the 'reading' to target advertisements.

Social media activities create emotional and social relations that are sometimes fully faceted and sometimes focused on a specific limited activity. Users' activities are mediated by a digital platform which records and analyses information about what users are doing in relation to other users, turning this information into the property of the platform owner. Monetisation comes primarily through targeted advertising that is built on data analysis provided by the platform which, in turn, can only be collected if the platform successfully creates a community engaged in different kinds of social interaction. Even at this stage, having looked only at search and social media, the idea of the 'user' was becoming complicated and defined not so much by words like community, emotion, sociality or culture, but by the nature of the actions users can take and how those actions relate to collective actions (Nieborg and Poell 2018).

Disintermediators focus on an existing service which usually has a defined regulatory and institutional context. That context is then disintermediated through a platform that introduces new mediations between the service users and the service providers. While disintermediators clearly produce collectives based on activities, whether those of users or providers, in comparison to social media these activities are socially and emotionally attenuated. Monetisation is integrated into the service that is offered by taking a portion of the funds flowing between user and provider.

The 'free' or non-monetised practices also produce platforms, users and collectives, and while some monetisation may occur this is secondary and not essential to the practice. The platform still mediates actions and defines the nature of the information flowing across it as a particular property, but usually in a distributive rather than exclusive form. This also leads to more distributed platforms but also to coordination problems that have to be solved.

Finally, we saw that gaming brings together all these monetisation strategies in a hybrid context where economic practices familiar from manufacturing and retail are also present. Again, platforms define the value in the action users can take, while mediating relations between players and between players and game become key processes allowing players and their collectives to partially frame and form the game.

Users who take actions that they value then repeat what they are doing, thereby creating collective actions. This will be so even if a platform is itself complex, and is not made of one integrated hardware/software system. Nieborg and Poell have called such processes the 'platformization of cultural production', and they explore the relationship between platforms and cultural industries arguing that 'Platformization ... marks the reorganization of cultural production and circulation, rendering cultural commodities contingent' (Nieborg and Poell 2018; see also Gillespie 2010). In a similar vein, Srnicek claims there is a platform capitalism which is both a specific sector and the driving force of twenty-first-century capitalism (2016: 3–8). While the term 'platform' has been used liberally in the preceding chapters, it should be noted that it is always defined in relation to the digital economic practices that are being analysed. As Nieborg and Poell suggest, a platform is the space for the organisation of production and circulation within the digital economy. Collectives of action can reform and affect the platform while the platform itself has the power to read these collectives and use that reading in two broad ways: to build the platform and its user base, and to identify and implement monetisation strategies. Two causations flow through this economic practice: the value to users of their actions and activities, and information defined as a property.

Two Causations in the Digital Economy

A recurrent feature in tracing digital economic practices has been that specific activities were offered in each digital economic practice: searching for information, sending pictures that will disappear in seconds, becoming a sorcerer in play with others, multiple means of exhibiting an emotional life, taking a cab and so on. At the simplest level, these activities *are* the reason why users take up a practice. As these activities were explored, it became increasingly difficult to pin them down with existing concepts, particularly because the same activities could be described with contradictory concepts: as both play and work, free and paid, leisure and labour. When examining the theory of free labour the same issue arose of contradictory concepts being used to understand the same activity. This was exacerbated in theories of both free labour and exploitation through a presumption that any activity was already labour, to the extent that for some theorists all life has become labour. This is a problem of words and concepts. In a different context, Stuart Hall identified a similar issue: 'This is the problem of coming at the end of a language rather than the beginning: none of the words will work for you any longer!' (Hall cited in Bird and Jordan 1999: 203–4).

Jarrett's use of feminist concepts of housework as labour pointed to a way out of this dilemma and toward a language more appropriate to digital economic practices. Drawing on theories of domestic labour, she argued there can be dual understandings of the same action:

> For users ... Facebook is experienced primarily as an exchange of use-values. The site can only convert the labour-power of user experience into the commodified form of user data (labour-time) after its experience as inalienable use-value by the user. And because it remains use-value, the affective intensity associated with exchanges on Facebook does not lose its capacity to build and sustain rich social formations even as it almost simultaneously enters the commodity circuit. (2016: 123)

Like Coté and Pybus, Jarrett points out that the uses to someone on social media of their platform-mediated social relations are simultaneously retained by them as emotional and affective even while they are being converted by the platform into labour on its behalf. Jarrett's claim that the same action can be both affective for the user and labour for the platform opens up the possibility of exploring ideas beyond labour.

To see beyond the divisions so often applied to activities in digital economic practices means seeing the various actions offered by different platforms for the activities in-themselves. The idea of a subject producing these actions need not be assumed, since it is possible to see the actions-in-themselves without having to explain them in relation to an originating subject. In her analysis of visibility Woodward offers a way of interpreting actions in digital economic practices that encompasses the psyche and the social, and which integrates seeing how different kinds of subjectivities around race, gender, sexuality, labour and more are always-already being constructed through such actions. She takes up the feminist theory of the 'gaze' to argue that:

> The gaze offers one way of thinking about this process of looking and highlights the interactive, relational aspects of what is involved in making things visible and invisible which connects personal, inner worlds of feeling and social worlds of social systems, structures and institutions and culture, including technologies of representation … Relationality is central to the politics of in/visibility and to my rethinking of the gaze … especially in challenging the oversimplification of experience and processes through which people make sense of the world. Relationality involves connections, and sometimes disconnections, of different forces which are in play in exploring what is seen and unseen and how the politics of in/visibility works. (2015: 148–9)

I interpret the gaze, as Woodward understands it, as being similar in its nature to activities in digital economic practices, in that both are constituted by a relationality between things done, technologies, emotions and affects, and social relations, all of which are constituting each other and are constituted in each moment that they occur. In parallel to Woodward's discussion of who is visible and what that means, it is useful to see the ability to participate in inter-related actions on a complex digital platform as equivalent to creating a visibility. This also means that each kind of platform-related action will not only constitute things like search, free software and so on but will also create gendered, raced, classed and other positions connecting the actions to wider social forces. Based on Woodward, the point becomes not what the activities are according to pre-existing categories but what activities become in multiple contexts.

Actions can thus be understood on the model of the gaze as constitutive of subjectivities and socialities. The causal motion to be followed here is not based on a presumption that activities become labour, but argues that they can be transformed, as Jarrett demonstrates, into something different depending on their position within the multifarious relations of an economic practice. Humans or their humanity are not deformed or presumed in these processes but are created in them. For example, the activity of posting on social media becomes part of an inter-relationality in which it may be multiply constituted as the expression of an emotional or social life, as a pure form of leisure, and as a bit of information available to be correlated with other bits of information, thereby constituting a small piece of labour for the platform. The key point is to follow the activities of a particular economic practice and see how they are constituted at different points in different contexts with different meanings; how are activities caused? This means foregoing the idea that the action itself has a unitary meaning and seeing it instead as relationally constituted. The same seemingly single action – such as posting a photo on a social media site, doing a search for book reviews, or entering into combat in a game – can be constituted in multiple ways and contexts. The accumulation of such actions will form subjectivities and patterned social relations with each action potentially multiply constituted by different contexts. If someone only becomes known when they do something iteratively, such as posting news items to their friends on social media or writing succinct software code, then an entirely different understanding of these actions may reconstitute that person's habits in different ways; for example, as representative of a particular demographic with specific interests that can be targeted with the appropriate advertisements (Jordan 2013: 141–8).

In the formation of subjectivities appropriate to a particular digital economic practice, different kinds of raced, sexed, gendered, classed and greened subjects will be integrated into that practice. This reveals the intersection of forms of power in digital economic practices and the key ways they may generate raced, gendered, and so on forms through both algorithms and cultures. There are many examples here, such as the discovery that Google's algorithm routing different job advertisements to different people was sending higher-paying jobs to men more frequently than to women; or crime prediction models that predict higher than appropriate crime rates depending on the racial composition of specific areas; or credit schemes and insurance companies that automate their decisions using algorithms that reveal a preference for white males or presumptions that women must have dependents (Cossins 2018; Noble 2018; Eubanks 2018). No digital economic practice will be indifferent to the multiple centres of power and exploitation in society, but will modulate, rely on and form itself around (as well as form) the politics of our worlds. These politics are here integrated into this first form of causation in digital economic practices, in which activities are transformed according to different contexts and meanings.

The first form of causation in digital economic practices then lies in the way in which an action may be formed and reformed in multiple settings and with multiple meanings and uses for different actors and actants, and without presuming that these diverging meanings and uses can be reconciled in a single consistent, unified moment or action. We need to determine what is causing activities to be created and what they mean: what causes the actions characteristic of a particular digital economic practice to be formed into moments of beauty, of sociality, of commerce, of sexuality, of labour and more? When examining a particular digital economic practice it is important to trace the ways that activities in that practice are formed repeatedly with different meanings and effects, without assuming that each activity or moment has a single meaning. The causality of actions and activities follows the ways in which labour, leisure, paid, unpaid, play and work are all formed secondarily to the initial activity within a digital economic practice.

The second form of causation relates to information, and is integral to seeing what is done on platforms as involving actions that are generative rather than fully formed. These are informational actions (Jordan 2015: 12–20), moments in which information is generated and moved. They are, in Woodward's terms, enfleshed actions because they are embodied by a finger tapping on a phone or tablet, by a body seated at a computer, by the electricity animating code running through a computer's CPU, by a voice on a chat channel and so on. This is not a segregation to bodiless virtual actions, the actions are material and embodied, but as de Beauvoir argued 'the body is not a thing, it is a situation: it is our grasp on the world and the outline for our projects' (de Beauvoir 2010: 46; Woodward 2015: 145). Information is what is developed and transmitted in these bodily, material and affective moments of action on platforms; for example the information in a status update, in a posted video or photograph, or in a piece of code, and so on. A key causality in relation to information in digital economic practices is property. What kind of property is the information on a platform, and who asserts ownership of this information-as-property?

Information is a difference we pay attention to because that difference has a context which makes it significant among the myriad differences that any context offers. For example, if a group of country walkers have two maps, then the difference between them that one is held by one person with a hat on and a second is held by another with no hat, that the maps exist in different spaces related to different hat-states, is not much commented on. But if one map shows a walking trail leading to a cliff and the other does not, then that is a significant difference that is likely to be picked up on as important information about the planned walk. In any context there are essentially infinite differences that might be significant, but information only results from the difference whose context makes it significant. Because information results from a 'competent difference' it is in principle available simultaneously to all who are competent in the context and to the full significance of that information (Jordan 2015: 12–18). All the walkers can look at the two maps and all can ponder the information they receive by noting the trail and cliff present on one map and absent on the other. Every difference is also a material one: the walker's information is only available to those who can see the maps. Even an idea in someone's mind has to be materialised in the brain's neurons. The possibility that everyone can at the same time know the same information and know it to its full extent, what can be called simultaneous complete use, depends on how the information is materialised. The rise of digital information, both natively digital and the massive digitalisation of prior existing information (such as music in iTunes' or Spotify's vast libraries, or books in Google Books), leads to a situation in which simultaneous complete use becomes ever more possible due to the ability to copy and distribute digitised information. Economists have usually treated the ability to share information as a lack, calling information goods 'non-rival' that have to be made rival in order to be economically traded. The causes of information becoming non-rival or of realising simultaneous complete use underpin the processes that make information into a property in digital economic practices.

As each digital economic practice comes from a series of activities that result in information – posts, likes, deaths and resurrections in a game, travel from A to B – the flow of such information is crucial to the constitution of each practice. As these are digital contexts, it is possible that all information might be made available to all and be equally usable by all, and how information is formed will direct it toward exclusive use by some or complete use by all. How information is treated will fundamentally be an issue of what kind of property it is formed as. A key causal mechanism within each digital economic practice is how the information that the activities in that practice produce is treated as a property.

Broadly, there are three different ways in which information can be formed as a property: as public domain, as private property and as distributed property. What combination or variation of these three types is implemented on a platform and underpins a digital economic practice is key to understanding that practice. These three types also need to be thought of as strategies, because how information is defined as what kind of a property is a form of causation that needs to be understood in each practice. Property will also be defined within regulatory regimes at regional, national and international levels and, though this complexity cannot be explored here, understanding what has to be asked about information as a property within each regulatory context will be important. Information can be in the public domain and so available to anyone to use and to change, including reverting it to a different kind of property (such as private). Information can be claimed as private property, and combinations of materiality and legality can be employed to ensure that information is used in ways defined only by those who own it. Finally, there is the inversion already discussed in relation to free software, in which exclusive ownership is claimed by the producer of some information who then inverts exclusive into distributive property by specifying that the information has to be openly shared and any changes to it also returned to everyone to share. Any examination of a digital economic practice has to follow how the information flowing through it is turned into a property and who benefits from this; any analysis will have to tease out these three kinds of information-as-property, which may be mingled together.

Information as a property is not solely a legal issue but also an organi-sational, cultural and social one. Asserting a kind of ownership is often subject to forces in addition to the legal, and we have seen examples of this in all the practices looked at so far. Google takes the openly available infor-mation about who links to what on the Web and privatises that information when it transforms it into the ability to respond to search queries. Facebook traces who its users link to and how, turning that into information about what types of people are interested in what kinds of topics. Free software distributes information in the form of code, allowing it to be legally fully and simultaneously available but effectively only available to change if you can read the relevant programming language. Games implement changes by fiat, coding them into the game, but often have to respond to players, among whom a negative enough response can lead to a reversion of the changes. These practices can be messy and fuse different processes together. For example, the Android mobile operating system was created by teams at Google on the basis of the free software Linux system, meaning it has to implement a version of information as distribution. Google's response is to make Android available but also to work so much on it, and often integrate it with other Google programs, that it becomes practically very difficult to take the system and repurpose it (though this is still possible, as some Chinese companies have shown, largely because Google services like search and maps are banned in China). In other words, while legally Android is open, effectively it is quite closed (Amadeo 2018a). Each platform through which a digital economic practice is realised will have legal and cultural processes that define the information on that platform as a property. Both digital economic causations – of activities transformed and information made property – will integrate politics from multiple centres of power, but how information results from an activity (or is that activity) and is caused to become a type of property, and how this then helps determine the nature of a digital economic practice, is particularly formative of information as a type of power. Specific kinds of information power have to emerge around digital economic practices (Jordan 2015).

Overall, there are two flows of causation that can be abstracted from the case studies of digital economic practices: activities that turn into categories such as labour and leisure, and information as open domain, exclusive or distributed property. I have used the term 'platform' for the complex sets of technologies and cultures that create the activities and information in a particular digital economic practice. The term has become a popular one for describing digital institutions and has been applied to a range of digital and internet-enabled contexts (Gillespie 2010; Jordan 2015). In the context of digital economic practices, the platform sometimes seems obvious with things like Google search and its connections to its backend that delivers search results and ads, or WeChat and its app, which is coordinated with servers creating message exchanges and connections to financial services. Distributed platforms also appeared when examining non-monetised digital economic practices, with free software relying on central services like a repository to monitor code, but also being framed by decision-making mechanisms and cultural commitments to sharing, aesthetics and judgements about whether a code 'runs'. As material realisations of digital economic practices, platforms both set the limits of a practice and define control in terms of who organises and directs the nature of its activities and how information becomes what kind of property. As I have argued elsewhere, in a digital and internet-enabled context, networks and protocols are the two necessarily linked concepts needed to understand this kind of (dis)organisation (Jordan 2015: 64–80).

Platforms both network together those who take up the activities on the platform, allowing users to connect to each other, and set protocols defining what is required to join the network and the nature of that networking. These are common organisational principles for networked technologies generally, underpinning the internet among other information technologies. Within digital economic practices some kind of platform has to be brought into existence to materialise a specific practice in the world. In this materialisation particular protocols will define who can access a network and what can be done on it, while the network will offer the means for users undertaking activities to inter-relate. For example, usernames and passwords are nearly ubiquitous on these platforms and are the most obvious example of protocols defining whether someone can join a network or not.

Platforms both establish the boundaries of a practice and define who controls which elements of that practice. Even in distributed platforms that are defined as much by cultures of participation as they are by passwords and usernames, the boundary of the practice is brought into existence through the performance of these cultures. Platforms are then complex; even in those that seem most obviously bounded, like social media, there are connections between parts of a platform, for example between the app and the WWW interface, and external connections such as any other activities that can be logged into by using a social media account as an entry pass. Platforms also create control; again this may be distributed through cultures but it can also simply turn on whether someone has access to a platform or not. Failure to pay a subscription to WoW will lead to the inability to play the game. Repeatedly entering false information on Wikipedia can lead to a user being banned from editing. Free services like social media can and will ban people who transgress the rules. Whether what is being done is or is not acceptable on a platform can be enforced by its cultures, such as Wikipedia's culture of requiring entries to be impartial and objective, as well as by protocols rendered in code including such things as passwords and usernames.

The organisation of a platform blends into a company's institutional form, and both will follow from how information has been formed as a property. Centralised and hierarchically controlled platforms within companies will tend to draw on information as an exclusive property. The logic of such organisations leads to the kinds of structures adopted by many digital companies which restrict control to a small number of people. Google and its parent company Alphabet are the exemplars of this as they are structured so that the founders retain control even while offering shares in the company to investors. Platforms that oversee information as a distributed property are far more likely to be a distributed platform themselves, with elements that are not integrated into one hierarchical whole, even if there are hierarchical organisations within the platform. These are not absolute processes and the institutional and organisational forms will aim not just to rely on a particular kind of information but also to form information as a property. These institutional forms will be the means through which information will be caused to become a particular kind of property and will rely on that kind of property.

The two causations of digital economic practices move from being general and abstract to specific and material through their instantiation in a platform. A platform has to be created which can bound and control the activities that are offered and the information that flows from those activities. A platform may be open and offer the ability to form activities and openly access the information that is being generated or, at the other end of the spectrum, activities can be controlled by the platform and the information created there kept privately, only seen and worked on by the platform's workers. Organisational forms will have a strong tendency to follow these forms of information, even as they aim to create information as a specific kind of property. An understanding of the dynamic forces that flow through digital economic practices is made possible by defining these two forms of causation – activities transforming into different possibilities and information defined as a form of property – and then following how they are made real by being instantiated in a platform. The next section will take these dynamics of causation in digital economic practices and model them as a sectoral economic form.

Digital Economic Practice

A digital economic practice is distinct from other economic practices and is defined by the creation of a community of activities the 'reading' of which offers an opportunity for monetisation: from lols to bags of gold. Each digital economic practice is created through a platform that manages how activities become paid, unpaid, leisure, labour, play, work or some other form, and how the information resulting from activities is turned into private property or is shared freely. These processes will be modelled through three linked divisions: value, property and profit. The modelling will be deliberately schematic, laying out elements while acknowledging the complexity of digital economic practices encountered in everyday life. These divisions can be represented in the accompanying figure, whose components will be discussed in turn.

The first division of this schematic is value. Each digital economic practice creates a kind of value for users. Each involves not a product but an activity of value to some people. The value of the activity is created through collective activities, not through straightforward offers of products, including service products, to consumers. Uber, for example, does not offer cab rides but a platform that mediates between those who need a cab ride and those who can provide one. The result is a platform that bounds and controls the value being offered by creating collectives based on activities. Four key elements build value into a platform, though the creation of any specific platform may come from varying emphases on and connections

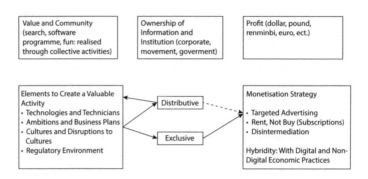

Figure 8.1. Digital Economic Practices

between these elements: technicians and technologies; business plans and ambitions to create something valuable; existing cultures and disruptions to cultures; and avoiding or complying with specific regulatory and governmental regimes. Further, while aspects of each of these elements might be found in other economic practices, it is the particular way they fit together, with the other parts of property and monetisation, that specifies a model of digital economic practice.

Technologies and technicians need to be assembled, offered incentives, and put into spaces that allow coding. Code has to be given an environment it can be animated in, such as servers. An array of actors appears here, from the Marxists employed to create Twitter's first iterations (Bilton 2014) to the recurrent arguments in each particular digital platform over which computer language is best suited to a given platform. Particular forms of labour are also relevant, especially the kind of labour seen in cultural and creative industries, theorised by, for example, Neff as 'venture labour'. These are not the activities of users, but the skilled labour of programmers, designers and other workers who are enticed into intensive labour often with minimal wages and benefits but with the lure of working on team projects that may 'change the world', and the admittedly lottery-like chance of becoming rich by being paid in stock if a platform is one of the rare ones to become highly successful (Neff 2012; Hesmondhalgh 2010). This labour is inextricably connected to the labour of machines such as servers, assembled in server farms, connected through code, and launched onto the internet to become accessible to users.

These technologist and technological actors are driven by, and can sometimes inform, ideas about what kind of value is going to be offered to users. The intention is not always realised, and numerous technologies shift under use to reveal the value most valued, but they always drive toward some kind of value to a user which is in turn linked to often grandiose visions of a better world and speculative business plans, themselves often only succeeding through a version of the network effect that results from attracting a large number of users. However, whether intended in advance or adopted during development, a conception of the value of a platform to users will be present.

This conception of value will drive both the technologies and the technologists, who will confront the sets of cultures that surround that 'value'. These will be many layered. There will be different cultures of interaction over the internet that will have to be addressed. For example, it is worth considering the difference between online interaction in the 2000s, conducted primarily through desktop and laptop computers, and that of the 2010s onward with its complex soup of apps on mobile devices that have intersected with and sometimes displaced personal computers. There will be cultures of backend development, for example in the way 1990s digital economic practices tended to invent and implement their own server farms compared to the 2010s when renting cloud space might be more attractive. There will also be cultures associated with the value itself that may have to shift: searching a library card catalogue is different to searching on Google and booking an Airbnb room is different to asking a travel agent to book a hotel. Through these processes of attempting to implement some value, the nature of the existing cultures related to that value will be shifted and, in turn, the process of creating that digital value will be affected.

As a counterpoint to cultures carried through collective practices and habits, formal regulatory and governmental environments will be encountered. Sometimes they will be wilfully or accidentally ignored, only to assert themselves and have to be worked with – it is not hard to think of the disintermediators here. For example, the tax arrangements of many digital economic companies seem designed to take advantage of the internet-wide reach of the value they offer to find the haven least likely to tax the platform's income. But the regulators may still come calling, as when city officials in Philadelphia demanded that 'ride sharing' companies pay the same tax as regular cabs when servicing that city's airport, or when European regulators demanded Google stop bundling its services, such as search, together with Android as an operating system. The significant human labour of moderating each platform will appear here as a platform seeks to manage the activities taking place on it, and especially as these activities take unexpected turns.

These four elements all have to be realised and articulated in order to create the value that is essential to a digital economic practice. Doing so produces the first division of a digital economic practice in the 'value' that a platform offers to users which, when successful, turns users into sets of collective activities. Within and encompassing this focus on value are questions of ownership that have to be designed and decided but also need to be separated from the creation of the digital value, because ownership in digital contexts has highly different possibilities to ownership when the value is dependent on a specific material object. Ownership is the second division of a schematic of digital economic practices.

Ownership is driven in digital economic practices by the possibilities of exclusive or distributive property rights, and organisation of the platform and of any company generally follow and are implied by the nature of information as a property on that platform. These need not be definitively one or the other but may consist of different intertwined property rights, as for example when Google and IBM use free software in contexts in which they also claim exclusive property rights over other forms of information. Further, legal property rights can be mediated, if not in some cases overturned, by the cultures that are present. For example, the way Google dominates Android effectively creates an organisationally and culturally based exclusive right over a nominally distributed information property. Each digital economic platform has to formally implement one or some combination of three kinds of property rights, which will be influenced by the underlying forms of information embodied in these rights.

The three kinds of possible property rights implemented on information within a digital economic practice are those already outlined when analysing free software: openly distributed, distributed with a licence, and exclusive. These different kinds of property are possible because when information becomes a commodity it is not essentialised by its material form; that is, information's property form is not predestined by its material form. A car or television can only be used one at a time and that means it can obviously and simply be made into property that is ownable exclusively by one. Commodities that are essentially information, like music or ideas or a book, have to have choices made about how many will be allowed access to the information's value, because in digital environments it can in principle be made available to everyone. This means that for information to be made exclusive and legally restricted the relevant information has to be formed in such a way that those rights are possible. Openly distributed in a digital and internet context is one form as it just means releasing all the information that is generated. Distributed with a licence may impose certain restrictions, such as open distribution on condition that the originator of the information is acknowledged, but it is most importantly a means of ensuring legal enforcement of distribution, particularly to prevent anyone taking distributed information and making it exclusive. The last kind of rights are exclusive information property rights that can be asserted and enforced through digital rights mechanisms, such as obfuscation of code, and legal mechanisms, such as prosecuting anyone not respecting ownership of that information.

Underlying these different choices are two principles related to the nature of information. First, information has the capacity to be simultaneously available to everyone who can access it. This radical possibility of simultaneous complete use underpins, among many things, the sharing of code in free software and the wide, licit or illicit, sharing of personal information. One principle that should be applied to the social meaning of a digital economic practice is the way it manages this possibility. Second, information can be subject to recursive processes in which the feeding of output from an information manipulation process back into that same process as input means infinite amounts of information can be produced from finite amounts. Whoever owns the information created in a digital economic practice and can manipulate it recursively will accordingly gain tremendous amounts of information about their practice and its social meaning. They are also the creators of new information by building recursions with the information about users that has been collected. Further, the development of information in this way can mould and form the particular value a practice is based upon, offering those who can manipulate the information the chance to alter the nature of whatever is being valued by its users. Again, in determining its social value and meaning, any digital economic practice should be examined in terms of who has access to the recursive processes that allow for the manipulation of the practice and its particular value.

The issue of property extends from how information is formed as a property to how the property of the platform itself is defined within the overarching company, foundation or other such institution. A correlation between information that is held exclusively and hierarchical integrated companies that contrasts with a correlation between information that is held distributively and a range of foundations, digital platforms and other elements suggests a simple relationship. This relationship should, however, be understood less as determinative and more as an underlying drive that will colour institutional structures. All three kinds of information as property may be associated with hierarchical and with peer-to-peer organisations; however, within exclusive forms of property there will be a constant pressure to secure that property with a range of company mechanisms, while a distributive form of property will tend to escape simple hierarchies and be more easily overseen through standards, cultures and a range of groups and organisations.

One further comment about property and information as the second division of any digital economic practice is in order, because for many such practices the decision to exercise exclusive property rights over information is taken early and almost invisibly – it appears to be the obvious, almost natural, choice. This will tend to be the case for those practices that aim to monetise information for profit. In an opposite way, practices that refuse profit will tend to have to decide how they will handle information's nature as a property. These non-profit strategies have often been thought of as weird or in need of explanation both for being non-profit and for not seeking exclusive ownership, because profit-making and working for pay are for many an implicit expectation of economic practices as such. Though such non-profit strategies have become better known, as seen in the plethora of initiatives with 'open' in their title, the tendency to fuse profit with exclusive ownership is often reflected in the quizzical analyses of non-profit digital economic practices. The fundamental point, however, is not which choice is the 'natural' one, but that all digital economic practices must confront the same underlying possibility of information being distributed, that is, being available for simultaneous complete use, or not.

The link between the creation of values through collective digital activities and the choice of information as property is that both will contribute to defining the way each practice will convert freely given time, emotion and action into labour and work. This is the point at which the one action can bifurcate into two (or more) values without any change in the action itself. If information is privatised and alienated from whoever produced it, then that information can unproblematically and often invisibly become another bit of labour on which revenue and profit might be based. The action may remain one of beauty, wonder or grief for the user – it may remain free, entertaining, and full of affective connection with none of these aspects compromised for the user – but the way in which the action results in information privatised to the platform will also ensure that it counts as labour for the platform controller. The conceptual dilemmas surrounding the notions of free, paid and unpaid, leisure and work are resolvable at this point as each action may be all of these things, just not for everyone all at once: beauty, wonder and grief for the user, profit and labour for the platform. In practices that do not privatise information from activities but return it to the users active on the platform, the information is not alienated in the same way as it is in for-profit practices, even if the actions here may also still be split into categories such as leisure and labour. What is returned to a user in a free digital economic practice shifts from being an individual action because what is returned is the result of many people's actions. For example, a voluntary contributor to Wikipedia may enjoy their editing while also enjoying the results not only of their own labour but also of that of whoever else has also leisured over either the page or on other parts of Wikipedia. Not-for-profit digital economic practices still involve actions that are different things depending on the context, and often fully return an activity to the user as labour that is only alienated from them in the sense that it is mingled with others' labour, all of which is returned. The obvious example is a free software programmer having the program they have acted on returned to them with many people's changes to the code included. The processes governing this intersection of actions and information as property may be complex, as already discussed in relation to the networks and protocols that structure free digital economic practices and which may lead to exclusions and forms of control. Information as a property encounters the transformation of activities and is resolved in different ways depending on the nature of each digital economic practice.

This leads to the third division (or section or pillar) of digital economic practices, that of monetisation or profit. Schematically there are four elements to this division: to go for profit or not; which monetisation strategy to adopt when profit is sought; hybridity within and without digital practices; and fear of the collective.

Whether to be for-profit or not has been discussed particularly when examining free digital economic practices and in establishing that monetisation is a choice consequent on the particular value a platform organises. While practices can mix profit and non-profit collective activities, it remains the case that most, including pretty much all those discussed so far in this book, fall heavily on one side or the other. It is true that Google oversees Android and that Richard Stallman and other free software advocates have sold copies of free software programs, but in both cases these are adjuncts to the primary focus of those involved. The companies with most balanced profit and non-profit practices might be those that support and sell free software while also making it freely available, making buying it akin to buying the support that comes with it. Red Hat, for example, offers a range of software services, primarily to corporate customers, using Linux and other free software. In 2017, Red Hat had $2.7 billion in revenue and $247 million profit, and was also the third largest contributor of code to the Linux kernel's development. Red Hat was bought by IBM in late 2018 for $34 billion, with the promise that it would be kept as a separate division (S. Gallagher 2018; Corbet 2017; Red Hat 2017). Though such a large company will have inevitable complexity, Red Hat was at its core a non-profit digital economic practice allied to a non-digital economic practice of selling services. I will return to this hybridity shortly, but it should be underlined that the key point about monetisation and profit is that it is a choice.

If profit-seeking is to be embedded in a digital economic practice, if seeking profit is added to the collective activities that create the value of the platform and which rely on information as a property, then a range of monetisation strategies are available. Monetisation requires finding a way to draw revenue from the collective activities and value offered by a platform and the information those activities both produce and depend on. Three broad strategies have emerged: targeted advertising; rent not buy (subscriptions); and competitive advantage through digitally driven disintermediation. This is not to say these are the only possible strategies, and others may emerge or be emerging, but they are the key three strategies after at least thirty years of digital economic practices. If they often build on prior non-digital economic practices, such as advertising or subscriptions, these will be adjusted in relation to the value, activities and information that a digital economic practice creates. The three monetisation strategies have been discussed when tracking practices earlier so they will only be briefly summarised here.

Targeted advertising relies heavily and most obviously on tracking the information offered by the collective practices that are attracted to and create whatever value the practice offers. Such platforms can offer their value for free and then control the information that flows from users taking up the activities to target advertising. In a number of cases this has been so spectacularly successful in generating profit that sometimes when the digital economy is spoken of this practice is the only one discussed (for example, in Zuboff (2019), where it is not only the only strategy discussed but has become the new form of capitalism). Rent not buy also covers subscriptions as both rely on controlling access to a value that is offered whether through a paywall or one-off payments allied to the ability to withdraw the service. One strategy of 'rent not buy' is to seem to offer buying something but in fact what is paid is more like a subscription, albeit often a one-off and not ongoing one, with the digital company able to close access to whatever the buyer thought they owned. A related strategy is straightforward subscriptions. Both strategies sometimes fail in the face of expectations of free value provided on the internet (somewhat ironically these are expectations fuelled by other digital economic for-profit practices, especially advertising) and sometimes succeed spectacularly, for example in some online games. Finally, companies may use disintermediation in contexts where there is already established economic activity to create a competitive advantage. Setting themselves up as a new intermediary and shifting the mediations between a service and its users in their favour allows a practice to dip into the revenue flowing between service providers and users.

Hybridity is the third aspect of monetisation and refers to the use of multiple strategies to gain revenue. Defining abstract monetisation strategies does not mean that each such strategy has to be pursued individually, rather hybrid forms emerge. Such hybridity can point in two directions. First, it might mean employing several digital economic strategies at once. For example, a platform offering an ad-free subscription and an ad-laden free version of the same service is not uncommon and it brings together two different strategies. Second, hybridity can mean using both digital and non-digital economic practices. This may occur when a primarily digital company employs relatively well-known retail practices, for example an MMOG that also sells boxed versions of its games, or when a non-digital company moves into using digital economic practices. Such connections will need to be carefully traced to identify where there are intersections and which revenue flows companies are primarily relying on, in order to grasp the nature of the digital economy as a sector.

Last, it should be emphasised that any successful digital economic practice will produce collective activities, what I have sometimes called communities of action, that emerge around a digital platform and the value it offers. These activities are an existential issue for a digital economy company because without them the company cannot create revenue. Locking in collective activities by creating a network effect so strong that users cannot avoid a specific platform for access to a specific value will then be a major goal for a digital economy company. To this end, the generation of more and more information, reused in recursive processes and continually seeking to draw in new and retain existing users, will be an ongoing dynamic in the digital economy. It will also be an ongoing fear for such companies that their users and collectives will simply move to another platform. Companies built on digital economic practices will simultaneously desire and fear their community and do both with the intensity of an existential need.

In summary, the model of digital economic practices consists of three interconnected divisions: value, property and profit. Value is created for users who realise that value in collective activities and is made from four components: technicians and technologies, business plans and ambitions, existing cultures and disruptions to cultures, and existing regulatory and governmental contexts. Property concerns the different ways in which the information generated by collective activities may be determined through exclusive or distributive property rights. Profit is consequent on the formation of a value that attracts users and the definition of what information means as a property; in digital economic practices monetisation is added to whatever value an information platform creates. These can be hybrid forms of monetisation that include connections to non-digital economic practices, and will revolve around at least one of three main strategies: targeted advertising, rent not buy, and disintermediation.

Conclusion

The model of the digital economy as a sector is formed by digital economic practices that link value, property and profit across the two causations of activities transformed and information as property. This schematic allows common aspects to be put into causal relationships to identify an economic dynamic, without reducing that dynamic to targeted advertising. What the modelling identifies is that the collective activities of users are the core and essential economic motor of digital economic practices.

This model and schematic builds on previous work but presents a different view. For example, Nieborg and Poell's (2018) account of the platformisation of cultural production has many resonances with that offered here. Kerr's (2016) approach to games also registers similar forces to those integrated into digital economic practices.

> The general characteristics of the new production logic can be summarised as the development of a 'free service' that is reliant on the continuous, dynamic and almost real-time flow of data between users, intermediaries, content creators and other parties, to support both indirect and direct forms of monetisation and customization. ... The 'central broker' in this new production logic is not the publisher or developer of the content, it is the intermediary distributor or platform owner. (Kerr 2016: 69–70)

In these and other similar arguments the platform often becomes the central economic player. This is heavily emphasised in Srnicek's work on 'platform capitalism', in which the digital economy is defined through the platform which then becomes the driving force of capitalism (Srnicek 2016; Srnicek and Williams 2016). The proposed model of digital economic practices builds on such work, but also displaces the platform from being the repository or main constituent of the digital economy to being an element within the practices that create the digital economy. The platform is important, but is not the central factor and can only be understood when it is seen as part of complex digital practices constructed out of value, property and profit.

The digital economy creates activities that users value, often in the process transforming existing activities that range from the cab ride to loving a friend and draws information from these activities potentially creating monetisation. It is not platforms that drive the digital economy. Platforms are one of the mechanisms needed to create practices, no more and no less. It is not free labour that drives the digital economy. Free labour may be created from activities but does not encompass them. It is not profit that makes the digital economy. However large some profits are, as important are some of the programs created in free digital economic practices. The digital economy is driven by practices that draw information about communities through a platform, offering opportunities for private profit or for sociality through information sharing. Collective activities, communities of action, are what make the digital economy a distinct economic sector.

9   Principles for Digital
       Economic Policy

Proposing a schematic or model of economic practices specific to the digital is a basis for consideration of policy for the digital economy. As the nature of the case studies given and schematic of the digital economy both attest, any such policies that are implemented will need to be situated in specific regulatory and cultural contexts. Given the wide range and diversity of such environments, this might be taken as a reason to think that proposing policies for the digital economy is impossible. Nevertheless, while acknowledging that identifying specific policies for particular times and spaces is not possible here, some general principles can be identified. These principles allow the identification of policy questions that should be addressed when examining or proposing policy for the digital economy.

There are three areas that stand out from the foregoing analysis: labour practices, taxation and alternative economic forms. However, running through each is the issue of jurisdiction, or the location of a digital economic company for the purposes of regulation. I will address this issue first because, although an exhaustive definition of specific jurisdictions is impossible, some of the key issues relate to the nature of digital economic practices and so are worth explicating. The policy principles proposed here then reflect what can be concluded from the first thirty years of digital economic practices, and will have to be further developed as these practices change.

Jurisdiction and Digital Economic Practices

Where can a set of digital economic practices, with either a platform and corporation or a platform and non-profit organisation, be located? The in-principle difficulty for digital economic practices is that the communications infrastructure of the internet, an existential precondition for digital economic practices, crosses regulatory boundaries and inter-connects activities from different regulatory contexts. We should not overestimate this, however, since many nations have implemented significant controls over internet traffic crossing their borders; long gone are the days when, as was once tried in the UK, someone thought it was a good idea to defend watching illegal material on their computer on the basis that the material was located on servers in a different country. The problem is also not resolved just because most corporations have a headquarters somewhere – some famous like the Googleplex in Mountain View or Apple's Infinite Loop – because such locations can be varied through complicated legal schemes. Even taking into account controls over the internet and the ability to locate headquarters, the underlying pressure that the flow of information puts on locating a digital economic practice for regulatory purposes remains. Putting aside issues that occur for all corporations and non-profit institutions in meeting regulations, what can be done here is to explore how the model of digital economic practices suggests a way of locating those practices and thereby establishing jurisdiction over information that often flows across regulatory boundaries.

The problem of companies crossing borders and so mixing regulatory authorities – opening up the possibility of manipulating tax, labour and other factors – is strongest after a digital economic practice platform has privatised the information flowing across it. In this case, all the information runs through the digital companies' platform, which allows that information or the rights to that information to be sent wherever suits the company running the platform. For example, as Fuchs (2018) points out, a not uncommon claim made by digital companies is that the value generated by their platform comes from its algorithms and software, leading to the claim that the income from activities is placeless as it is the result of the value created in the platform's software, which can be licensed wherever the company wishes. If digital economic corporations can base their taxable value on the information flowing through their platforms after that information has become private property, then by appealing to intellectual property rights they can define that information as their source of value and license that value anywhere in the world. This issue only arises with for-profit companies relying on exclusive property rights. If the information is distributed then by definition it is available for examination by all and not subject to hidden manipulation by the platform.

Corporations in many other sectors may try to manipulate where they are taxed and regulated, but often the nature of their practices ensures that their activities can be located – a mineral must be mined somewhere, a pair of shoes bought somewhere, and so on. Digital economic practices inherently obfuscate their locations because they deal primarily in information that is only visible within a platform and in this way is visible to the platform controller but not outside it. Alongside the various tricks all companies can employ, some digital economic companies have an additional and particularly informational way of manipulating the location of their revenue and profit. One of the most famous cases is the now discontinued 'double Irish' method of manipulating taxation, which worked for many kinds of economic practices but achieved a particular potency in relation to companies for which information is the central property.

The 'double Irish' was a tax arrangement specific to US companies that was closed in 2014, though companies were given four years to transition from it. The arrangement was not illegal (McDonald 2014). A US company can develop something informational, such as software, and then sell this, at cost, to a company based in somewhere like Bermuda (which has a zero corporate tax rate). Once the intellectual property was located in Bermuda the company there could revalue upward the intellectual property asset, paying no tax on its increased value. The Bermuda company then licenses the software, say advertising algorithms, to a company in Ireland. A second Irish company has to be formed (hence double Irish) due to certain local regulations and the first Irish company licences to the second. This explains why Ireland was probably chosen as Irish regulations allowed a company not to pay tax in Ireland if it was fully controlled elsewhere even if it was legally incorporated in Ireland. The second company in Ireland sells a service elsewhere in Europe and pays the first company, there was no tax liable in Ireland on transfers between companies in Europe. This Irish company in turn pays to the Bermuda-based company the royalty that company is owed for licensing the intellectual property rights. The money thus travels through two companies to rest in a third in Bermuda, which has zero tax rate, and zero tax is paid. Most, if not all, of the European advertising income for Google or Facebook was funnelled in these ways, with such companies asserting strongly that all their sales business was done by the Irish companies (HOCCPA 2013). There were other complex twists on such manipulation of regulations to reduce tax, in this case close to zero, while remaining within the law. What is useful for considering policy on the digital economy is to note how the centrality of the value of the information – the software measured by its intellectual property rights valuation – offers the chance for a company to move its value around. The corporation still requires a base in at least one country to start the process, but where its revenue is actually based can be put to one side and become irrelevant for tax purposes with profits, losses and revenue located with the holder of the intellectual property rights (HOCCPA 2013; Thorne 2013). Though now removed, the double Irish arrangement remains a good example of how information, once privatised, can allow a company to play with location. This is in contrast to the activities of users, which are located in one place.

If digital economic companies that privatise information gain an additional means of manipulating the location of their profit-making activities, then the word 'activities' suggests a way this can be countered. If information may flow in ways only the platform can see, offering the platform ways to manipulate location to wherever best suits the company, then the activities in which the platform's value is realised and from which information arises will always be located at the users. The digital economy is not virtual in the sense of being nowhere, as every user is locatable; that is to say, every user will have an internet protocol (IP) address that will indicate their location. All computers connected through the internet have to have a number address, called their IP number, that allows information to be routed to and from that computer. IP numbers allow a measure of activity and of its location, consequently also of how much value is derived from any location, with location definable at whatever level is appropriate. Such a view is not unlike existing sales tax regimes, where the tax is levied on a particular activity (buying) at the point that activity takes place. What is different is that a purchase, as an activity, comes with a price, a percentage of which can be taxed, but activities in digital economic practices are often monetised separately to the action. Activities allow jurisdictions to be defined but not what can be done; they locate a company at the levels at which regulation occurs by locating activities in the same area as a regulatory authority. Regulation of digital economic companies has a way through activities of ensuring an accurate understanding of where value is generated by any company, on condition that such companies are forced to give up the information about the location of their users (which may in turn have privacy implications).

The argument here has similarities with Fuchs's proposal for an online advertising tax. Fuchs's argument derives from treating all activities as labour (a significant difference to the argument presented here), and locates value with the labour in activities on a monetised digital platform (somewhat similar to the argument here). As Fuchs does not see activities as pre-labour and able to be determined later as such, there is a divergence with my argument, but it is important to see that whether coming from the view put here that not all human activities on digital platforms should be considered labour under capitalism or agreeing with Fuchs's point of view, the result is similar in noting that the value of activities is derived by users in specific locations that are traceable. In my argument, recognising that activities always have a place only addresses the problem of locating a digital economic practice for the purposes of jurisdiction, whereas Fuchs, by starting with labour and following the profit made from it, can move directly to taxation on ads related to activities.

It is also worth noting that the European Union has developed a proposal to try to situate companies through a comparative calculation of their location-based sales, salaries, employees and capital assets. The main concern for the EU was to find a way to tax companies, particularly digital ones, that have income from a nation or region but do not have a headquarters or an official office in that nation or region. This is also a concern when companies move their offices around to ensure the lowest tax while still drawing revenue from regions where they are paying minimal or no tax. Again, the issue here is one of jurisdiction: what sets the boundaries to a location within which the revenue and profit of a company can be determined and the appropriate tax rate set by governments within that location? For some companies this EU proposal may have merit, but for companies drawing substantial revenue from free services it remains a difficult base from which to work, as their revenue and value are not necessarily reflected by locally based revenue, capital and employment. Further, such a calculation remains open to being 'gamed' by any information-based company, because the activities may continue through employment and offices situated outside a particular location (European Commission 2017).

A last example of such efforts – which taken together indicate the attention starting to be paid to the problems digital economic practices pose for taxation – is the UK government's October 2018 budget, which included plans for a 'digital services tax'. Though not to be implemented until April 2020, this was a direct response to arguments that large digital companies like Facebook were not paying appropriate levels of tax. The plan was to levy a 2 per cent tax on 'revenues from those activities that are linked to the participation of UK users', on companies with global revenues of over £500 million per annum and with a minimum £25 million per annum allowance (HM Government 2018: Section 3.26). Details of the tax plan were not available, but the focus on activities is notable.

Fuchs's, the EU's and the UK government's approaches reflect a fundamental issue in relation to many digital economic practices in knowing what is actually going on within national, regional or supranational boundaries. By understanding the way digital economic practices work and their dependence on activities, a way of determining locations and hence jurisdiction is made clear. The key way to achieve definition of jurisdictions is to follow user activities, whether free or paid, because this information is both collected and allows users to be located.

An exception to the problem of location and jurisdiction comes with digital economic practices using disintermediation. These can be located in the same way based on activities, but they tend already to be heavily tied to particular regulatory regimes. The early and ongoing battles of the first big two disintermediators, Uber and Airbnb, have tended to be with city regulators, for the very good reason that disintermediation means locating economic practices within already existing regulatory regimes and then remediating those regimes to the companies' advantage, and these regimes tend to be at city level. National or supranational advertising or rent-not-buy revenue strategies may require jurisdiction definition, but cab rides and apartment rentals are so obviously located that regulators should know where to call.

Defining jurisdiction is inherently possible in digital economic practices by focusing on users, their activities and their IP (or other similar) addresses. Privacy issues may arise if companies are forced to give up data, but this would seem to be an issue of implementation as data anonymised for individuals but not for areas would serve for the purposes of defining jurisdiction. Not only is location through activities possible through requirements to disclose, for some governments the data is quite likely already in their control, given the revelations from Edward Snowden and others about the huge data gathering exercises routinely undertaken by some state intelligence services (Harding 2014). In the following sections, jurisdiction will be treated as a solvable problem requiring only political will and competent implementation.

Tax and Digital Economic Practices

Taxing digital companies has become a significant issue as it has emerged that some of the best known have been reporting large profits while paying little tax in most nations and regions. Sadly, this is not to suggest that digital companies are doing more or less in terms of paying or avoiding tax than other kinds of companies. Scandals like the Panama Papers reveal highly complex schemes which all tend toward pushing legal requirements to their limit to reduce tax bills for the rich to a minimum (Obermaier and Obermayer 2017). It is not within this book's remit to cover all such schemes, the point here is simply whether there is anything specific about digital economic practices in this general context.

Based on the definition of jurisdiction given in the previous section, some policy questions in relation to tax follow. Assuming that jurisdiction is defined in relation to activities, tax may then track the relationship between activities and either revenue or profit. That is, the policy question to be considered is: given the level of activity measured in a particular practice, what revenue and/or profit is being generated and what is the appropriate tax rate for this? Such a tax would be unavoidable for any digital economic practice because the level of activities is recorded and can be aggregated – knowing the activities and their relationship to profit is a matter of implementing systems not of principle. The question then remains of the relationship between activities, revenue and profit. Concerns here would again have to do with implementation and with what each regulatory body felt was an appropriate level to tax which stream of money. Rising levels of activity do not necessarily lead to revenue or profit, as proven by many digital companies. The alternative of taxing revenue or profit directly opens up the problem that these arguments seek to solve, as it is essentially the same problem of defining jurisdiction and again offers companies the ability to manoeuvre their finances. While activities are a way to measure how much economic activity a company has, this has to then be related to revenue and/or profit in order to define taxation.

Calculating a user's worth to a digital company has not gone entirely unnoticed, with a number of websites and apps offering ways of rating this. Though it was discontinued in 2016, the anti-virus software company AVG for a while added a calculator to its privacy tool. In 2014 you could use AVG's PrivacyFix to see its estimate of what over a year your online activity had contributed to some digital companies. For example, one journalist reported the app as estimating their worth to Facebook as $20.57 annually and to Google as $223 (Delo 2014). The privacy company Abine offered a quiz to determine how much a user is worth to Facebook (and to reinforce the need for privacy by revealing how much Facebook knows about a user) (Freeman 2012). There are also more than a few articles that attempt to determine the average value of a user based on aggregate data. For example, in 2016 Gibbs calculated that on average a user was worth $3.73 per financial quarter to Facebook, and when looking regionally North American users were worth $13.54 compared to Asia-Pacific users at $1.59 (Gibbs 2016). Such calculations are often rough, but they demonstrate in principle the ability to combine information about individuals with aggregate data and come up with an individualised contribution figure.

All these rough numbers are examples of the possibilities when looking at digital companies from the side of users and their activities, and particularly the possibility of taxing digital companies rather like a sales tax is levied, by focusing on the activities that earn a company money. This may be a simplification of how a sales tax works but it is relevant as a broad principle. There is no obvious reason why relating the activities on a digital platform – which are of course all recorded and available for analysis – to the income generated by that platform cannot open up forms of taxation on income which is incontrovertibly located in particular places and times. Consideration might be given to how activities generate income from advertising: when does a click on a link lead directly to income? Following income on activities is one strategy; however, it would miss the enormous value to platforms of all the activities recorded on them, whether they lead immediately to ads or income or not, because all that information allows for the refining of profiles and targeted advertising. The value of activities that do not directly produce revenue but do produce information that a platform can use to then produce revenue, through ads for example, can be indicated by Google's rumoured plans to charge phone makers for the use of its Android operating system if they unbundle Google's services from Android and so stop producing an information flow to Google. This move was forced by the European Union over concerns that Google's practice of bundling its services, like Google Maps, with Android, even when Android was used by another company as its phone or tablet operating system, was monopolistic. Leaked Google documents suggested the company would charge $40 per unbundled device because, though Google did not lose revenue by unbundling its services, it would lose the information flow on which its ad revenue is based (Amadeo 2018b). Finally, because of the disconnection between activities and income, consideration would have to be given to ensuring digital companies are taxed in the same way as non-digital companies on profit or revenue, since taxation based purely on digital activities could lead to tax demands where neither revenue nor profit were being realised, even potentially of free digital economic practices. Implementation would then have to consider the value of all activities, the activities that lead to income, and a control, similar to other forms of taxation, on when taxation should start on a company.

From this basic proposal two paths open up. One is to consider aggregate taxation. If a company's total revenue for a region that has tax-raising powers is estimated, and that estimation relates revenues to activities, then tax can be levied on that amount. For example, based on Facebook's accounts it is thought that the company gained revenue of £842 million in the UK in 2016 and paid £5.1 million in tax (a rate of less than 1 per cent). If Facebook's revenue had been taxed at the equivalent rate to the UK's version of sales tax (VAT) of 20 per cent, then the tax bill would have been just over £168 million.[1] In Australia the goods and services tax (GST) would have required 10 per cent (PA 2017). The previously mentioned UK government proposal of a 2 per cent tax would have raised close to £17 million. The point here would be to relate the amount raised in a particular region to the activities in that region.

A second route would be to consider the possibility of micro-transactions in the context of taxation. With an appropriate model there is in principle no reason why individual activities associated with income could not be taxed as the activities progress, in a way that considers both actual income and the value of the information being privatised by the platform.

Micro-taxation would produce results based directly on actual activities and their location that benefit a digital company. This raises an associated possibility that micro-taxation could be considered alongside micro-income to users in which the same calculation that defines revenue-per-activity ensures a percentage of that revenue flows both to government and to the individual user. Such schemes would require controls to prevent automated 'farming' of a site, not entirely unlike how content farms seek to drive users to their sites to gain income from ad clicks. This would potentially be problematic for micro-income and micro-taxation if citizens tried to maximise tax or income however they could. Implementation would then have to control such gaming of the system, possibly most usefully by ensuring valid connections between activities and revenue, so that even if activities are driven by users trying to raise tax or income they are also only a percentage of increased revenue for the company. On the other hand, as will be considered in the discussion of the commons below, this also opens up possibilities for collectivised income from a platform that is controlled by its users rather than privatised for the profit of a few.

In conclusion it should be emphasised that taxation based on activities only relates to certain strategies for monetisation of digital economic practices. For example, subscription-based services applying 'rent not buy' strategies might more easily and authentically to the economic practice be taxed straight on the exchange between renter and rentee, with jurisdiction based on the location of the rentee. The fundamental policy principle that addresses all digital economic practices is not micro-taxation or micro-transaction or some other such form, but that taxation should derive from activities as they relate to the revenue and profit of a digital economic corporation.

Labour and Digital Economic Practices

Labour and the digital economy has recurred as a theme and become one of the main questions asked of the broader 'social good' of digital economic corporations. Research demonstrating the poor income of Uber drivers, often below minimum wage levels, and the profit digital companies are drawing from the freely given activities of their users, are just two of the controversies that have arisen in both academia and the popular press about labour in the digital economic sector. From the perspective of the model of digital economic practices, there are two policy principles that recurrently pose problems in relation to labour: freely given activities that are monetised, and disintermediation as a monetisation strategy.

The question of free labour has been discussed at length already, and here we need only draw out some of the ethical issues implicit in the debate and consider what policy questions might follow. The conclusion, putting things Red Queen backward, is that this is primarily an issue of defining information as a property for profit or for sharing. The problem many see is that some digital economic practices connect freely given time and effort by users on a privately owned platform to significant financial profit. The two and two equals outrage here is that individuals' labour, that is their time and freely given effort, is being stolen and not paid for by a company that then profits, sometimes to huge benefit (and sometimes while paying little tax). Some of the complexities and confusions of the debate around free labour come from the controversy generated by this connection of stolen labour and gross profit. My analysis has suggested that treating the activities on a platform as stolen labour is not a reliable position, both conceptually and when the empirical evidence from those undertaking the activities is examined. Yet there remains an issue here, as there is no doubt that companies benefit financially from being able to take information from their users' activities.

The underlying issue is the point at which the information from activities is turned into a property and what kind of a property. Further, it is often not the information derived directly from activities themselves that leads to profit, which instead comes from that individualised information being reworked through a platform to create insights that are only available to the platform controllers. What is implied in criticisms of privatising the information from individuals' activities on a platform is that information is a private property. Many critiques of such platforms assume or assert that the information a user has to input to gain access to a platform is the property of the user: age, gender, location and so on. This is then considered stolen without recompense. However, if this is taken to be the definition of information as property then there is cause for concern, because it is also the case that any new information created from that collected on the platform is by the same principle owned by the platform. All the key recursions, all the complex correlations and complex understandings that fuel targeted advertising, do not exist prior to the platform inter-connecting the information given or extorted to it. In short, if someone considers information about themselves to be their private property then, to be consistent, they have to grant the same ownership rights to the platform over information that is native to that platform, because, just as age, gender and so on are considered the possession of whoever has them, the correlations are only ever in the possession of the platform that creates them (Jordan 2015: 200–7).

The ethical question is then, what definitions of property should be employed in these contexts? This opens up two policy questions. First: is the relationship between users and companies an ethical one, in which the initial giving up of information is clearly understood and appropriately recompensed in activities? The bargain here is one of exchanging information for access to free activities, and there is no reason why that bargain should not be examined, just as any such exchange that has a wide social impact can be. The companies are in no position to judge if the relationship is ethical, given the benefits that accrue to them from gaining as much information as possible. Further, though the company is providing a service and may argue that the swap of information for that service is ethical, it is also not uncommon for access paid for with information to become a form of blackmail. For example, if it is very difficult for someone not to use a platform – such as a social media site on which all the other members of their family communicate – then they will have to give up their information whether they wish to or not. In general, the drive within digital economic practices to create more benefit for a company by creating ever more information will undermine that company's capacity for ethical consideration of this issue. Here is one of the reasons Google's famous 'don't be evil' slogan turned into its 2018 'you can make money without being evil' (one of Google's 'ten things we know to be true'). Moreover, as discussed in the previous section in relation to taxation, it is possible to consider ways in which users could be recompensed with more than just access to a site by offering micro-income.

The second policy question is whether the information companies hold and the services they provide amount to a social good and should be considered as such (Havalais 2009: 1–5). Are the data and algorithms that a search engine company uses to produce search results a social good? At what point does the information held by a digital company as their private property need to be reconsidered as a necessary social good which cannot be left to one private company? The fact that it is impossible to deal with the huge amounts of information produced in our twenty-first-century societies without some means of searching it has delivered a potentially extraordinarily important social good into the hands of private companies. Similarly, the fact that companies like Twitter and Facebook have become key players in the distribution of news has been questioned as possibly undermining democracy in the face of their management of news feeds. There are potentially wide social benefits but also potential damages from some digital economic practices. The more radical policy question then concerns who should own information, and according to what principles. What kind of property is information if we view it from the point of view of society as a whole, and insist it should benefit society as whole?

What is clear here is that out of the free labour debate policy issues emerge concerning the ownership of information and broad conceptions of social good. What a more innovative response to this might be will be touched on in the next section on the information commons. In regard to issues of free labour and the privatisation of information by platforms that offer activities, questions should be asked about the ethics of the relationship between a user and a platform and between society and a platform.

The second set of policy questions around labour arises in relation to disintermediating digital economic practices.[2] As argued earlier, disintermediators develop digital platforms that create practices connecting service users with service providers in ways that remove various regulations or constraints imposed on existing service providers, replacing them with new mediations controlled by the platform. Connecting users and providers allows disintermediating digital platforms to monetise their practice primarily by taking a percentage of the money flowing between users and providers. As many of the advantages the digital company creates flow from its removal of regulations or other costs that fall on existing service providers, it has an inherent interest in not taking responsibility for either users or providers. This refusal opens up the recurrent issue of whether users and providers of such services are being exploited. The image Airbnb presents is of allowing people to occasionally rent out a bedroom or their house or flat while on holiday, which glosses over the importance of multiple landlords to its revenue, as the previous analysis of New York and Barcelona suggested. Uber presents itself as allowing many to gain a further income stream from an asset they already have, their car, but analysis suggests that the transfer of costs to the driver means they end up working long hours for remuneration at best close to, and often less than, the minimum wage (Molla 2018; Cherry 2015).

The pressure within this digital economic practice is to keep users and providers outside of the responsibility of the company, while also maintaining various new forms of control over them. This raises policy questions that face in two directions. First, the effects on users and providers of the standards and risks associated with their service being mediated by a platform, often controlled by algorithms, needs consideration. In particular, the almost hidden loss of all kinds of risk controls that are part of existing regulation needs examination. Users need protection from the risks of getting into someone's car or staying in someone's flat, such as hidden or exorbitant costs and so on. Providers also need consideration of the risks to themselves and their assets, particularly with regard to such things as health insurance, while their effective wage levels also need consideration (Scholz 2017). Second, policy needs to address the broader effect on society of these various disintermediations and reintermediations. The troubles in a number of cities over whether Airbnb is driving out local residents in favour of tourists is an example of an issue that is not so much about risk control and disintermediated regulation as it is about the consequences of disintermediation on life in a given place. Policy makers will also need to examine whether the new practices bring benefits, for example easier and cheaper cab rides, particularly because some services may be popular, which may well affect the ability of regulators to make changes (especially when a local populace is mobilised by a digital corporation).

In both policy directions, the point is not how evil the effects of a disintermediating digital practice are assumed to be but assessing how those effects will be highly variable in different parts of a local population. What cab drivers might find problematic and threatening to well-established livelihoods, cab passengers might find highly attractive. What needs to be especially considered is the cynicism of companies in trying to mobilise, particularly with financial backing, that part of the population in favour of their activities, and the ability of digital companies to hide their workings within proprietary platforms. The latter is a specific advantage digital corporations often have, and will need consideration in terms of whether the information they gather and their use of it should be under closer scrutiny. Uber's use of algorithms to try to prevent investigators from taking a ride in one of its cabs is as clear an example as possible of a company using its obscured software practices to manipulate regulation in its favour (Bradshaw 2017). Policy makers, whether government or community based, may need to force platforms to open their information resources and manipulations, much as New York regulators did when forcing Airbnb to disclose details on their landlords, revealing that larger landlords were a major income source.

It is clear that there are policy issues around activities that are turned into labour by digital companies, and policy issues relating to disintermediation as a strategy for monetisation in digital economic practices.[3] As with the analysis of tax issues, the wider social impact of such practices will be relevant when considering policy questions in the digital sector. The final section of this chapter will look at a more radical and more socially oriented set of policy questions.

Commons and Digital Economic Practices

If digital economic practices are both those practices that draw on the collective activities of users and are practices that need not be monetised, then it is possible to consider different kinds of economic organisation than privatised and profit-seeking ones. Moreover, such consideration is essential as it draws on the most beneficial to the most people possibility of information by making use of information's capability for simultaneous complete use. Taking inspiration from enterprises like free software and Wikipedia, the idea of some kind of information commons has been an obvious and much discussed possibility, particularly for reinvigorating or even reinventing a left that too often seems caught intellectually in ways of thinking tied to industrial societies (Bollier and Conaty 2014). The possibility of commons-based social organisation, drawing on the powers of digital and internet platforms to enable a society based on open, peer-to-peer sharing, has been widely discussed and connected to shifts in particularly European politics such as the Podemos movement in Spain, the Stir to Action campaign in the UK (www.stirtoaction.com), or more generally to what has been called 'left populism' (Gerbaudo 2017).[4] While I cannot cover this wide field here, what can be done is to note what analysing digital economic practices may open up as radical possibilities that could be integrated into existing discussions, such as Scholz's arguments for 'platform cooperativism' (Scholz 2016).

The underlying issue is the possibility of creating platforms that fully embrace information's capacity for simultaneous complete use, like a Pirate Bay for social, cultural and economic schemes. The many 'open data' projects that various galleries, libraries and governments have developed, and the pressure on academia to make its research available as open access, are in part responses to this possibility, which, though it has always been present within information, achieves a scope and reach through digital and internet socio-technologies that previous technologies such as books or the radio could not match. Making all information available and returning all the uses of that information to the commons opens up the potential for broad social good. Any implementation of such schemes, for example a search engine run on these principles, will have to face important questions about limits: Should medical information about everyone be made available to everyone? Should credit histories and financial details? Privacy advocates would immediately understand the huge risks of a totally open system, raising the policy question of limits. But this is an implementation issue rather than a fatal issue of principle. The key principle is to turn information from being an exclusive property to a distributive one; though limits are important, platforms may be designed that are inherently distributive, with some restrictions, instead of being inherently restricted, with some distribution. It is also a principle that can be applied by any organisation with the resources to create a platform.

In this context the possibility of micro-transactions as a means of sharing returns is relevant. This may look like a matter of simply creating platforms with a monetisation strategy to share the income, and such a strategy should not be dismissed out of hand, but the broader possibility would be to reconsider what value is being generated by a platform and seek ways of redistributing it. For example, the strategy of disintermediation could lead to cooperation in which a service can be collectively operated because the information is available to all users and providers. Platforms such as CouchSurfing (prior to its shift toward greater managerial ownership and control), or the many book-sharing apps and schemes, point to ways in which sharing might allow the benefits of such platforms to be managed and shared by those who use the platform.

A different form of digital industry emerges in this shift from profit-based industries and information as private property to community-beneficial industries and information as distributive property. Policy questions here must address the issue of 'who benefits' from these different formations of information in digital societies. Within digital industries the principles of exclusion or distribution pose a stark difference for the current 'big' players, as a policy change toward information as distributive would require that the Googles and Facebooks distribute their billions and their information. Mechanisms that would reward users from a fund based on a collectively generated value that can be monetised are possible. This would not mean the end of rent or value-extraction, just as copyleft in free software did not end exclusive forms of property but built on them to invert privatised information into collectivised information. Policy will then turn on the question of 'who benefits' from inverting monetisation so that profit is not exclusive but distributed. Ads may not end on a social media site conditioned as a distributive digital platform, but an owner's exclusive billions could be turned into distributed incomes. The possibilities of an information commons are radical in their inversion of profit-making digital industries into collective practices of wider social benefit.

Conclusion

The policy discussion in this chapter has addressed general principles that will need consideration by any community or government in which digital economic practices emerge. These principles may be split into two general areas: those relevant to issues that are within, very broadly understood, current economic and social arrangements that digital economic practices may extend or disrupt; and those relevant to the emergence of new social and economic practices that break with profit-taking in favour of social development. The issue of jurisdiction is key, particularly because sometimes it is assumed rather than analysed. Deciding jurisdiction is essential to gaining any kind of hold over companies built on digital economic practices. Definition of place, and hence of jurisdiction, can be resolved by focusing not on moveable information complexes but on the activities of users of platforms. It then becomes a matter of choice whether any regulatory body wishes to establish exactly what income raising is done by a digital company and where. With the definition of jurisdiction, tax and labour become areas in which a number of further policy principles emerge for integrating digital economic practices into societies. This integration could involve greater tax transparency and responsibility for labour, or restraining the unfettered self-interest and obsession with profit that have contributed to the twenty-first century's record of rising economic inequality (Piketty 2014). What the present discussion offers are some of the questions that need to be asked of digital economic practices to ensure they are part of building just societies and not just disrupting them.

The discussion of information commons-like possibilities strongly argue for the general benefits to society, to all life, that could flow from turning digital economic practices away from profit-making and toward collective goods. Digital economic practices that freely distribute information to many, and demand in return that any further information generated is also freely released, offer significant resources for practices that value social life in all its aspects beyond just its financial ones. The potential for information, in an information age, to be available to all, simultaneously and to the full extent of its usefulness, offers resources for radical change. How then does this analysis relate to a wider understanding of societies and their possible futures? The concluding chapter will take up this final consideration for understanding digital economic practices.

10 Digital Economic Practices and the Economy

Digital Economic Practices and Capitalism

Capitalism is a word that, in these pages, has been more absent than is usual when discussing the digital economy. Reading any discussion of the digital economy will generally mean finding 'capitalism' repeated, all too often as though it is self-evidently clear what it means, with that assumed self-evidence rooted in the politics of economies. Does capitalism refer to an assumption of all the good that the free market brings? As is obvious with a little contemplation, there is no such thing as a free market as all markets are regulated in some way, for example even if only to enforce private property. Is capitalism assumed to be an evil that ruins society? Exchange still has to occur in society and the theory of this evil is often unstated in many accounts, while those that are explicit often succumb to a deep complexity usually related more closely to early twentieth-century socio-economies than the digital economy. 'Capitalism' has all too often become little more than a swear word or rallying call. This book has avoided using it as a broad term in order to focus on seeing digital economic practices in action and then modelling the digital economy. We can now look at the wider significance of those practices, particularly their reliance on cultures and collective actions.

Seeing what is new and what is the same is not always easy. For example, when discussing rent or exploitation in the digital economy some argue that the analysis of for-profit digital economic platforms confirms the Marxist analysis of capitalism as exploitation, with only a small step needed to affirm that nothing is fundamentally new here. Identifying what is new in digital economic practices does not mean asserting that a whole new economy has arisen; the argument here has been for an explicitly sectoral analysis, but with specific dynamics in hand we can now turn to the wider effects of those digital economic practices. While this might seem an exclusively economic issue, I agree with those who argue that sociology, politics and culture are essential to understanding economics (and vice versa) (Piketty 2014: 32–3, 574–5; Du Gay and Pryke 2002; Hesmondhalgh and Baker 2013; Conor et al. 2015). Culture is crucial because digital economic practices rely on collective activities, communities even, and cultural and social analysis must then be integrated with economic to see such economic activity's full scope. The injection of cultural and social analysis into the economic has been progressed from a number of directions, including drawing on feminist analyses of the importance of domestic labour and on contributions from those analysing the cultural and creative industries.

Digital economic practices create and feed on collective activities, on the kinds of necessarily group interactions that build communities, cultures and societies. Others have noted the ability of social media to directly monetise social relations, often referring to it as the direct monetisation of humanity, life and emotion (Stark 2009: 206–10; Dean 2012: 131–4; Zuboff 2019). But social media and targeted advertising are only one example of how digital economic practices make themselves into industries of beauty, wonder and grief, even if they seem the most commented on. Turning all kinds of activities into a form of labour is a process that digital economic practices undertake. This process can make the exact same events, the same actions taken by someone, into leisure and entertainment for the user of the platform and information that benefits the platform and that effectively becomes labour for the platform. By collapsing activities into labour the critics of free labour assume what they criticise by turning everything that everyone does into labour for private profit, paid or unpaid. If the fundamental insight that social, cultural and emotional life is being monetised is asserted then that assertion depends on the collective activities and social relations that constitute and underpin life, or, for Zuboff, humanity. It is then important to understand these processes without assuming some pre-given identity or humanity, because it is not a matter of social, cultural and emotional life as pre-given, but of how these are formed through the activities and relations created and manipulated within digital economic practices.

While some have identified the link between such things as likes and posts on social media and the profits from advertising, fewer have identified that it is not a matter of life being monetised but of the components of collective life being created and formed within platforms. Digital economic practices create particular kinds of activities that may attempt to mirror or replicate existing social relations in digital contexts, but which instead form new activities of value to users who may or may not take them up. 'Friending' is an example, with the process of making a friend obviously pre-existing digital economic practices but being taken up by some platforms who rely on existing understandings of what it means to become a 'friend' and then recreate this in a new form (boyd 2006). Searching is similar, particularly when the way searches are personalised is understood. Personalisation ensures that many may ask the same question and receive different answers that are yet all answers to the same question, meaning that in many search engines what a question means has shifted from being articulated by the person asking it to being formed by the search engine that will deliver an answer (Feuz et al. 2011).

Digital economic practices are creating versions of life as beauty, wonder and grief that alter the nature of beauty, wonder and grief. This should not lead to an automatic condemnation of such practices, especially not if that condemnation assumes that physically based communication is superior to digital forms, and that any replacement of physical co-presence by digitally mediated co-presence will be negative. Many such changes produce differences, particularly in communicative forms, which may be appropriate to different contexts and cannot automatically be assumed to be negative (Jordan 2013). The point here is to recognise the ways in which many for-profit corporations, whose fundamental existential challenge is to make financial profit or die, are creating and manipulating the constituents of life by forming and reforming social and cultural collectivities.

The nature of emotion, the very nature of our connections to each other and to other beings, is integrated into and dependent on collective practices that have been formed for the purpose of profit-making. The reach of these is now great, from fitness apps and the quantified self, to dating and love, to dieting and personal regard, to making friends, searching for information, and more. Digital economic practices need to be examined, critiqued and contested for the ways they are remaking our affective emotional, social and cultural lives through the activities they offer, activities that realise something of value to people that often appears familiar, like making a friend, but is reformed into a digital activity that imbues it with new meaning. Neither can some ideal state prior to digital economic practices be identified that has since been corrupted; emotion and humanity are formed in practices – the question is, how are they being formed now in digital economic practices? While identifying how an economic practice forms society is not new – the relationship between the car industry and suburbanisation being one example of the way in which economic practices not only address existing activities but form them – what is new is the way in which the digital economy not only reforms and then forms society but extends this to our deeply personal lives.

Our collective actions and interior emotions, all intermingled and expressing fundamental relations to each other, even if sometimes a service relation, are the stuff digital economic practices feed on. This does not mean that life is turned entirely into labour, but that the way we live is being contested by many digital economic practices to form life as something that produces a profit. And some such practices have been monetised for monstrous profits worthy of the robber barons of the early twentieth century. Against this, the importance and power of non-monetised digital economic practices should not be underestimated; they offer hope for more collectively beneficial outcomes. The achievements of Linux as a free software operating system, or the WWW Consortium's curation of the protocols that hold the Web together, are significant. Deep concern is gradually being aired over some for-profit digital companies, for example Facebook's and Twitter's role in spreading news and false news. And this concern should extend to thinking more radically about the ways such companies have taken over areas of social life, from taxis to friends, and reformed them to their benefit, changing not just our access to cabs or ways of making friends but the very nature of cabs and friends. It is not just the headline profits of companies like Google and Facebook that are worthy of attention, but the wide range of their interventions that change the nature of our lives through the activities offered by each platform.

The combination of drawing revenue from information and user activities also suggests a particular relationship to the network effect for digital economic practices. The network effect occurs because in any network each node gains value exponentially as more nodes join, potentially reaching a point where the network has so much value, because it has so many connections, that it becomes dominant. We see network effects in platforms like Facebook in social media, Google and Baidu in search, Wikipedia for encyclopaedias and so on. Such network effects can lead to the dominance of a platform over a particular form of value, even if it offers free activities that users can always withdraw from. Such dominance can be hard to shift and is the equivalent of a monopoly in other economic sectors. Digital monopolies can be further entrenched by for-profit platforms if they successfully monetise, as this then gives them the financial power to buy up rivals. Facebook's purchase of other social media sites such as Instagram or the messaging service WhatsApp point to the way in which monopolies in digital economic practices may be entrenched, both by dominating information in those practices and, when that dominance results in profit, by using financial power to simply buy up or replicate any opposition. Such monopolies are an inherent potential within digital economic practices because the network effect means there will always be more value in information networks that are more complex and have more connections.

Capitalism, and the contemporary global economy, is being transformed by digital economic practices, and the dynamics just outlined are part of what is needed to understand the wider socio-economics of the twenty-first century. This book is not an attempt to explain the contemporary economy in total, nor does it try to redefine the existing economy of developed nations as a 'digital economy'. In this sense, though it shares some aspects with Srnicek's (2016) 'platform capitalism' or Zuboff's (2019) 'surveillance capitalism', the argument is different. The approach has been to follow practices to try to understand if digital and internet socio-technologies have brought shifts in economic practice to the extent that there is now a sector of the economy that is digital. Based on case studies and existing concepts, I have argued that there is such a sector, and its links to other sectors have been sketched in. These links can be seen in hybrid economic practices that bring together different kinds of practice. It is worth noting how these hybrid practices work in both directions, with some companies that seem originally digital taking up non-digital practices (such as Google selling products like phones and laptops) and some pre-digital companies taking up digital practices (as in Walmart's use of blockchain technologies). But understanding such interactions is only possible after identification of the dynamics of digital economic practices; given that identification, it is then possible to see where a company might be taking up digital practices or simply using digital technologies as part of existing economic practices. In short, it is not technology that defines a digital economic practice.

Unfortunately, fully connecting such conclusions about hybridity and the formation of specific company practices to the wider economic discussion is beyond the scope of this book. There has been no lack of analysts of the economy, particularly since the 2008 global financial crisis, and a future project would be to look at such overarching work and see how a sectoral approach might integrate the digital economy and what it tells us about economic life overall (Piketty 2014; Mason 2015; Skidelsky 2018). But this has been one of the points of this book's method: if you start with the big picture, if you decide this is capitalism of one sort or another, then do not be surprised if you find that the digital economy is a version of that big picture. There may be some value in such approaches, but this book has pursued a different method, one that recognised it was not clearly understood what the digital economy meant and then set about building such an understanding.

The End

Trying to understand the digital economy began with a confusion: can we really group Apple, Microsoft, Amazon, Google and Facebook together as digital companies, implying that they all share a similar kind of economic method? The answer to this question in the introduction was quizzical; now it is clearly no. Among the big five, there are different economic methods at work, something the source of their revenue makes clear given the difference between companies selling things they make, selling things other companies make, and selling users' identities.

The key feature of the preceding analysis is that it has been sectoral, only after which could the effect of the digital economy on the wider economy be analysed. Sometimes the rather awkward phrase 'digital economic practices' has been retained, where using 'digital economy' might have been easier. But this phrasing was chosen to underline that this is not an analysis of the economy, digital or otherwise, but of the specific dynamics of economic practices that are dependent for their existence on digital and internet socio-technologies. Socio-technologies here should not be read as implying a technological determinism, but as registering the complex intersection of cultures, social relations and technologies. These digital economic dynamics are sectoral and abstract; they will exist in the world in multiple relations and hybrid combinations of attempts to profit or to build freely available resources. Understanding digital economic practices requires identifying their nature in the linking of value, property and profit in relation to informational resources that result from activities undertaken by many users on digital platforms that may or may not be monetised.

The digital economy is made from practices that find ways to mine the emotions, socialities and cultures of digitally dependent communities of action by forming and managing those emotions, socialities and cultures. The danger is that in its creation of an industry of beauty, wonder and grief, the digital economy is also recreating for its own benefit what beauty, wonder and grief mean and how we experience them. The analysis of digital economic practices highlights the need to reclaim our relations to each other, not to exclude or remove the digital (I love online gaming!), but to assert the right of all of us to both know what is happening to our fundamental relations and have a collective right to influence how they are developed. The digital economic practice of beauty, wonder and grief only exists because of our experiences of these things that are fundamental to who we are and to what we can experience and do. The industry has to recognise, or be forced to recognise, that its dependence on our collective emotional, social and cultural activities gives us rights over its development of our lives.

The digital economy is ultimately a vampire and must be staked by a democratised digital culture.

Notes

Chapter 1

1   The *Financial Times* methodology can be found at www.ft.com/content/1fda5794–169f-11e5-b07f-00144feabdc0. The Fortune 500 gives the most recent available numbers but ranks companies by revenue. The figures come coded to thirty-eight economic sectors according to the FTSE/Russell Industry Classification Benchmark, a scale that is mirrored in the Fortune ranking (FTSE/Russell 2016). To decide on the top-level sectors I compared the classification used by FT and Fortune to other influential classification models: the United Nations International Standard Industrial Classification, the related European Union Statistical Classification of Economic Activities, and Standard and Poor's Global Industry Classification Standard. I distilled from this analysis six top-level categories: digital, financial, manufacturing, extractive, retail and services. Following this I reviewed all the 500 companies and their existing classification, allocating companies that clearly seemed to fit a broad understanding of the digital economy to the digital category.

2   These years were chosen for several reasons in addition to the datasets being available, in a context where such datasets may be sold for greater sums than academic budgets allow. First, they offer a decade-long view of a stabilised digital economy after the 1997–2002 dot.com bubble and NASDAQ crash. Second, changes in data format make other years difficult to access and use. Third, 2017, though derived from a different ranking, was the most recent data available. In light of the definitional issues that this chapter will explore, a subsequent project would be to revisit and extend this statistical view based on a consistent and coherent definition of the digital economy.

3   All figures in the rest of this chapter, unless otherwise indicated, come from Fortune 2017.

4   This is not unlike Butler's account of the importance of iteration in performativity, or Derrida's of the impossibility of repetition – if something is an exact repeat then it is the same thing as the original, if it is not exact then it is not a repeat – both of which are solved, in complex ways, by noting that it is the cultural or social logic of a particular context that tells all those entangled that this is a repeated entanglement (Butler 1997: 150; Derrida 1988; Jordan 2013: 41–5).

Chapter 2

1 Technically, these figures are from Alphabet Inc., the conglomerate that controls Google and a number of other businesses. As Google is the largest of the companies in Alphabet I will avoid the distraction of referring to Alphabet and refer to the whole conglomeration as Google.
2 At the time of writing, Google was undergoing an internal controversy over creating a China-specific search engine that some employees objected to as they believed it would enable spying and censorship (Mayer 2018).

Chapter 3

1 There is a need for some caution about the jump in net income as this period covered tax changes (Facebook 2018).

Chapter 4

1 Anyone interested in Uber and its economics should look at Horan's articles available at the Naked Capitalism website, beginning with: www.nakedcapitalism.com/2016/11/can-uber-ever-deliver-part-one-understanding-ubers-bleak-operating-economics.html, or alternatively at Horan's own website: http://horanaviation.com/Uber.html.
2 DataHippo claim that they 'scrape' the data from the API of the platform. Their methodology is outlined in the FAQs at https://datahippo.org/en.
3 This analysis does not touch on the taxes the company may have paid overall – which for digital companies has been a source of great controversy – it only quantifies what should have been paid on these particular rentals (Booth and Newling 2016a).
4 I am deliberately shortening this outline of Bitcoin to focus on it as an economic practice; there are many details that can safely be left aside to avoid both the inexorable pull to technical detail and the impassioned politics Bitcoin produces. See Casey and Vigna (2018) for a strongly pro-Bitcoin view; Gerard (2017) for a just as strong anti- view; and Popper 2015 for something somewhere in between.

Chapter 5

1 For space reasons, I am going to avoid as much as possible the free software versus open source debate, which has been covered extensively elsewhere (Jordan 2008: 59–65). I will use the term free software as its key elements (free

in both financial and cultural terms, and built on a community) are important to understanding digital economic practices.

2 Several distinctions within software code are being elided here. The fundamental issue is whether someone can view and change the code, which is itself a written language, or whether they are presented with the code as a functioning object. Within this there are possibilities, such as macros, for changing the functionality of a software program without altering the basic codebase. The key point to understand about free software is how a specific coding that enables some activities – like adding up within a spreadsheet – is allied to the ability to share and alter this coding.

3 And something of an irony with Torvalds accused in 2018 of several years of abusive behaviour (Bright 2018).

Chapter 6

1 It was not possible to check the methodology for this figure as it comes from a private sale report too expensive for academic budgets; it should be treated with caution as it seems very high, and hardware bought for a personal computer for gaming may be difficult to distinguish from other uses. Further, the figure covers the period when PC graphics cards boomed in price due to their being used for Bitcoin mining, hence any figures that assumed that graphics card sales were primarily for gaming would in this period be highly suspect (Lee 2018).

2 US figures are used for comparison as only figures for the United States were available. Whether the film industry or games industry is bigger is a contested subject. For example, Kerr notes the many difficulties surrounding what to count (for example, if I've counted the hardware for games, should I also count sales of DVD/Blu-Ray players for film? What about streaming services like Netflix for movie income?) and argues that games are not a bigger industry than movies. The figures presented in this chapter are I feel a reasonable comparison that suggest the film industry is likely to be bigger than games, though not by a huge amount. In any case, both my analysis and Kerr's suggest that games are a major cultural industry (Kerr 2016: 31–4).

3 All figures, including those for pets and services below, are from July 2018, and taken from the Blizzard USA shop at https://us.shop.battle.net/en-us/family/world-of-warcraft.

4 And perhaps it is time for full disclosure: in MMOGs I have played *Rift* and *Warcraft*, as well as *Dark Age of Camelot* and *Warhammer Online*, fairly extensively.

Chapter 7

1   This footnote adds some background technical analysis that many will not need. Surplus value was held to be the extra value the owner of a factory, or a means of production, could extract by paying workers less than the full value of the products they create. Put crudely, if during their working hours a worker produces value embodied in goods that will exchange for ten dollars and is only paid six dollars, then the 'surplus' four dollars fall to whoever owns and organises the worker's work. This 'surplus' created by activity is not necessarily known by those who are active; the worker does not 'see' the value they produce and so cannot know there is a surplus being expropriated (Huws 2104: 152; Dyer-Witheford 2015: 22–5; Andrejevic 2013: 151–2).

2   Huws's cogent objection to Fuchs's argument is that without any idea of subsistence required to recreate labour, that is without any idea of the necessary labour and time required to reproduce labour, there can be no definition of surplus value, as the value of surplus is by definition differentiated through its relation to the labour required for subsistence (Huws 2014: 173–4). While not making this argument explicitly, Dyer-Witheford also notes the importance of 'socially necessary labour time' to defining the value of a commodity, an implication of which is the one Huws articulates, that without necessary labour time there can be no value to distinguish surplus value (Dyer-Witheford 2015: 22–4).

Chapter 9

1   Value Added Tax is not exactly equivalent to a straight sales-only tax, but is the most appropriate measure in this context for the UK. US measures are not used here as they tend to vary state by state.

2   An extensive review of the legal implications (albeit primarily for US law) of this ongoing tendency in disintermediating digital economic practices is provided in a special edition of the *Comparative Labor Law and Policy Journal*, 37(3) (2015).

3   A further possible policy area needing analysis in relation to labour is that even the problematic statistical analysis of the digital economy given in Chapter 1 suggested that the relationship between a digital company's valuation and its employee numbers might mean that digital economic practices produce high valuations and low employee numbers. Zuboff makes a similar point by comparing Google's and Facebook's market capitalisation and employee numbers to General Motors, stating that 'GM employed more people during the height of the Great Depression than either Google or Facebook employs at their height of market capitalization' (2019: loc. 9010). Following this book's analysis, a further project would be to code a digital sector for monetised companies and see how this compares to other sectors. My analysis of the FT

500 companies found that the digital sector had a particularly high value in terms of the relationship between profit and employee numbers, about equal with the financial sector. It is tempting to see here the dependence of a digital company on freely given activities that it then converts into labour for itself, as all such activities would not count as those of employees but would still add value to the company. However, as outlined in the opening chapter, such analysis suffers from a poor definition of the digital as a sector and accordingly produces untrustworthy statistics. It would need a subsequent project to produce a sound statistical base.

4   For anyone who wishes to pursue the broader debate, the work of the Peer to Peer Foundation is a useful resource: https://p2pfoundation.net. Similarly, the work of Dimitry Kleiner and the telekomunist manifesto: http://telekommu-nisten.net/the-telekommunist-manifesto. This work is not without its critics (for example, Rigi 2014).

References

Activision (2018) 'Activision Blizzard 2017 Annual Report', at https://investor.activision.com/annual-reports.

Airbnb (2017) 'Airbnb Fast Facts', at https://press.atairbnb.com/app/uploads/2017/08/4-Million-Listings-Announcement-1.pdf.

Airbnb (2018) 'What is the Airbnb Service Charge?', at www.airbnb.co.uk/help/article/1857/what-is-the-airbnb-service-fee.

Alphabet Inc. (2017) 'Press Release: Alphabet Announces Fourth Quarter and Fiscal Year 2016 Results', at https://abc.xyz/investor/news/earnings/2016/Q4_alphabet_earnings.

Alphabet Inc. (2018a) 'Alphabet Announces Second Quarter 2018 Results', at https://abc.xyz/investor/pdf/2018Q2_alphabet_earnings_release.pdf.

Alphabet Inc. (2018b) 'Alphabet Announces First Quarter 2018 Results', at https://abc.xyz/investor/pdf/2018Q1_alphabet_earnings_release.pdf.

Amadeo, R. (2018a) 'Google's Iron Grip on Android: Controlling Open Source By Any Means Necessary', *ArsTechnica*, at https://arstechnica.com/gadgets/2018/07/googles-iron-grip-on-android-controlling-open-source-by-any-means-necessary.

Amadeo, R. (2018b) 'Google to Charge Android OEMs as Much as $40 per Phone in EU After the EU Ruling', Ars Technica, at https://arstechnica.com/gadgets/2018/10/google-to-charge-android-oems-as-much-as-40-per-phone-in-eu.

Amin, A. and Thrift, N. (eds) (2004) *The Blackwell Cultural Economy Reader*, Oxford: Blackwell.

Anderson, C. (2013) *Makers: The New Industrial Revolution*, London: Random House.

Anderson, S. L. (2017) 'Watching People is Not a Game: Interactive Online Corporeality, Twitch.tv and Videogame Streams', *Game Studies*, 17(1), http://gamestudies.org/1701/articles/anderson.

Andrejevic, M. (2013) 'Estranged Free Labor', in Scholz, T. (ed.), *Digital Labor: The Internet as Playground and Factory*, London: Routledge.

Anthony, A. (2001) 'Where to, Guv'nor?', *Guardian*, at www.theguardian.com/theobserver/2001/mar/11/features.review7.

Apple (2017) 'Apple Reports Fourth Quarter Results', at www.apple.com/uk/newsroom/2017/11/apple-reports-fourth-quarter-results.

ASF (2017) 'The Apache Software Foundation Annual Report May 2016–April 2017', at https://blogs.apache.org/foundation/entry/the-apache-software-foundation-announces15.

Auletta, K. (2011) *Googled: The End of the World As We Know It*, London: Virgin Books.

Axon, S. (2018) 'Amazon Achieved a Market Valuation of $1,000,000,000,000', *ArsTechnica*, at https://arstechnica.com/gadgets/2018/09/amazon-achieved-a-market-value-of-1000000000000.

Balkin J. (2008) 'The Constitution in the National Surveillance State', Faculty Scholarship Series, Paper 225, at http://digitalcommons.law.yale.edu/fss_papers/225.

Banks, J. (2013) *Co-creating Videogames*, London: Bloomsbury.

Banks, M. (2017) *Creative Justice: Cultural Industries, Work and Inequality*, London: Rowman and Littlefield.

Barad, K. (2007) *Meeting the Universe Halfway: Quantum Physics and the Entanglement of Matter and Meaning*, Durham, NC: Duke University Press.

Barnes, B. (1988) *The Nature of Power*, Cambridge: Polity.

Bayer, J., Ellison, N., Schoenebeck, S. and Falk, E. (2016) 'Sharing the Small Moments: Ephemeral Social Interaction on Snapchat', *Information, Communication and Society*, 19(7), pp. 956–77.

Beaver, L. (2016) 'WeChat Breaks 700 Million Active Monthly Users', *Business Insider*, at www.businessinsider.com/wechat-breaks-700-million-monthly-active-users-2016–4?IR=T.

Benkler, Y. (2006) *The Wealth of Networks*, New Haven: Yale University Press.

Berners-Lee, T. with Fischetti, M. (2000) *Weaving the Web: The Original Design and Ultimate Destiny of the World Wide Web*, New York: HarperCollins.

Birchall, C. (2014) 'Radical Transparency', *Cultural Studies: Critical Methodologies*, 14(1), pp. 77–88.

Bilton, N. (2014) *Hatching Twitter: A True Story of Money, Power, Friendship and Betrayal*, London: Sceptre.

Bird, T. and Jordan, T. (1999) 'Sounding Out New Social Movements and the Left: Interview with Stuart Hall, Doreen Massey and Michael Rustin', in Jordan, T. and Lent. A. (eds), *Storming the Millennium: the New Politics of Change*, London: Lawrence and Wishart.

Bishop, T. (2017) 'New Numbers Show How Microsoft's Biggest Businesses are Really Doing in the Cloud Era', *Geekwire*, at www.geekwire.com/2017/new-numbers-show-microsofts-biggest-businesses-really-cloud-era.

Bitcoinchain (2018) 'Week Thursday 31st May to Wednesday 6th June', at https://bitcoinchain.com/pools.

Bollier, D. and Conaty, P. (2014) *A New Alignment of Movements?: A Report on Commons Strategies Group Workshop*, at www.bollier.org/blog/new-alignment-movements.

Booth, R. and Newling, D. (2016a) 'Airbnb UK Tax History Questioned as Income Passes Through Ireland', *Guardian*, at www.theguardian.com/technology/2016/dec/19/airbnb-uk-tax-history-questioned-as-income-passes-through-ireland.

Booth, R. and Newling, D. (2016b) 'Airbnb Introduces 90-day Annual Limit for

London Hosts', *Guardian*, at www.theguardian.com/technology/2016/dec/01/
airbnb-introduces-90-day-a-year-limit-for-london-hosts.

Botsman, R. (2017) 'Big Data Meets Big Brother as China Moves to Rate
Its Citizens', *Wired*, at www.wired.co.uk/article/chinese-government-social-
credit-score-privacy-invasion.

Bourdieu, P. (1977) *Outlines of a Theory of Practice*, Cambridge: Cambridge
University Press.

boyd, d. (2006) 'Friends, Friendster, and Top 8: Writing Community Into Being
on Social Network Sites', *First Monday*, 11(12), at http://firstmonday.org/
article/view/1418/1336.

boyd, d. (2011) 'Social Network Sites as Networked Publics: Affordances,
Dynamics, and Implications', in Papacharissi, Z. (ed.), *A Networked Self:
Identity, Community, and Culture on Social Network Sites*, London; Routledge.

boyd, d. and Ellison, N. (2007) 'Social Network Sites: Definition, History, and
Scholarship', *Journal of Computer-Mediated Communication*, 13(1), pp. 210–30.

boyd, d. and Marwick, A. (2010) 'I Tweet Honestly, I Tweet Passionately: Twitter
Users, Context Collapse and the Imagined Audience', *New Media and Society*,
13(10), pp. 114–33.

Bradshaw, T. (2017) 'Uber Vows to Stop Using "Greyball" Tool to Block
Officials' Rides', *Financial Times*, at www.ft.com/content/fd2137a2–0465–
11e7-aa5b-6bb07f5c8e12.

Brennan, M. (2017) '2017 WeChat Report', *China Channel*, at https://
chinachannel.co/1017-wechat-report-users.

Bright, P. (2018) 'Linus Torvalds Apologizes for Years of Being a Jerk, Takes
Time Off to Learn Empathy', *ArsTechnica*, at https://arstechnica.com/
gadgets/2018/09/linus-torvalds-apologizes-for-years-of-being-a-jerk-takes-time-
off-to-learn-empathy.

Bruns, A. (2008) *Blogs, Wikipedia, Second Life and Beyond: From Production to
Produsage*, New York: Peter Lang.

Burgen, S. (2017) 'Barcelona Cracks Down on Airbnb Rentals with Illegal
Apartment Squads', *Guardian*, at www.theguardian.com/technology/2017/
jun/02/airbnb-faces-crackdown-on-illegal-apartment-rentals-in-barcelona.

Burgen, S. (2018) 'Barcelona Airbnb Host "Manages Rentals Worth
£33,000 a Day"', *Guardian*, at www.theguardian.com/cities/2018/oct/22/
barcelona-airbnb-host-manages-rentals-worth-33000-a-day-report.

Burgess, M. and Woollaston, V. (2017) 'DuckDuckGo: What is it and How Does
it Work?', *Wired*, at www.wired.co.uk/article/duckduckgo-anonymous-privacy.

Bustillos, M. (2015) 'Inside the Fight Over Bitcoin's Future', *The New Yorker*, at
www.newyorker.com/business/currency/inside-the-fight-over-bitcoins-future.

Butler, J. (1997) *Excitable Speech: A Politics of the Performative*, London:
Routledge.

Cadwalladr, C. (2014) 'Wikipedia's Jimmy Wales: "It's True, I'm Not a Billionaire.
So?" – Interview', *Guardian*, at www.theguardian.com/technology/2014/feb/07/
jimmy-wales-wikipedia-interview.

Casey, M. and Vigna, P. (2018) *The Truth Machine: The Blockchain and the Future of Everything*, London: HarperCollins.

Castranova, E. (2005) *Synthetic Worlds: The Business and Culture of Online Games*, Chicago: Chicago University Press.

Cetina, K. K., Schatzki, T. and von Savigny, E. (eds) (2005) *The Practice Turn in Contemporary Theory*, London: Routledge.

Chen, M. (2012) *Leet Noobs: The Life and Death of an Expert Player Group in World of Warcraft*, New York: Peter Lang.

Cherry, M. (2015) 'Beyond Misclassification: The Digital Transformation of Work', *Comparative Labor Law and Policy Journal*, 37(3), pp. 577–602.

CIW Team (2017) 'China Search Engine Market Share in Apr 2017', *China Internet Watch*, at www.chinainternetwatch.com/20538/search-engine-market-share-apr-2017.

Coleman, G. (2012) *Coding Freedom: the Ethics and Aesthetics of Hacking*, Princeton: Princeton University Press.

Conor, B., Gill, R. and Taylor, S. (eds) (2015) *Gender and Creative Labour*, London: Wiley-Blackwell.

Consalvo, M. (2007) *Cheating: Gaining Advantage in Videogames*, Cambridge, MA: MIT Press.

Constine, J. (2017) 'Facebook Changes Mission Statement to "Bring The World Closer Together"', *Techcrunch*, at https://techcrunch.com/2017/06/22/bring-the-world-closer-together.

Constine, J. (2018) 'WhatsApp Hits 1.5 Billion Monthly Users. $19 Billion? Not Bad', *Techcrunch*, at https://techcrunch.com/2018/01/31/whatsapp-hits-1-5-billion-monthly-users-19b-not-so-bad.

Cook, J. (2014) 'Uber's Internal Charts Show How Its Driver-Rating System Actually Works', *Business Insider*, at http://uk.businessinsider.com/leaked-charts-show-how-ubers-driver-rating-system-works-2015-2.

Corbet, J. (2017) 'A Look at the 4.14 Development Cycle', *LWN*, at https://lwn.net/Articles/736578.

Corbet, J. and Kroah-Hartman, G. (2018) '2017 Linux Kernel Development Report', at www.linuxfoundation.org/2017-linux-kernel-report-landing-page.

Core (2018) 'CoreEcon: Economics For a Changing World', at www.core-econ.org.

Corneliussen, H. and Rettberg, J. (eds) (2008) *Digital Culture, Play, And Identity: A World of Warcraft Reader*, Cambridge, MA: MIT Press.

Cossins, D. (2018) 'Discriminating Algorithms: 5 Times AI Showed Prejudice', *New Scientist*, at www.newscientist.com/article/2166207-discriminating-algorithms-5-times-ai-showed-prejudice.

Coté, M. and Pybus, J. (2007) 'Learning to Immaterial Labour 2.0: Myspace and Social Networks', *Ephemera*, 7(1), pp. 88–106.

Couldry, N. (2004) 'Theorising Media as Practice', *Social Semiotics*, 14(2), pp. 115–32.

Cullen, D. (2016) 'Has the Way Universities Teach Economics Changed Enough?',

Guardian, at www.theguardian.com/higher-education-network/2016/apr/28/has-the-way-universities-teach-economics-changed-enough.

Davies, R. (2016) 'Uber Suffers Legal Setbacks in France and Germany', *Guardian*, at www.theguardian.com/technology/2016/jun/09/uber-suffers-legal-setbacks-in-france-and-germany.

Dean, J. (2012) *The Communist Horizon*, London: Verso.

de Beauvoir, S. (2010) *The Second Sex*, London: Vintage Books.

De Kosnik, A. (2013) 'Fandom as Free Labor', in Scholz, T. (ed.), *Digital Labor: The Internet as Playground and Factory*, London: Routledge.

De Kunder, M. (2018) 'The Size of the World Wide Web', at www.worldwidewebsize.com.

Deleuze, G. (1991) *Empiricism and Subjectivity: An Essay on Hume's Theory of Human Nature*, New York: Columbia University Press.

Delo, C. (2014) 'How Much Are You Really Worth to Facebook and Google?', *AdAge*, at http://adage.com/article/digital/worth-facebook-google/293042.

Derrida, J. (1988) *Limited Inc.*, Evanston: Northwestern University Press.

Doctorow, C. (2016) 'The World Wide Web Consortium at a Crossroads: Arms-Dealers or Standards-Setters?', *Electronic Frontier Foundation*, at www.eff.org/deeplinks/2016/11/world-wide-web-consortium-crossroads-arms-dealers-or-standards-setters.

Dogtiev, A. (2018) 'Snapchat Revenue and Usage Statistics', *Business of Apps*, at www.businessofapps.com/data/snapchat-statistics/#1.

DuckDuckGo (2018) 'Sources', at https://duck.co/help/results/sources.

Duffy, B. E. (2017) *(Not) Getting Paid to Do What You Love: Gender, Social Media, and Aspirational Work*, New Haven: Yale University Press.

Du Gay, P. and Pryke, M. (eds) (2002) *Cultural Economy: Cultural Analysis and Commercial Life*, London: Sage.

Dullforce, A. (2015) 'FT 500 2015 Introduction and Methodology: See How the Top Global Companies Were Ranked', *Financial Times*, at https://next.ft.com/content/1fda5794–169f-11e5-b07f-00144feabdc0.

Dyer-Witheford, N. (2015) *Cyber-Proletariat: Global Labour in the Digital Vortex*, London: Pluto.

Dyer-Witheford, N. and de Peuter, G. (2009) *Games of Empire: Global Capitalism and Video Games*, Minneapolis: University of Minnesota Press.

Elmer, G. (2004) *Profiling Machines: Mapping the Personal Information Economy*, Cambridge, MA: MIT Press.

ESA (2018) 'Essential Facts About the Computer and Video Game Industry', *Entertainment Software Association*, at www.theesa.com/wp-content/uploads/2018/05/EF2018_FINAL.pdf.

Eubanks, V. (2018) *Automating Inequality: How High-Tech Tools Profile, Police, and Punish the Poor*, New York: St Martin's Press.

European Commission (2017) 'Communication from the Commission to the European Parliament and the Council: A Fair and Efficient Tax System in the European Union for the Digital Single Market', at https://ec.europa.

eu/taxation_customs/sites/taxation/files/communication_taxation_digital_
single_market_en.pdf.

Evans, E. (2016) 'The Economics of Free: Freemium Games, Branding and the
Impatience Economy', *Convergence*, 22(6), pp. 563–80.

Facebook (2018) 'Facebook Reports Fourth Quarter and Full Year 2017 Results',
at https://investor.fb.com/investor-news/press-release-details/2018/Facebook-
Reports-Fourth-Quarter-and-Full-Year-2017-Results/default.aspx.

Facebook Business (2018) 'About the Delivery System: Ad Auctions', at https://
en-gb.facebook.com/business/help/430291176997542.

Farivar, C. (2018) 'San Francisco to Uber, Lyft: If Your Drivers Aren't Employees,
Prove It', *Ars Technica*, at https://arstechnica.com/tech-policy/2018/05/
san-francisco-to-uber-lyft-if-your-drivers-arent-employees-then-prove-it.

Feiner, L. (2019) 'Analysts Don't Know What to Make of Uber's $100 Billion
Valuation', *CNBC*, at www.cnbc.com/2019/04/13/analysts-dont-know-what-
to-make-of-ubers-100-billion-valuation.html.

Feuz, M., Fuller, M. and Stadler, F. (2011) 'Personal Web Searching in the Age of
Semantic Capitalism', *First Monday*, 16(2), at https://journals.uic.edu/ojs/index.
php/fm/article/view/3344/2766.

FLOSS Project (2002) 'Free/Libre and Open Source Software: Survey and Study:
FLOSS Final Report', at http://flossproject.merit.unu.edu/report/index.htm.

Fortune (2017) 'Fortune Global 500 2018', *Fortune Magazine*, at http://fortune.
com/fortune500.

Freeman, K. (2012) 'What Are You Worth to Facebook?', *Mashable*, at https://
mashable.com/2012/05/14/val-you-calculator-worth-facebook.

FT (2006) 'FT Global 500 2006', *Financial Times*, at www.ft.com/
content/19e214d6-f7c7-11da-9481–0000779e2340.

FT (2015) 'FT Global 500 2015', *Financial Times*, at www.ft.com/content/
a352a706–16a0–11e5-b07f-00144feabdc0.

FTSE/Russell (2016) 'FTSE/Russell Industry Classification Benchmark', at www.
ftserussell.com.

Fuchs, C. (2014) *Social Media: An Introduction*, London: Sage.

Fuchs, C. (2018) *The Online Advertising Tax: A Digital Policy Innovation.* Camri
Policy Brief, University of Westminster: London.

Fung, A. (2008) *Global Capital, Local Culture: Transnational Media Corporations in
China*, New York: Peter Lang.

Fung, A. (2018) *Cultural Policy and East Asian Rivalry: The Hong Kong Games
Industry*, London: Rowman and Littlefield.

Gallagher, B. (2018) *How to Turn Down a Billion Dollars: The Snapchat Story*,
London: Virgin Books.

Gallagher, S. (2018) 'This is Fine: IBM Acquires Red Hat', *Ars Technica*, at https://
arstechnica.com/information-technology/2018/10/ibm-buys-red-hat-with-
eye-on-cloud-dominance.

Galloway, A. (2004) *Protocol: How Control Exists After Decentralization*, Cambridge,
MA: MIT Press.

Gandolfi, E. (2016) 'To Watch or to Play, It Is in the Game: The Game Culture on Twitch.tv Among Performers, Plays and Audiences', *Journal of Gaming and Virtual Worlds*, 8(1), pp. 63–82.

Gates, B. (1976) 'An Open Letter to Hobbyists', at https://upload.wikimedia.org/wikipedia/commons/1/14/Bill_Gates_Letter_to_Hobbyists.jpg.

Gerard, D. (2017) *Attack of the 50 Foot Blockchain*, CreateSpace Independent Publishing Platform.

Gerbaudo, P. (2017) *The Mask and the Flag: Populism, Citizenism and Global Protest*, London: Hurst and Co.

Gibbs, S. (2016) 'How Much Are You Worth to Facebook?', *Guardian*, at www.theguardian.com/technology/2016/jan/28/how-much-are-you-worth-to-facebook.

Giles, J. (2005) 'Internet Encyclopaedias Go Head to Head: Jimmy Wales' Wikipedia Comes Close to Britanica in Terms of the Accuracy of its Science Entries', *Nature*, 438 (7070), pp. 900–1.

Gillespie, T. (2010) 'The Politics of Platforms', *New Media and Society*, 12(3), pp. 347–64.

Gillespie, T. (2018) *Custodians of the Internet: Platforms, Content Moderation, and the Hidden Decisions That Shape Social Media*, Yale: Yale University Press.

Gillies, J. and Cailliau, R. (2000) *How the Web Was Born: The Story of the World Wide Web*, Oxford: Oxford University Press.

Gittleson, K. (2014) 'Amazon Buys Video-Game Streaming Site Twitch', *BBC*, https://www.bbc.co.uk/news/technology-28930781.

Golumbia, D. (2016) *The Politics of Bitcoin: Software As Right-Wing Extremism*, Minneapolis: University of Minnesota Press.

Google Finance (2018) 'NYSE: Snap: Market Summary', at www.google.com/searc h?q=NYSE:SNAP&tbm=fin#scso=uid_hgb8WoSsJcjQgAbY2bpQ_5:0.

Graft, K. (2011) 'Interview: Trion's Debut Rift Closes in on One Million Sell-Through', *Trion Worlds*, at www.trionworlds.com/en/news/media-coverage/2011/06/gamasutra-rift-1m.

Grubb, J. (2018) 'NPD 2017: An Incredible Year for Games Leads to 11% Sales Growth', *Venturebeat*, at https://venturebeat.com/2018/01/18/npd-2017-an-incredible-year-for-games-leads-to-11-sales-growth.

Hall, S. (1986) 'The Problem of Ideology: Marxism Without Guarantees', *Journal of Communication Inquiry*, 10(2), pp. 28–44.

Haraway, D. (1991) *Simians, Cyborgs, and Women: The Reinvention of Nature*, London: Free Association Books.

Haraway, D. (2008) *When Species Meet*, Minneapolis: University of Minnesota Press.

Haraway, D. (2016) *Staying With the Trouble: Making Kin in the Chthulucene*, Durham, NC: Duke University Press.

Harding, L. (2014) *The Snowden Files: The Inside Story of the World's Most Wanted Man*, London: Guardian Books.

Havalais, A. (2009) *Search Engine Society*, Cambridge: Polity.

Helmore, E. (2017) 'Snapchat Shares Soar 44% to Value Loss-making Company at $28bn', *Guardian*, at www.theguardian.com/technology/2017/mar/02/snapchat-ipo-valuation-evan-spiegel-bobby-murphy-snap-inc.

Hesmondhalgh, D. (2010) 'User-generated Content, Free Labour and the Cultural Industries', *Ephemera*, 10(3–4), pp. 267–84.

Hesmondhalgh, D. and Baker, S. (2013) *Creative Labour: Media Work in Three Cultural Industries*, London: Routledge.

Higgin, T. (2009) 'Blackless Fantasy: The Disappearance of Race in Massively Multiplayer Online Role-Playing Games', *Games and Culture*, 4(1), pp. 3–26.

Hillis, K., Petit, M. and Jarrett, K. (2012) *Google and the Culture of Search*, London: Routledge.

Hjorth, L. and Richardson, I. (2011) 'Playing the Waiting Game: Complicating Notions of (Tele)presence and Gendered Distraction in Casual Mobile Gaming', in Greif, H., Hjorth, L., Lasen, A. and Lobet-Maris, C. (eds), *Cultures of Participation: Mediapractices, Politics and Literacy*, New York: Peter Lang.

HM Government (2018) *Budget 2018: Copy of the Budget Report October 2018 as Laid Before the House of Commons by the Chancellor of the Exchequer When Opening the Budget: HC 1629*, London: House of Commons.

HOCCPA (2013) *House of Commons Committee of Public Accounts: Tax Avoidance – Google; Ninth Report of Session 2013–14; HC112*, London: House of Commons.

Hollander, R. (2018) 'WeChat Has One Billion Monthly Active Users', *Business Insider UK*, at http://uk.businessinsider.com/wechat-has-hit-1-billion-monthly-active-users-2018-3.

Hook, L. (2018) 'Airbnb Marks First Full Year of Profitability in 2017', *Financial Times*, at www.ft.com/content/96215e16-0201-11e8-9650-9c0ad2d7c5b5.

Horan, H. (2017) 'Will the Growth of Uber Increase Economic Value?', *Transportation Law Journal*, at https://papers.ssrn.com/sol3/papers.cfm?abstract_id=2933177.

Humphries, M. (2012) 'EA Won't Green Light Any Single-Player Games', *Geek. Com*, at www.geek.com/games/ea-wont-green-light-any-single-player-only-games-1513693.

Huws, U. (2014) *Labor in the Global Digital Economy: The Cybertariat Comes of Age*, New York: New York University Press.

IBM (2017) 'IBM Reports 2017 Fourth Quarter and Full Year Results: Press Release', at www.ibm.com/investor/att/pdf/IBM-4Q17-Earnings-Press-Release.pdf.

IFPI (2018) 'Global Music Report 2018: Annual State of the Industry', International Federation of the Phonographic Industry, at www.ifpi.org/downloads/GMR2018.pdf.

Jarrett, K. (2016) *Feminism, Labour and Digital Media: The Digital Housewife*, London: Routledge.

Javed, B. K. (2018) 'Microsoft: Bing Ad Revenue Up 15%', *Campaign*, at www.campaignlive.co.uk/article/microsoft-bing-ad-revenue-grew-15/1456212.

Jenkins, H. (2006) *Convergence Culture: Where Old and New Media Collide*, New York: New York University Press.

Johnson, M. R. and Woodcock, J. (2019) 'It's Like the Gold Rush: The Lives and Careers of Professional Video Game Streamers on Twitch.tv', *Information, Communication & Society*, 22(3), pp. 336–51.

Jordan, T. (2005) 'Virtual Economics and Twenty-First-Century Leisure, *Fast Capitalism*, 1(2), at www.fastcapitalism.com.

Jordan, T. (2008) *Hacking: Digital Media and Technological Determinism*, Cambridge: Polity.

Jordan, T. (2013) *Internet, Society and Culture: Communicative Practices Before and After the Internet*, London: Bloomsbury Academic.

Jordan, T. (2015) *Information Politics: Liberation and Exploitation in the Digital Society*, London: Pluto.

Joseph, D. (2018) 'The Discourse of Digital Dispossession: Paid Modifications and Community Crisis on Steam', *Games and Culture*, 13(7), pp. 690–707.

Juul, J. (2013) *The Art of Failure: An Essay on the Pain of Playing Video Games*, Cambridge, MA: MIT Press.

Kant, T. (2015) 'FCJ-180 "Spotify Has Added an Event to Your Past": (Re)writing the Self through Facebook's Autoposting Apps', *Fibreculture*, 25, at http://twentyfive.fibreculturejournal.org/fcj-180-spotify-has-added-an-event-to-your-past-rewriting-the-self-through-facebooks-autoposting-apps.

Karmali, L. (2012) 'EA's Peter Moore: Free-to-Play is an "Inevitability"', *IGN UK*, at http://uk.ign.com/articles/2012/06/21/eas-peter-moore-free-to-play-is-an-inevitability.

Kelty, C. (2008) *Two Bits: The Cultural Significance of Free Software*, Durham, NC: Duke University Press.

Kerr, A. (2016) *Global Games: Production, Circulation and Policy in the Networked Era*, London: Routledge.

Keynes, J. (1938) 'Letter to Roy Harrod, 4th July 1938; 787', in Besomi, D. (ed.), *The Collected Interwar Papers and Correspondence of Roy Harrod, Electronic Edition*, at http://economia.unipv.it/harrod/edition/editionstuff/rfh.346.htm#.

Kirkpatrick, G. (2010) *The Facebook Effect: The Inside Story of the Company That is Connecting the World*, New York: Simon and Schuster.

Kline, S., Dyer-Witheford, N. and De Peuter, G. (2003) *Digital Play: The Interaction of Technology, Culture and Marketing*, Montreal: McGill-Queen's University Press.

Knight, S. (2015) 'World of Warcraft Loses Another 1.5 Million Subscribers Ahead of New Expansion', *TechSpot*, at www.techspot.com/news/61642-world-warcraft-loses-another-15-million-subscribers-ahead.html.

Lashinsky, A. (2015) 'Netscape IPO 20-year Anniversary: Read Fortune's 2005 Oral History of the Birth of the Web', *Fortune Magazine*, at http://fortune.com/2015/08/09/remembering-netscape.

Lashinsky, A. (2018) 'This is Uber's Biggest Problem', *Fortune Magazine*, at http://fortune.com/2018/02/14/uber-2017-financial-results.

Latour, B. (2007) *Reassembling the Social: An Introduction to Actor-Network-Theory*, Oxford: Oxford University Press.

Lazzarato, M. (1996) 'Immaterial Labor', *Generation Online*, at www.generation-online.org/c/fcimmateriallabour3.htm.

Lee, T. (2018) 'Declining Cryptocurrency Prices are Making Graphics Cards Affordable Again', *ArsTechnica*, at https://arstechnica.com/gaming/2018/07/declining-cryptocurrency-prices-are-making-graphics-cards-affordable-again.

Levy, S. (2011) *In the Plex: How Google Thinks, Works and Shapes Our Lives*, New York: Simon & Schuster.

Lih, A. (2009) *The Wikipedia Revolution: How a Bunch of Nobodies Created the World's Greatest Encyclopedia*, London: Aurum Press.

Lin, H. and Sun, C.-T. (2011) 'Cash Trade in Free to Play Online Games', *Games and Culture*, 6(3), pp. 270–87.

Lunden, I. (2016) 'Activision Blizzard Closes Its $5.9 Billion Acquisition of King, Makers of Candy Crush', *TechCrunch*, at https://techcrunch.com/2016/02/23/activision-blizzard-closes-its-5–9b-acquisition-of-king-makers-of-candy-crush.

McDonald, E. (2017) 'Newzoo's 2017 Report: Insights Into the $108.9 Billion Global Games Market', at https://newzoo.com/insights/articles/newzoo-2017-report-insights-into-the-108–9-billion-global-games-market.

McDonald, H. (2014) 'Ireland to Close "Double Irish" Tax Loophole', *Guardian*, at www.theguardian.com/business/2014/oct/13/ireland-close-double-irish-tax-loophole.

McDonald, K. (2006) *Global Movements: Action and Culture*, Oxford: Blackwell.

Machekovech, S. (2018) 'An MMO Goes Full Circle, Promises to Bring Subscriptions *Back* This Year', *ArsTechnica*, at https://arstechnica.com/gaming/2018/01/free-to-play-mmo-will-test-a-paid-branch-minus-mtx-and-loot-boxes-in-2018.

Mager, A. (2012) 'Algorithmic Ideology', *Information, Communication and Society*, 15(5), pp. 769–87.

Makuch, E. (2012) 'Rift Revenues Reach $100 Million in 2011', *GameSpot*, at www.gamespot.com/articles/rift-revenues-reach-100-million-in-2011/1100–6348954.

Marshall, A. (1890) *Principles of Economics*, 8th edition, Indiana: Liberty Fund, at http://oll.libertyfund.org/titles/marshall-principles-of-economics-8th-ed.

Marx, K. (1978) 'The German Ideology', in Tucker, R. (ed.), *The Marx-Engels Reader*, 2nd edition, New York: W. W. Norton.

Mason, P. (2015) *Postcapitalism: A Guide to Our Future*, London: Penguin.

Massanari, A. (2015) *Participatory Culture, Community and Play: Learning From Reddit*, New York: Peter Lang.

Matney, L. (2017) 'YouTube Has 1.5 Billion Logged-In Users Watching a Ton of Mobile Video', *Techcrunch*, at https://techcrunch.com/2017/06/22/youtube-has-1–5-billion-logged-in-monthly-users-watching-a-ton-of-mobile-video.

Mayer, D. (2018) 'Google Employees Outraged Over Its Chinese Search Engine Are Just Doing as They're Told', *Fortune Magazine*, at http://fortune.com/2018/08/17/google-china-search-employees.

Milward, S. (2018) '7 Years of WeChat', *TechinAsia*, at www.techinasia.com/history-of-wechat.

MmogChart (2005) 'MMOG Active Subscriptions 120,000+', access via Internet Archive, at https://web.archive.org/web/20051214203354/www.mmogchart.com:80.

Modine, A. (2008) 'World of Warcraft Upkeep Costs Only $200 Million' *The Register*, at www.theregister.co.uk/2008/09/18/world_of_warcraft_upkeep_200m.

Moffit, J. (2014) 'The Differences Between Google and Bing SEO Algorithms', *Elvin Web Martketing*, at https://onlinemarketinginct.com/2014/07/10/differences-google-bing-seo-algorithms.

Molla, R. (2018) 'Half of US Uber Drivers Make Less Than $10 an Hour After Vehicle Expenses, According to a New Study', *Recode*, at www.recode.net/2018/10/2/17924628/uber-drivers-make-hourly-expenses.

Nash, K. (2018) 'Walmart Requires Lettuce, Spinach Suppliers to Join Blockchain', *Wall Street Journal*, at https://blogs.wsj.com/cio/2018/09/24/walmart-requires-lettuce-spinach-suppliers-to-join-blockchain.

Neff, G. (2012) *Venture Labour: Work and the Burden of Risk in Innovative Industries*, Cambridge, MA: MIT Press.

Newzoo (2018) 'Top 25 Public Companies by Game Revenues', at https://newzoo.com/insights/rankings/top-25-companies-game-revenues.

Nieborg, D. (2014) 'Prolonging the Magic: The Political Economy of the 7th Generation Console Game', *Eludamos: Journal for Computer Game Culture*, 8(1), pp. 47–63.

Nieborg, D. (2015) 'Crushing Candy: The Free-to-Play Game in Its Connective Commodity Form', *Social Media + Society*, 1(2), pp. 1–12.

Nieborg, D. and Poell, T. (2018) 'The Platformization of Cultural Production: Theorizing the Contingent Cultural Commodity', *New Media and Society*, at http://journals.sagepub.com/doi/full/10.1177/1461444818769694.

Noble, S. (2018) *Algorithms of Oppression: How Search Engines Reinforce Racism*, New York: New York University Press.

Obermaier, F. and Obermayer, B. (2017) *The Panama Papers: Breaking the Story of How the Rich and Powerful Hide Their Money*, London: Oneworld.

O'Brien, C. (2015) 'CEO Evan Spiegel in Cannes to Pitch Snapchat's Ad Platform: "We Care About Not Being Creepy"', *Venturebeat*, at https://venturebeat.com/2015/06/22/ceo-evan-spiegel-in-cannes-to-pitch-snapchats-ad-platform-we-care-about-not-being-creepy.

OECD (2011) *OECD Guide to Measuring the Information Society 2011*, Paris: OECD Publications.

OECD (2014) *Measuring the Digital Economy: A New Perspective*, Paris: OECD Publications.

O'Neill, M. (2009) *Cyberchiefs: Autonomy and Authority in Online Tribes*, London: Pluto.

Orland, K. (2016) 'After Blizzard Shutdown, Legacy World of Warcraft Server Returns This Month', *Ars Technica*, at https://arstechnica.com/

gaming/2016/12/after-blizzard-shutdown-legacy-world-of-warcraft-server-returns-this-month.

Orland, K. (2017) 'As PC Sales Shrink, the Gaming PC Market Grows Faster Than Expected', *Ars Technica*, at https://arstechnica.com/gaming/2017/01/as-pc-sales-shrink-the-gaming-pc-market-grows-faster-than-expected.

Orland, K. (2018) 'Four Publishers Must Change In-game Loot Boxes to Avoid Dutch Gambling Laws', *Ars Technica*, at https://arstechnica.com/gaming/2018/04/dutch-government-rules-some-loot-boxes-count-as-illegal-gambling.

PA (Press Association) (2017) 'Facebook UK Pays Just £5.1 Million in Corporation Tax Despite Jump in Profit', *Guardian*, at www.theguardian.com/technology/2017/oct/04/facebook-uk-corporation-tax-profit.

Page, L. and Brin, S. with Motwani, R. and Winograd, T. (1999) 'The PageRank Citation Ranking: Bringing Order to the Web', *Technical Report Stanford Infolab*, at http://ilpubs.stanford.edu:8090/422.

Papacharissi, Z. (ed.) (2011) *A Networked Self: Identity, Community and Culture on Social Network Sites*, London: Routledge.

Park, K. (2005) 'Internet Economy of the Online Game Business in South Korea: The Case of NCsoft's Lineage', in Kehal, H. and Singh, V. (eds), *Digital Economy: Impacts, Influences and Challenges*, London: Idea Group.

Pasquinelli, M. (2008) *Animal Spirits: A Bestiary of the Commons*, Amsterdam: NAi Publishers, Institute of Network Cultures.

Perzanowski, A. and Schultz, J. (2016) *The End of Ownership: Personal Property in the Digital Economy*, Cambridge, MA: MIT Press.

Phillips, A. (2015) 'Headshots, Twitch Reflexes, and the Mechropolitics of Video Games', *Games and Culture*, 13(2), pp. 136–52.

Piketty, T. (2014) *Capital in the Twenty-First Century*, Cambridge, MA: Harvard University Press.

Popper, N. (2015) *Digital Gold: The Untold Story of Bitcoin*, London: Penguin.

Pryke, M. and Du Gay, P. (2007) 'Take an Issue: Cultural Economy and Finance', *Economy and Society*, 36(3), pp. 339–54.

Qiu, J. (2016) *Goodbye iSlave: A Manifesto for Digital Abolition*, Urbana: University of Illinois Press.

Raymond, E. (2001) *The Cathedral and the Bazaar: Musing On Linux and Open Source By an Accidental Revolutionary*, Sebastopol, CA: O'Reilly.

Reckwitz, A. (2002) 'Toward a Theory of Social Practices: A Development in Culturalist Theorizing', *European Journal of Social Theory*, 5(2), pp. 243–63.

Red Hat (2017) 'Red Hat Reports Fourth Quarter and Fiscal Year 2017 Results', at www.redhat.com/en/about/press-releases/red-hat-reports-fourth-quarter-and-fiscal-year-2017-results.

Reynolds, M. (2017) 'Debate Rages Over Controversial Standard For the Web', *New Scientist*, at www.newscientist.com/article/2126513-debate-rages-over-controversial-copyright-standard-for-the-web.

Rigi, J. (2014) 'The Coming Revolution of Peer Production and Revolutionary Cooperatives. A Response to Michel Bauwens, Vasilis Kostakis and Stefan

Meretz', *Triple C: Communication, Capitalism and Critique*, 12(1), at www. triple-c.at/index.php/tripleC/article/view/486.

Ross, A. (2013) 'In Search of the Lost Paycheck', in Scholz, T. (ed.) *Digital Labor: The Internet as Playground and Factory*, London: Routledge.

Rutherford, S. (2018) 'Snapchat's Unskippable Six-Second Ads Have, Sadly, Arrived', *Gizmodo*, at https://gizmodo.com/snapchats-unskippable-six-second-ads-have-sadly-arriv-1826038714.

Samuelson, P. (2006) 'IBM's Pragmatic Embrace of Open Source', *Communications of the ACM*, 49(10), pp. 21–5, at https://scholarship.law.berkeley.edu/facpubs/2372.

Schatzki, T. (2008) *Social Practices: A Wittgensteinian Approach to Human Activity and the Social*, Cambridge: Cambridge University Press.

Schneiderman, E. (2014) 'Airbnb in the City', New York: Office of the Attorney General of the State of New York, at www.ag.ny.gov/pdfs/AIRBNB 20REPORT. pdf.

Scholz, T. (ed.) (2013) *Digital Labor: The Internet as Playground and Factory*, London: Routledge.

Scholz, T. (2016) *Platform Cooperativism: Challenging the Corporate Sharing Economy*, New York: Rosa Luxemburg Foundation.

Scholz, T. (2017) *Uberworked and Underpaid: How Workers are Disrupting the Digital Economy*, Cambridge: Polity.

Schroeder, S. (2018) 'Hacker Steals Coins From Cryptocurrency Verge With a "51 Percent" Attack', *Mashable*, at https://mashable.com/2018/04/05/ verge-crypto-hack/?europe=true#N6V0CEMqQiqP.

Shu, C. (2015) 'Traditional Red Envelopes Are Going Digital Thanks to China's Largest Digital Companies', *Techcrunch*, at https://techcrunch.com/2016/02/08/ smartphone-hongbao.

Skidelsky, R. (2018) *Money and Government: A Challenge to Mainstream Economics*, London: Allen Lane.

Smith, A. (1982) *The Wealth of Nations*, London: Penguin.

Smith, C. (2019) '55 Amazing Twitch Stats and Facts', DMR Business Statistics website, available at https://expandedramblings.com/index.php/twitch-stats.

Snap (2018) 'Snap Inc. Reports Fourth Quarter and Full Year 2017 Results', at https://investor.snap.com/news-releases/2018/02–06–2018–211639653.

So, S. and Westland, J. C. (2010) *Red Wired: China's Internet Revolution*, London: Marshall Cavendish Business.

Sproull, L. and Keisler, S. (1993) 'Computers, Networks and Work', in Harasim, L. (ed.), *Global Networks: Computers and International Communication*, Cambridge, MA: MIT Press.

Srnicek, N. (2016) *Platform Capitalism*, Cambridge: Polity.

Srnicek, N. and Williams, A. (2016) *Inventing the Future: Postcapitalism and a World Without Work*, London: Verso.

Stark, D. (2009) *The Sense of Dissonance: Accounts of Worth in Economic Life*, Princeton: Princeton University Press.

Statista (2017) 'Worldwide Search Market Share of Bing as of August 2017,

By Country', *Statista*, at www.statista.com/statistics/220538/bing-search-market-share-country.

Statista (2018a) 'Global Box Office Revenue From 2005 to 2017', *Statista*, at www.statista.com/statistics/271856/global-box-office-revenue.

Statista (2018b) 'Global Unit Sales of Current Generation Video Game Consoles From 2008 to 2017 (in Million Units)', *Statista*, at www.statista.com/statistics/276768/global-unit-sales-of-video-game-consoles.

Steam (2019) 'Steam and Game States', https://store.steampowered.com/stats.

Steinkuehler, C. (2006) 'The Mangle of Play', *Games and Culture*, 1(3), pp. 199–213.

Stone, B. (2017) *The Upstarts: Uber, Airbnb and the Battle for the New Silicon Valley*, London: Penguin Random House.

Sullivan, D. (2016) 'Google Now Handles at Least 2 Trillion Searches Per Year', *Search Engine Land*, at https://searchengineland.com/google-now-handles-2–999-trillion-searches-per-year-250247.

Tapscott, D. (2015) *The Digital Economy: Rethinking Promise and Peril in the Age of Networked Intelligence*, 20th Anniversary Edition, New York: McGraw Hill Education.

Taylor, T. L. (2009) *Play Between Worlds: Exploring Online Game Culture*, Cambridge, MA: MIT Press.

Taylor, T. L. (2012) *Raising the Stakes: E-Sports and the Professionalization of Computer Gaming*, Cambridge, MA: MIT Press.

TDF (2016) 'The Document Foundation Annual Report 2016', at https://blog.documentfoundation.org/blog/2017/07/21/annual-report-2016.

Terranova, T. (2000) 'Free Labour: Producing Culture for the Digital Economy', *Social Text*, 18(2), pp. 33–58.

Thorne, D. (2013) *The Double Irish and Dutch Sandwich Tax Strategies*, LLM Research Paper, Wellington: Faculty of Law, University of Wellington.

Throsby, D. (2014) *Economics and Culture*, Cambridge: Cambridge University Press.

Tkacz, N. (2014) *Wikipedia and the Politics of Openness*, Chicago: University of Chicago Press.

TN (2018) 'Top Selling Video Titles in the United States 2017', *The Numbers*, at www.the-numbers.com/home-market/packaged-media-sales/2017.

Toffler, A. (1970) *The Third Wave*, New York: Random House.

Topping, A., Kassam, A. and Davies, L. (2014) 'Angry Cab Drivers Gridlock Europe in Protest at "Unregulated" Taxi App', *Guardian*, at www.theguardian.com/uk-news/2014/jun/11/cab-drivers-europe-protest-taxi-app-uber-london-madrid.

Touraine, A. (2002) 'The Importance of Social Movements', *Social Movement Studies*, 1(1), pp. 89–95.

Turrow, J. (2011) *The Daily You*, Yale: Yale University Press.

@twitterir (2018) 'Q4 and Fiscal Year 2017 Letter to Shareholders', at http://files.shareholder.com/downloads/AMDA-2F526X/6251558451x0x970892/

F9B4F616–659A-454B-89C6–28480DA53CCA/Q4_2017_Shareholder_ Letter.pdf.

Vaidhyanathan, S. (2012) *The Googlization of Everything (and Why We Should Worry)*, Updated edition, Berkeley: University of California Press.

Vaughan-Nichols, S. (2018) 'Google Moves to Debian For In-house Linux Desktop', *ZDNET*, at www.zdnet.com/article/google-moves-to-debian-for-in-house-linux-desktop.

Vercellone, C. (2005) 'The Hypothesis of Cognitive Capitalism', Presentation, Birkbeck College and SOAS, London, at https://halshs.archives-ouvertes.fr/halshs-00273641.

Vercellone, C. (2006) 'Wages, Rent and Profit: The New Articulation of Wages, Rent and Profit in Cognitive Capitalism', *Generation Online*, at www.generation-online.org/c/fc_rent2.htm.

Viega, F., Wattenberg, M. and Dave, K. (2004) 'Studying Cooperation and Conflict Between Authors with History Flow Visualizations', CHI Conference on Human Factors in Computing Systems, Vienna Austria, at https://web.archive.org/web/20061102220229/http://alumni.media.mit.edu/~fviegas/papers/history_flow.pdf.

VGChartz (2018) 'VGChartz Yearly Chart Index', at www.vgchartz.com/yearly.

Wark, M. (2013) 'Considerations on A Hacker Manifesto', in Scholz, T. (ed.) *Digital Labor: The Internet as Playground and Factory*, London: Routledge.

Weber, S. (2004) *The Success of Open Source*, Cambridge, MA: Harvard University Press.

WeChat (2015) 'TechTip – Your Guide to WeChat Moments', at http://blog.wechat.com/2015/06/12/tech-tip-your-guide-to-wechat-moments.

Wikimedia Foundation (2018a) 'Annual Report 2016–17', at https://annual.wikimedia.org/2017/index.html.

Wikimedia Foundation (2018b) 'Frequently Asked Questions', at https://wikimediafoundation.org/about/#How_is_the_Wikimedia_Foundation_funded?

Wikipedia (2014) 'Wikipedia: List of Wikipedians by Article Count', at https://en.wikipedia.org/wiki/Wikipedia:List_of_Wikipedians_by_article_count.

Williams, S. (2002) *Free as in Freedom: Richard Stallman's Crusade for Free Software*, Sebastopol, CA: O'Reilly.

Woetzel, J., Seong, J., Wei Wang, K., Manyika, J., Chui, M. and Wong, W. (2017) 'China's Digital Economy: A Leading Global Force', McKinsey Global Institute Discussion Paper, at www.mckinsey.com/featured-insights/china/chinas-digital-economy-a-leading-global-force.

Woodward, K. (2015) *The Politics of In/Visibility: Being There*, Basingstoke: Palgrave Macmillan.

Zoepf, S. (2018) 'The Economics of Ride-Hailing, Revisited', Centre for Energy and Environment Policy, MIT Working Papers, at http://ceepr.mit.edu/files/papers/2018–005 20Authors 20Statement.pdf.

Zuboff, S. (2019) *The Age of Surveillance Capitalism: The Fight For a Human Future at the New Frontier of Power*, London: Profile Books.

Index